THE REFLECTIVE WORKBOOK FOR PARENTS AND FAMILIES OF TRANSGENDER AND NON-BINARY CHILDREN

Your Transition as Your Child Transitions

D. M. Maynard

Jessica Kingsley Publishers
London and Philadelphia

First published in Great Britain in 2020 by Jessica Kingsley Publishers
An Hachette Company

4

Copyright © D. M. Maynard 2020

A CIP catalogue record for this title is available from the British Library and the Library of Congress

ISBN 978 1 78775 236 8
eISBN 978 1 78775 237 5

Printed and bound in the United States by Offset Paperback Manufacturers Inc.

Jessica Kingsley Publishers' policy is to use papers that are natural, renewable and recyclable products and made from wood grown in sustainable forests. The logging and manufacturing processes are expected to conform to the environmental regulations of the country of origin.

Jessica Kingsley Publishers
73 Collier Street
London N1 9BE, UK

www.jkp.com

This workbook is dedicated to you, the parents and families who serve as role models to all by unconditionally supporting and loving your children throughout their gender journey, for your voices matter and must be heard as you advocate for the human rights and respect every child deserves!

CONTENTS

ACKNOWLEDGMENTS

First and foremost, I want to thank all of the parents, children, and other family members who have honestly voiced their thoughts and experiences with me, and I especially extend a heartfelt appreciation to them for entrusting me to share personal pieces of their own stories.

To my supportive cheerleaders—Marlene Arvan, Yolana Cumsky Winick, Pat Dakis, Sam Eber, Hakan Eber, Michael George, Burim Konjusha, Mary Marino, Gail Moskowitz, Martha Murphy-George, Maureen O'Brien, Ronnie Ruderman, Eli Strock, Leah Strock, Jonathan Sutton, and JoAnn Wright: thank you all for your sincere encouragement and belief in my abilities.

To Mom, Dad, Aunt Sue, Uncle Steve, and my sister Stacy: as always, I write with all of you as the angels on my shoulders.

To Mia and Andreia: thank you for being pioneers, wise beyond your years, and my courageous teachers.

To the Jessica Kingsley Publishers Team: thank you for this glorious opportunity, for all of your creative talents, and for making another lifelong dream of mine come true.

To Andrew James, my incredible and supportive Editorial Director: thank you for always making yourself available to talk with me, for showing me endless respect, and for your constant collaborative spirit...you are fantastic in every way!

To Emily Badger, Yojaira Cordero, Giuliana di Mitrio, Kath Mackrill, Isabel Martin, Adam Peacock, Victoria Peters, Julia Zullo, and most especially Emma Holak, my Bonus Team at JKP: thank you for your professional guidance, valuable touches, and passion for publishing.

To Christie Block, David Bradlee, DO, Jonathan Lyons, and Chris Straayer: thank you for generously extending your specialized knowledge to me when I needed it most.

To Stephen Terzuoli and Wendy Yalowitz: thank you for listening with your heart and for helping me as I completed this workbook.

To Simon Langer and Hakan Eber: thank you for being willing to offer your gifted skills to capture the essence of who I am through the lens of your camera and artistic abilities.

To Randi Kaufman, PsyD, Aidan Key, Jean Malpas, LMHC, LMFT, Elijah C. Nealy, PhD, MDiv, LCSW, and Katherine Rachlin, PhD: thank you for your devotion and nurturing of trans and non-binary individuals and their families, whom you have selflessly served and will continue to do so as they all navigate their own paths, for your work has been an inspiration to me, as well as countless others.

To my 2MaPaSis—Barbara Baughan and Maria Riccardi: thank you for reminding me to float, loving my meatballs, and knowing how to make me laugh!

To my chapter reader editors—Rosemary Capelle, Briana Cribari, Teresa Dawber, Nancy Ekloff, Christine Izquierdo, Denise Lasiuk, Mary LoCascio, Cheryl Minsky, Katherine Rachlin, PhD, Benay Shear, and Dee Wojis: thank you for caring enough to share your outstanding editing skills (even when you were overwhelmed with your own lives), being as true blue as humanly possible, and for loving me unconditionally...your precious friendships mean the world to me and having you all in my corner makes my heart sing!

To my multiple chapter reader editors—Barbara Rachlin, PhD, Kevin Johnson, MD, and Donna Restivo: thank you for your dedicated hours, attention to detail, and the kindness you warmly offered in every loving suggestion!

To my brilliant advisors and 24/7 shoulders to lean on—S.J. Langer and Pat Molloy: thank you both beyond words for carrying me across the finish line, offering me your extensive expertise, endless time, intellectual insight, faith in this project, and abundance of assistance throughout the entire process of writing this workbook. Your tenacious input truly made the difference and I am eternally grateful to both of you!

To my husband: thank you for always believing in my ideas, helping me through the sleepless nights, for being a power of example in more ways than I could ever express loudly enough, and for choosing me to be your life partner...I love you completely and forever my CB!

AUTHOR'S DISCLAIMER NOTES

- Whenever the words *parent* or *parents* are used, they will be the umbrella term for and will also refer to: parent/s, caregiver/s, guardian/s, other family members, and families, which can include, but not limited to, siblings, cousins, aunts, uncles, and grandparents.

- The usage of *parent* or *parents* is meant to enable the reader to comprehend the workbook more easily; therefore, the words *parent* or *parents* will be used throughout most of the workbook for both clarity and efficiency. However, it must be acknowledged that this resource is intended for parents AND all other family members who seek to navigate their own journey as their child or relative—18 years of age or younger—has transitioned or is considering transitioning.

- Though the title and above disclaimer suggests that the use of this workbook is pertinent for parents and families of transgender and/or non-binary children, it also applicable for parents and other family members of transgender and/or non-binary youth and/or adults, regardless of their age.

- The word *trans* will be used throughout most of the workbook and will serve as the umbrella term to include every and all gender identities and/or gender expressions a child, youth, and/or adult feels aligns with their affirmed gender that is different from their gender assigned at birth.

- The inclusive use of the word *trans* is embedded within and will incorporate , but not limited to, these words and/or terms: transgender, trans-identified, in transition, gender non-binary, non-binary, questioning, gender questioning, questioning their gender, genderqueer, gender fluid, gender diverse, gender expansive, gender creative, gender nonconforming, intersex, transgender/gender diverse (TGD), transgender non-binary (TGNB), transgender nonconforming (TGNC), and identifying on the transgender spectrum. It should be noted that children and adults may hold more than one of these identities at the same time, over a certain time period or over their lifetime.

- These terms will be interchangeable and understood as inclusive of, but not limited to, any of the possible singular and/or multiple ways a child may prefer to identify; therefore, whenever the word *child* is used, it refers to any child who considers themselves as: transgender, trans-identified, in transition, gender non-binary, non-binary, questioning, gender questioning, questioning their gender, genderqueer, gender fluid, gender diverse, gender expansive, gender creative, gender nonconforming, intersex, TGD, TGNB, TGNC, and on the transgender spectrum.

- When questions appear in this workbook and use the word *child* and/or *child's*, it should be understood that *family member* or *family member's*, can be substituted for *child* and/or *child's*.

- Please note that for the purposes of this workbook, the phrase "in their affirmed gender" is used more often. However, it is understood that some individuals can prefer to use the phrase "as their affirmed gender." Acknowledging that language related to gender in TGNB communities is continuously evolving and quite expansive, readers should feel free to substitute whichever one of these phrases is more comfortable for them.

- The words and/or phrases *transition, the transition, in transition, transition process*, and *transitioning* shall be used throughout the workbook and will be both interchangeable with and refer to, but not limited to, the phrases gender questioning and questioning their gender, and may also be part of the gender-affirming process for those children who identify as transgender, trans-identified, in transition, non-binary, gender non-binary, questioning, gender questioning, questioning their gender, genderqueer, gender fluid, gender diverse, gender expansive, gender creative, gender nonconforming, intersex, TGD, TGNB, TGNC, and on the transgender spectrum.

- In reference to pronouns: *they/them/their* will be used as a singular pronoun throughout the workbook, as well as *he/him/his* and *she/her/hers*.

- All the names in the Sampler Shares section have been changed to preserve the anonymity of those who have generously and candidly offered to share their experiences and thoughts. Whenever possible, the gender and sexuality of the contributor has also been kept private in order to ensure an extra layer of confidentiality. However, if names or initials are used, they are altered to conceal the actual identities, names, and initials of those who participated, as well as those of their family members. The first initial is a letter I assigned to those who responded to the questions and the second letter represents P (parent), S (sibling), and G (grandparent). In addition, this clarification of terms should be noted and will be referred to within the workbook, especially in the Sampler Shares section: Assigned Female At Birth (AFAB) and Assigned Male At Birth (AMAB). Moreover, whenever the pronouns she/her/hers, he/him/his, and they/them/their appear in the Sampler Shares section, they will align with the pronouns the child prefers to use at the moment the responses were submitted but they may change over time. To clarify, the views and thoughts of those who participated in the Sampler Shares section are meant to express diverse opinions of various parents and other family members, but may not necessarily all be in alignment with the author's views or thoughts.

- For some children and adults, the transition process continues throughout their lifetime; for others, the transition is considered over once all the social and/or medical interventions desired are completed. For the parent/s and/or other family members, the duration of the transition process of their child can be connected to one of these two circumstances or based on the period when the major focus of their time is concentrated on the transition, in its varied forms. Many parents I know or who have attended my workshops refer to their relationship with their child in terms of before, during, and after the transition or the time it took to navigate their child's affirmed gender, referring to "after" as the period when the topic of the transition is no longer front and center on a daily basis. Therefore, some of the questions that include periods of time may use the phrase "before, during, and after." You may choose to respond in terms of this sequencing or elect to answer only in terms of "before and during." This disclaimer is included to acknowledge and honor those for whom the transitioning period is never over; for whom the term "after" may never apply.

· It is recognized that more than one person in the family can identify as, but not limited to, transgender, trans-identified, in transition, gender non-binary, non-binary, questioning, gender questioning, questioning their gender, genderqueer, gender fluid, gender diverse, gender expansive, gender creative, gender nonconforming, intersex, TGD, TGNB, TGNC, and on the transgender spectrum. Though recognizing this, the workbook is meant to help you focus on your feelings and thoughts only from the point of view as a parent and/or family member whose child or relative is exploring living in their affirmed gender.

· The workbook is offered to give voice from the perspective of the parent/s and other family members who are related to a child in the family who is affirming their gender. It is intended to help anyone who is searching for a reflective resource with regard to any aspect of their child's social or medical transition as they are, but not limited to, in transition, having transitioned, questioning their gender, identifying as non-binary, or are living in their affirmed gender.

· In reference to the stage your child is at this moment, this workbook is intended to be useful for those parents and other family members whose child or relative is beginning any aspect of the transition process, is questioning their gender, or is discovering what they need to feel whole in relation to their affirmed gender. The focus of most of the vignettes, questions, tools, and exercises contained within this workbook is for those parents and other family members before and during the transition process. However, several of my workshop attendees have expressed that the workbook could be useful for those parents and other family members who still need to navigate their own journey post any medical or social aspects of their child's transition or gender questioning.

· LGBTQ (lesbian, gay, bisexual, transgender, queer, or questioning), LGBTQ+ (lesbian, gay, bisexual, transgender, queer, or questioning plus others), and LGBTQQIA+ (lesbian, gay, bisexual, transgender, queer, questioning, intersex, allies, plus others), or other variations, will be used as inclusive terms for anyone who identifies on the continuum; the term used is never meant to exclude or offend any person or group that prefers one variation of this umbrella term over another. Its usage will reflect the details of the story or something specific to the passage it is contained within. The key is that the parents and other family members' needs, best interests, and perspectives are the focus in each and every instance, in addition to honoring the child's need to live in their affirmed gender.

- *This book does not provide medical or legal advice.* The information contained in this book is for informational purposes only. The opinions expressed in this book are those of the author, and any ideas or suggestions contained in the book are based solely on the author's experiences. This book is not intended to be a substitute for professional medical, mental health, or legal advice. Always seek the advice of your physician or other qualified healthcare/mental healthcare provider with any questions you may have regarding a medical condition, diagnosis, or treatment and before undertaking a new healthcare regimen, and never disregard professional medical advice or delay seeking it because of something you have read in this book. In addition, you should seek the advice of legal counsel familiar with the subject matter and authorized to practice in your jurisdiction before acting or relying on the opinions and information presented in this book.

Chapter 1

YOUR PRIVATE SPACE: AN INTRODUCTION

Did you have a boy or a girl? How many times has this question been asked once someone finds out that a baby is born? In many cultures, it is one of the major questions posed to parents and other family members, along with: What's the baby's name? How much does the baby weigh? How long is the baby? Is everyone healthy? It is quite clear that the baby's visible genitalia determine the child's gender assigned at birth and, more often than not, a massive amount of the child's future will be based on this assumption. The baby's gender will become of such central importance to some that reveal parties, extravagant events, particular colored clothing, bedroom decor, and baby showers will all be dictated by this fact. In addition, an abundance of other milestones will be affected and categorized for the lifetime of the child. Often this destiny begins when a sonogram is performed and is celebrated while the child is still in utero! This mere labeling, which is influenced by the child's gender assigned at birth, even prior to meeting the baby, can have a major impact on a parent's reaction when and if they learn that their child is now identifying as transgender, non-binary, and/or is questioning their gender. For some parents, love and care for their child's well-being will immediately triumph over the pressures that society can easily impose on them based on cultural constraints; total acceptance will occur without any hesitation. For other parents, the knowledge of their child's need to question their gender is confusing and concerning. In a multitude of instances, even the most supportive parent and vocal advocate of their child's needs may have to process specific aspects of their child's gender journey, for they may discover that some changes are difficult for them to absorb. It is not uncommon for one family member to feel one way about the transition, while another may feel quite differently. This disparity is likely to create stress within the family. The varied possibilities of a parent's stance in relation to their child's transition can be overwhelming, and more than one internal response may be present within the same family member immediately or over time.

When a child in the family begins to socially and/or medically transition, the dynamics of the family unit can start to shift. For certain family members, this change may affect their daily life in a peripheral manner, but for others in the same family unit, it can feel as if their world is turning upside down. Yet, for some families, very little may be affected other than the way a child is verbally addressed and presents. We all enter and experience our place in a family differently, and the relationship we have with the one in transition can influence our reaction to such changes. As a result, family members may not be aligned or in agreement. Furthermore, the role that the child who is in transition represents within the family circle may play a major part in the way each family member approaches the possible shifts. In reality, the different ways in which this all affects and feels for everyone in the family need to be honored and respected in a compassionate manner. It must be stated that there can be specific cultural and religious practices where publicly acknowledging a child's need to live in their affirmed gender can cause them and/or other family members grave harm and create an unsafe environment for all within their family. However, if a parent feels or thinks they cannot support their child's transition, for whatever reason, this does not mean they should try to prevent their child from exploring their own needs and ability to move towards living their authentic life. Should this be the case, it is vital that someone else takes the initiative by coming to the child's aid. The lack of this assistance can have dire consequences for all involved.

The histories within the family unit and what the transition represents are often invisible factors that can influence each family member's thoughts and feelings in reference to a child's transition. The experiences of the families in this book are based on Western culture. With this knowledge and having a clear understanding of the critical intersectionality of their multiple identities such as, but not limited to, race, religion, and socio-economic status, alongside cultural beliefs, parents and families will need to face an essential question: "How can I support my child's transition?" The answer to this question will provide significant meaning in the path a child may take and how they will proceed.

During my tenure of more than 30 years as an educator, I had the pleasure of teaching and working alongside students ranging in age from 3 to 18 years old. Throughout my career, I have experienced numerous students who did not identify as cisgender or had a diverse gender expression. I did not know if these children would eventually identify on the transgender spectrum or not. Many parents and other family members of these same children disclosed their thoughts and feelings to me about how their child was presenting privately at home. Some spoke of their own fear of being judged, and the shame of their child's secret life at home, or wanted to know if I had witnessed any of the same behaviors during the school day. Other parents simply asked for help and guidance on how to support their child's transition.

First and foremost, I am a teacher! Implicit in the title of educator was a need to protect and nurture those who were under my care. Ensuring a space that fostered tolerance and was free of judgment afforded my students an opportunity to grow from every situation they encountered and feel safe to be true to themselves. As a classroom teacher, my mission was to embrace the child as a whole and support all aspects of the child as an individual. Though my primary daily focus was on my students, the well-being and care of their family members, especially their parents, was always taken into consideration.

Parents and families are often the pioneering heroes behind the child who is transitioning. Most resources in reference to children focus on the child, whereas the materials for parents and families usually place emphasis on how the parent and other family members can help or support their child in a variety of ways. Rarely, if ever, is there space for the needs and feelings of the parents and other family members, either supportive and/or conflicted. Parents and families deserve a tool which offers them a private place to discover their own voices as they recognize how the possibility or actuality of the transition can alter their personal relationships and may impact legal and financial matters. After hearing the experiences of the parents and other family members, who bravely confided their concerns to me, I felt it was critical for me to provide a workbook that addressed the unique needs of parents and families as they navigated their child's gender exploration.

This workbook offers parents and families a structured safe space to explore their own necessities and wants, while enabling them to sort through all the chaos in a non-judgmental manner, as they navigate their own social and emotional transition in relation to their gender diverse child. As a result of the transition process, parents and families can be conflicted with the duality of being supportive of their trans-identified child and their own uncertainties. This resource was created for each family member, especially the parents, to unleash their often overlooked and unheard voices. Each member of the family deserves a private space where they can process and question the transition as they approach their own level of comfort and acceptance, on their own timeline. Providing this place can be one of the most valuable tools in helping a family member work through and embrace their own fears, doubts, and questions without judgment or stigma. There is more than one track to acceptance, regardless of the perspectives of those involved. This dignified and long overdue self-help workbook focuses on all the knowns and unknowns, while providing a personal tool for the parents and other family members to express these ambivalences.

Knowing this, whenever something occurs in a person's life, it is often suggested they ask themselves: What are the lessons embedded within the moment? This is always followed by self-reflection, which may enable the individual to draw their own conclusions. Sometimes adults need to become the student, so that they can navigate where they are going and the journey they will follow in order to move forward. This self-reflective workbook is born from what I have learned during my experience as an educator and is based on a multitude of requests from the parents and other family members who have taken my workshops at conferences throughout the world. I have compiled and incorporated all the questions, exercises, and tools that were used during these workshops, which families expressed were helpful. This resource has something for everyone, but not every part will be necessary for every family member. Take what you want and leave the rest behind. There are no rules or absolutes in reference to which exercises, tools, or questions to reply to, now or if ever. Respond to those that speak to you and your needs.

My greatest hope is that the journeys of the parents and other family members who have so bravely shared their stories with me will bring you a sense of comfort and the knowledge that you are not alone. Each voice is simply the path of a family member combined with the experiences of others and is not intended to suggest that your route will necessarily be the same as anyone else's. Moving through the transition may not be easy or painless for many parents and/or other family members. There can be moments when you may be embarrassed by your thoughts, actions, or words, but more often than not there will likely be far more times when you will be courageous, caring, protective, and present. In time, for many parents and other family members, more days will be filled with pure joy and celebrations, than not. There is no script or perfect way to travel this road as the passenger, while the child you love deeply finds their destiny during the transition process, as they question their gender.

Though the chapters are presented in the workbook in a specific sequence, it should be stressed that you may choose to use the chapters out of order, for each stands independent of the others. As part of your process, it does not matter the order in which you journal the questions you opt to answer from each chapter. You may not be ready for some portions, be past others, or you may be right on time for exactly what is being offered. Skip those that do not apply to you at this moment. Some questions may become more relevant later on during the transition, while others may never be necessary for you to answer. If you find a later chapter discusses a topic that addresses your needs, move on to that chapter. Besides a plethora of questions, this self-help workbook includes anecdotes, communication tools, exercises, glossaries, and graphic organizers. Each chapter will contain heartfelt passages based on the feedback I received from parents and families I interviewed, conversations that were had, and workshops I attended or led. The last chapter will provide a list of resources that are pertinent to parents and families.

Remember to take breaks when you feel it is necessary, and know that it is possible to return to any question when you feel refreshed. Make time to go for walks, watch television, or do other things that comfort you. Keep in mind that journaling can be very helpful, provide clarity, and be extremely cathartic; it can also be exhausting, foster ambivalence, and be extremely emotional. Knowing this, I have included a Deserving De-Stressing Delights section in each chapter, offering specific ways to refocus your energy from the transition and channel it towards finding a place of inner peace and calmness.

Do what feels right and helpful to you. You cannot make a mistake and your thoughts can remain private. No one ever needs to know your entries; however, if at some point you feel comfortable discussing your journaling with another family member, your child, a therapist, or spiritual mentor, the option is available to you. The routes you will take and even the wrong turns you feel you may have already experienced are all part of the journey that has led you to this workbook. In fact, the life lessons you hope to develop over time can be communicated to others or not; it is your choice. The purpose of this journal is simple: to create a space that feels safe, right, and nurturing for all parents and family members as your child maps out their own path throughout this process. The questions posed and the exercises and tools provided within this workbook are intended for you. The answers are already inside you, waiting to be written down!

CONTENTS OF THE CHAPTERS

1. Your Private Space: An Introduction

This chapter serves as an introduction that will explain the structure and purpose of the book. The workbook offers a place free of judgment for parents and families to journal their own journey and support their process throughout the transition. It is a self-reflective, private space where you can voice any of your thoughts, feelings, fears, concerns, worries, confusions, joys, and celebrations in writing. Each of the following chapters focuses on one or two critical aspects of the transition that may affect the life of the parents and families.

2. Unexpected and Confused

The specific questions, exercises, and vignettes focus on the possible initial fears, thoughts, worries, and concerns that parents and families can experience once they learn their child may transition. The tools are based on such topics as safety issues, the validity of the family roles, self-doubts, and the unknowns.

3. Who Are You?

This chapter confronts the challenges some parents and families experience when asked to address their child in a different way. These questions, exercises, tools, and vignettes refer to the possible need to use another pronoun or name, and are intended to help navigate when photos and memories of the past may no longer be celebrated or visible. This chapter helps parents and families learn how to incorporate the new pronoun and name within the family interactions, during moments of tension or unease, and at social events.

4. Grief May Apply

This chapter examines the reality that many parents and families express feelings of loss and find that a mourning period applies as they process their child's transition. This section focuses on the five stages of grief: denial, anger, bargaining, depression, and acceptance (Kübler-Ross & Kessler, 2005). Through reflective inquiry, parents and families explore how this might pertain to the relationship they experience as their child or relative transitions. As grieving can be a non-linear process, so the path may be for parents and families throughout the transition.

5. It Can Be a Foreign Language

This part of the workbook tackles the often overwhelming world of new vocabulary. Parents and families respond to questions and exercises that assist them in unraveling various label options and their own comfort level of implementation. Exercises are included to help parents and families understand appropriate ways and times to incorporate the nuances and culture of this new language.

6. Social and Medical Options: Sorting It Out!

This chapter explores some of the challenges of medical choices facing the parent and families with respect to the surgeries, preserving fertility, hormones, and the possible side effects of these options that the child in transition may need to consider in the future or desire to have access to now. This chapter will offer parents and families specific questions, exercises, tools, and vignettes to help them discover how to talk about these decisions as a family. It can assist them in determining what areas of the medical and/or social transition, if any, they may comfortably participate in and support when their child realizes they identify on the transgender spectrum. For example, family members will need to determine to what extent they will be involved with the medical options, such as attending doctor appointments or assisting with post-surgical recovery.

7. Friends and Family: Will They Stay, or Will They Go?

This chapter assists parents and families in dealing with the possible reactions of friends and other family members to the transition. Trying to understand what, when, why, and how to engage with others before or during the time when parents and families are themselves adjusting can be extremely overwhelming and isolating. In addition, specific tools assist parents and families to gauge their comfort or ability to discuss the transition with siblings or young relatives. Lastly, parents explore the possibility of joining new social circles or creating a family of choice should those who are in their life not be supportive.

8. Work: In or Out?

This chapter explores the importance of when, why, or, indeed, if one shares the transition with employers and co-workers. It provides a reflective space to discover whether parents and families elect to work with human resources personnel at their workplace and to gain an understanding of what legal rights they have at work. Financial security and medical insurance policies at work can become compromised when parents and families may need to disclose that their child is transgender, in order to access medical insurance for hormones and/or surgery, as well as possibly requesting time away from their job.

9. Insurances, Gender Marker, and Documents... Oh My!

The chapter discusses the options that some parents and families may need to investigate with respect to legally changing their gender marker and/or legal name. Altering your child's name and/or gender on birth certificates, passports, financial and health insurance policies, bank accounts/trusts, social security card, school forms, school/college diplomas, and transcripts can be an exhausting job. These suggestions for parents and families offer a way to cope with the overwhelming reality of all these changes. Each state and country often has its own laws and policies; therefore, parents and families' best approach to these time-consuming undertakings must be carefully thought through as their child transitions.

10. Privilege: Loss or Gain?

This chapter explores how one's privilege is or has been affected through the intersections of patriarchy, misogyny, racism, transphobia, feminism, and male privilege. Will parents, their child, and other family members feel a loss of equality, such as being invited to specific social events, or being offered possible future opportunities? In contrast, will parents, their child, and other family members experience positive gains such as an increase of physical safety due to the transition? In addition, will there be sports team involvement, club memberships, and gendered parties that will foster an inherent loss or gain of participation? Learning how to accept these potential changes can positively impact parents, their child, and other family members' self-worth and confidence on many levels.

11. Let's Talk About Finding a Therapist

Many times, concerns can be alleviated if parents and families connect with a knowledgeable and experienced therapist. For some, the search for an appropriate therapist can be time-consuming and/or critical. Through journaling their needs and the guided support provided by the tools offered in this workbook, parents and other family members can learn how to find the path that is best for them.

12. The World of Schools

This chapter focuses on the role school policies play in the life of a child who is exploring their gender identity and expression. Parents and families will learn in what manner they can intervene when school practices negatively affect the daily life of their child, as they move towards living in their affirmed gender. Parents and families will learn means to determine which guidelines are acceptable throughout their child's transition and how to approach school district personnel to promote the safety of their child while at school. By journaling, parents and families are given tools to help navigate procedures that accommodate and communicate their child's personal needs in the classroom in order to support the process as their child transitions and/or affirms their gender.

13. Celebrations Come in Different Sizes

This chapter assists parents and families in understanding how they can move forward as the child's transition may evolve. The answer to this inquiry can be fluid and vary from day to day, month to month, and year to year. In addition, this chapter addresses the topic of how parents and families can respond, should they be asked inappropriate questions by others. Whether your child fully transitions or not, the process deserves to be acknowledged and celebrated by those parents and other family members who have helped their child embrace where they now identify on the transgender spectrum.

14. Where Are You Now?

This chapter reflects on the pulse of parents and other family members' journey by asking them to re-evaluate, honestly and continuously, their thoughts, feelings, concerns, worries, and confusions. The parents and other family members are asked to focus on their future and examine how they have transitioned due to their child's transition. Additional questions, exercises, and vignettes are included for the child, parents, and other family members in order to help them communicate openly as a family and live a life that embraces the transition.

15. You Are Not Alone (Resources, Glossary, and Answer Keys)

The last chapter offers articles, books, websites, support groups, and more that focus on the needs of parents and families. It will also include all of the answer keys for Chapter 5.

SET-UP

Each chapter contains most, if not all, of these sections:

1. Anecdotal Affirmations

Poetic affirmations appear throughout each chapter and were created for you. They are meant to inspire, comfort, and empower you when you need them most. Their presence is intended to set the tone and intention before you begin the chapter. They are meant to embrace you in any way that soothes your heart. The affirmations may be used as a springboard for writing or as a conversation starter with someone else.

2. Vital Vignettes

These vital vignettes serve as an introduction to the questions. The vignettes are included to help you gain some insight from the unknowns that parents and other family members have navigated as their child's transition unfolded. Providing these passages as a precursor to the questions is meant to offer reflective thoughts of those who freely, but anonymously, shared their stories with me during the interviews and workshops that I have led and attended. They represent some of the experiences parents and other family members have provided in hopes of having pieces of their journeys told.

3. Graphics Galore

Most chapters in this book contain graphic organizers, which can be used to assist you in visually expressing your thoughts without having to write them in a narrative format. In order to serve you best, they may be placed in a different order within each chapter. Every graphic organizer can be used for various purposes, but if you find one type works best for you, use it as often as you like.

Bar Graph is an image that can be viewed to observe the ranking of data, which is translated into bar-like structures to display findings on a topic or question. Through illustrations of the gathered information, the user can evaluate the comparison of the bars to reach their own conclusions in reference to a single topic or question. This graphic organizer encourages you to assess the importance or value of these topics, independently of other topics, based on a personal rating system of 1–10. In contrast to the Pie Graph graphic organizer—though both organizers enable the user to view topics in comparison with the others—the bars of the Bar Graph do not need to add up to 100 or 100 percent.

Box is a format for notes or can be used as a place to store information connected to one topic or subject, which compartmentalizes or assesses a situation. It is visually comprised of multiple boxes to create a framework.

Pie Graph is a visual representation of percentage showing the comparison of various categories based on a single subject, question, or circumstance in the shape of a pie. Some think of it as a pizza pie with each slice standing for a different component of the topic. The total composition of all the parts is summed to 100 or 100 percent. Each part or section is assigned a percentage based on its user's point of view. The goal is to exhibit a quick way to prioritize or place a value on every critical factor that affects the outcome of the subject, question, or circumstance in relation to the other topics.

Splash should be imagined as if you took a liquid, such as water or paint, and splattered it on a blank canvas. It is intended to let your juices flow as you brainstorm with no judgment or organizational care. Respond to the statement or inquiry with a word or short phrase and quickly splatter your reply. By creatively splashing words and short phrases, attempt to express your responses randomly by scattering them on paper. When you have completed the graphic organizer, it should almost look as if you created a canvas of words by squirting them on the page. It encourages you to elicit a reaction that is visceral and has a desire to be released on paper.

T-Chart can be used to show different perspectives in relation to the same topic or question. There are many versions of this graphic organizer that can host two, three, or more columns. The two-column graphic usually lists or states two aspects of a problem, unknown, or dilemma. A three-column T-Chart format can assist the user in deciding by comparing and contrasting the positive, negative, and equal/neutral (+/−/=) options in response to an inquiry, conflict, or situation. Another variation is KWL, which houses what a person "Knows," "Wants to know or learn," and then does "Learn."

Timeline is sequential and helps record the order or timing of a situation or event that has occurred or will occur. Though not used in its traditional formatting, it assists in creating a tentative time frame to complete a current or future task that may be time sensitive with numerous factors or parts.

Venn Diagram is a comparison graphic organizer that aids in comparing and contrasting a situation or an inquiry. Once a question is posed, the upper left ring (#1) of the connecting circles is filled in with the reader's response. Then the upper right ring (#2) of the diagram is completed with the responses of the child. The lowest central ring (#3) is to be filled in with a third family member's response. The next step is to notice if any of the replies overlap between any two of the individuals from any two rings (#1 with #2, #2 with #3, and #3 with #1) and then remove these responses from the rings and place them into the overlapping location to easily view the common responses. This step should occur three times based on the numbers stated in the previous sentence. Once this is completed, the last step is to remove any common responses from all three new overlapping portions, #4, #5, and #6, and fill in any common responses in the interlocking central overlapping portion (#7) of the Venn Diagram based on all three responses. To further clarify, the overlapping of #1 and #2 is #4, the overlapping of #1 and #3 is #5, the overlapping of #2 and

#3 is #6, and the overlapping of #4, #5, and #6 is #7. The outcome is visually seeing where the responders agree and where they differ.

Webs are often described as visually presenting a topic and its subtopics in the way that a spider's web scatters branch-like patterns, which generate from a central source. Every part of the growing web is connected to an initial word or phrase. Once the beginning word or phrase is placed in the center position, the user's associated words or phrases are placed in the outer connecting circles in response to the central statement. This pattern continues until the web is completed or the response to the question or statement is personally finished.

4. Reflective Responses

There are several ways you can partake in the questions posed in this workbook, but ultimately the hope is for you to use them in the manner that works best for your needs. Some individuals may only choose to write their responses to a select group of questions in each chapter, whereas others may reply to each and every question. You may even elect to repeat this process more than once throughout the transition process. Each chapter poses questions that are intended to help you discover where you stand with regard to processing the transition and what is comfortable for you. Your responses may remain the same for a long period of time or they may evolve as you explore your options and have time to digest all that you are experiencing and feeling. Each and every path has its own value and purpose.

5. Deserving De-Stressing Delights

Each chapter offers structured ways to release any stress from the transition and direct your energy towards de-stressing and rewarding yourself in a loving and tender manner. Intentionally allowing time to simply stop, breathe, and rest from journaling and processing is essential for your well-being. This section reminds you to carve out space to engage in activities that restore and rejuvenate you through self-care, which will help you feel pampered and nurtured.

6. Empathy-Embracing Exercises

This exercise is meant to help you gain an awareness of the importance of speaking your truth, regardless of the consequences. It is intended to aid in diminishing your own possible pain and confusion while strengthening your acceptance level, as your child transitions or considers doing so. Perhaps thinking of a private and difficult experience from your past or in the present will create a deeper understanding of the emotional process your child may be experiencing. Its presence in the workbook is to encourage you to view the transition through the lens of your child, while honoring your needs and helping to better prepare you for the process.

7. Sampler Shares

These samplers create a space where some parents and other family members share their own responses to questions posed in this workbook. All participants' names have been changed to respect the privacy of parents, their child, and other family members. The responses are included simply to open your mind to a variety of ways others approached the writing based on their situation. Their replies are placed at the end of the chapter, but please keep in mind that if these testimonials become intrusive or prevent your own process from evolving, feel free to refer to them at a later time or not at all. However, some parents and other family members found the guidance of these "Sampler Shares" especially helpful when they had a block as they were journaling or were unsure that the question was one they wanted to answer. There are no absolutes when using this workbook, only offerings to help you gain a greater understanding of your own needs and wishes.

8. Communication Corner

This exercise is also presented in the form of a graphic organizer. Through the use of a list of these questions, parents, their child, and other family members will be given a tool that supports communication within the family circle. Parents, their child, and other family members are invited to initiate a discussion in relation to the transition, when comfortable, by sharing their thoughts and concerns with their child and other family members through an open dialogue. The questions posed in this section are intended to help start the discussion. Many families may find comfort in doing this exercise as they engage in these private and personal conversations.

QUESTION #1

Before you proceed to Chapter 2, I invite you to respond to the following question:

What do you hope or expect to learn or gain from reading and journaling in this workbook?

....

....

....

....

....

....

....

....

....

....

....

....

....

....

....

UNEXPECTED AND CONFUSED

VITAL VIGNETTE

For some parents, finding out your child identifies as transgender, non-binary, and/or is questioning their gender can be a time celebrated with prideful excitement and a welcome relief. This awareness can create a special bond with your child and an opportunity to embrace all that is to come in the future. For others, being told that your child is transgender, identifies as non-binary, and/or is questioning their gender, especially when you were unaware of this fact and never expected the possibility, can be initially confusing, induce worry, and foster concerns. Sometimes, a parent can experience a combination of all of these emotions, even if they are accepting and supportive. It is critical that you do not judge your response to the information you have been told, but rather reflect on all of the thoughts that are in your mind and heart. Every parent brings their own history to this realization and may react or internalize this knowledge in a way that is unique to their own circumstance. There is space enough for everyone's journey and for every emotion that arises! Some parents need time to process in solitude, while others can have a desire to research and gather as much information as possible. Some may want to discuss a few of the details with their child, whereas others may find it more suitable to process this new reality with another family member, a close friend, spiritual mentor, or therapist. The challenge, if any, is deciding which choice works best for you.

> ANECDOTAL AFFIRMATION
>
> *I don't understand,*
> *How did I*
> *Not know?*

While some parents will adjust quickly without any inner turmoil and eagerly embrace these changes on day one, others may not. Each reaction must be honored and respected. Although controversial, your need to process this news may not be aligned with the wishes of your child. As a result, this can cause a great deal of conflict within these relationships. Each person's needs must be considered, communicated, and valued. Sometimes outside professionals can play a critical role in the next steps to assist each person as they find their own voice. Ideally, those involved in the transition will be in sync and have enough clarity to reach a consensus that is acceptable and in the best interest of the child. However, the truth is that, in some cases, this process can be extremely painful for parents, and even for the child as they seek to feel whole.

Accepting what your child is telling or showing you can create a great inner struggle for some or be a very natural flow for others. For some parents, though the exploration is an easy passage, obvious and painless, certain aspects of the transition may be or become overwhelming, filled with levels of internal conflict.

At times, some parents can be at odds with what to do if family members or others in their life feel they, as parents, should not support their child's transition. If this happens, and it sometimes does, many parents often make the decision to choose the needs of their child above their own and those family members who do not validate the transition. This may be a case of life or death for some children, and the effects of not supporting your child, as well as not being their advocate, can result in consequences that can be tragic for many children and families.

For those parents who clearly identify themselves as being at ease with learning that their child is transgender (trans), you may choose to skip certain exercises and not answer or complete every option offered in this workbook. You may be able to process the transition in a way that is not confusing, worrisome, or concerning. Perhaps your mindset is due to the geographic area you live in, the history you have experienced within the LGBTQ+ community, or the time period in which you have grown up. Maybe your experiences have enabled your child's transition to be one that is not filled with questions or opposition from you. If this is the case, simply use this journal as a tool to assist you in housing your written thoughts, and respond to whichever questions and exercises that best serve your needs.

For the portion of those parents who identify themselves as confused, worried, and concerned with learning of the transition, this workbook can be a major form of support at a time when you can no longer recognize yourself and/or your family dynamics, your own needs, and what your next steps may be in the near future. Discovering anything unexpected can be difficult, especially when you have come from an environment where the word "transgender" was not a part of your vocabulary. Trying to sort out all of the unknowns and hundreds of questions that may be racing in your mind can baffle and numb the thought and language processes of even the most insightful and articulate individual, within a very short span of time. As challenging as life may be, once you are told this information, it can be extremely empowering and helpful to write down everything that is happening. Simply documenting the when, how, and what of a situation enables you to process all you are experiencing and feeling. Later, when you are able to think more clearly and express your feelings in words, having a detailed diary of your thoughts, fears, or questions may foster the clarity that, in time, will return once again. The frenetic racing of thoughts can be never ending. Documenting when and how you found out your child is trans can help you to recall the considerations and feelings that were going through your mind as you received the information.

Journaling the specifics of your journey may also be useful for clarity, should you choose to relay your process to a therapist or confidant in the future. Some people are unsure of how they feel when realizing their child is trans. It is recommended that you answer what you can, but to pace yourself. It is not a test and there is no right or wrong answer. Feel free to peruse other sections or chapters in this workbook at any time. You are in charge of how to navigate this journey of exploration in the hope of discovering how to fulfill your needs. In truth, as you may be figuring this all out, your previous life commitments and the transition process are occurring simultaneously. This fact may compound your daily life. Carve out time and a place to journal about your confusions, fears, and thoughts in a safe space, and remember to record your celebrations, hopes, and progress. These tools are for all those who have learned their child is now trans-identified, and will aid in leading them to live in their affirmed gender. Certain questions within this workbook may hold more significance or feel more relevant than others. Make this resource work for you, as you navigate your own course of understanding!

GRAPHICS GALORE

Splash

Can you jot down all the emotions you feel or felt when you learned about your child's need to transition? By creatively splashing words and short phrases, quickly attempt to express your answers randomly with as many responses as possible scattered on the paper. (Examples: angry, very content, scared.)

GRAPHICS GALORE

Web

Although the transition may be unexpected and confusing, now that you know, this is a space for you to share the range of emotions you are experiencing. Exploring positive and exciting thoughts, as well as those that are baffling, can be extremely cathartic. Select one concerning thought or celebratory feeling and write it down in the center of the web. Then branch out and write the specific thoughts in the outer circles, which connect and relate to the central emotion.

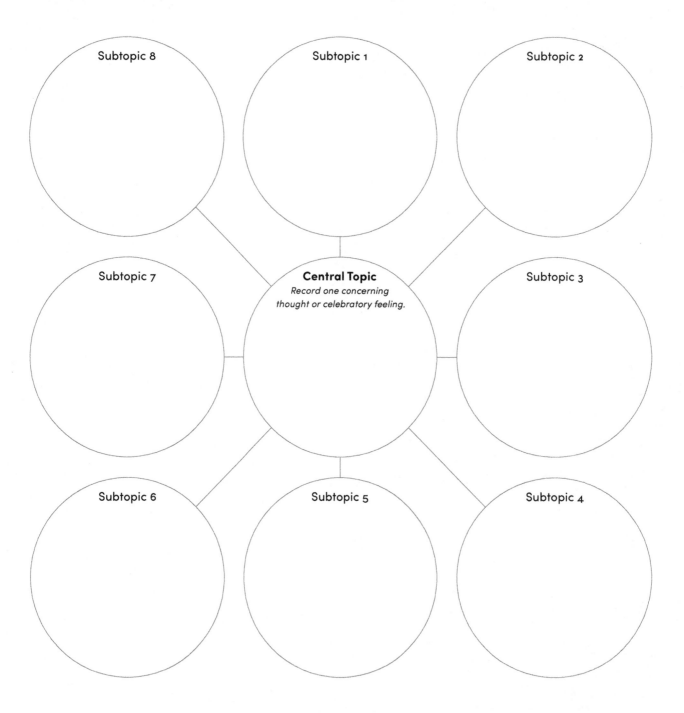

REFLECTIVE RESPONSES

1. How and when did you discover your child was trans?

   ....

   ....

   ....

2. What do you think it meant when your child told you they needed to transition?

   ....

   ....

   ....

3. How do you feel about the possibility or reality of your child transitioning?

   ....

   ....

   ....

4. Now that you think about it, can you recall any situation, event, activity, or moment that might have indicated that your child would need to transition?

   ....

   ....

   ....

5. If your child transitions, how do you believe your life will remain the same and/or be different?

   ....

   ....

   ....

6. Are there any concerns going through your mind about the possibility or perhaps reality that your child or family member may transition, and if so, what are they?

. . . .

. . . .

. . . .

7. Do you fear that your child and other family members will not be allowed around other children, now that your child is trans, and if so, what are they?

. . . .

. . . .

. . . .

8. What are your concerns, if any, should your child's school become aware that they are trans?

. . . .

. . . .

. . . .

9. How do you plan on responding if anyone rejects your child for transitioning?

. . . .

. . . .

. . . .

10. Do you feel it is appropriate to ask your child if it is necessary for them to transition now, if they can delay the process, or if it is possible for them never to transition? Why or why not?

. . . .

. . . .

. . . .

11. What concerns can you share with your child in relation to the transition?

....

....

....

12. What concerns can you share with others in relation to the transition?

....

....

....

13. What concerns can you not share with your child in relation to the transition?

....

....

....

14. What concerns can you not share with others in relation to the transition?

....

....

....

15. What can or should you do if you resent your child because of their need to transition?

....

....

....

16. How can you help and show support for your child as they are transitioning?

....

....

....

17. What safety issues do you envision for your child before, during, and after they transition, especially when using public bathrooms, at the home of others, attending school, or on the street?

....

....

....

18. What do you need to do to ensure that both of you and other family members are safe at your home, at the home of others, and on the street throughout the transition, while in the company of your child?

....

....

....

19. How do you feel about your child dressing in their gender-affirming clothing?

....

....

....

20. How do you think the transition will affect or change your relationship with your child?

....

....

....

21. How do you think the transition will affect or change your relationship with others?

....

....

....

22. How do you feel your expectations of your child will be affected or change throughout their transition?

....

....

....

23. What do you think your parental options are if your child begins to socially transition?

....

....

....

24. What do you think your parental options are if your child begins to investigate any part of medically transitioning?

....

....

....

25. How much are you willing to be a part of your child's transition process?

....

....

....

26. How do you think your family living conditions will be affected and/or changed throughout the transition?

. . . .

. . . .

. . . .

27. How do you think you will feel if others are able to or not able to tell that your child is trans?

. . . .

. . . .

. . . .

28. What can you do to take care of yourself while much focus is now on your child, and as the other demands of life also consume your time?

. . . .

. . . .

. . . .

29. Do you believe your child will request to change their name and/or pronoun that they were assigned at birth and how do you think this will affect you emotionally?

. . . .

. . . .

. . . .

30. Do you think there are other parents whose child is going through this type of transition? If so, will you try to find them and how will you begin this process?

. . . .

. . . .

. . . .

GRAPHICS GALORE

Venn Diagram

What are five of your greatest concerns in regard to the transition and what are they for your child and/ or other family members? It is helpful to explore whether you share any of the same concerns in order to address them. It is equally important to understand which concerns your child and the other family members need to discuss or are thinking about at this present time.

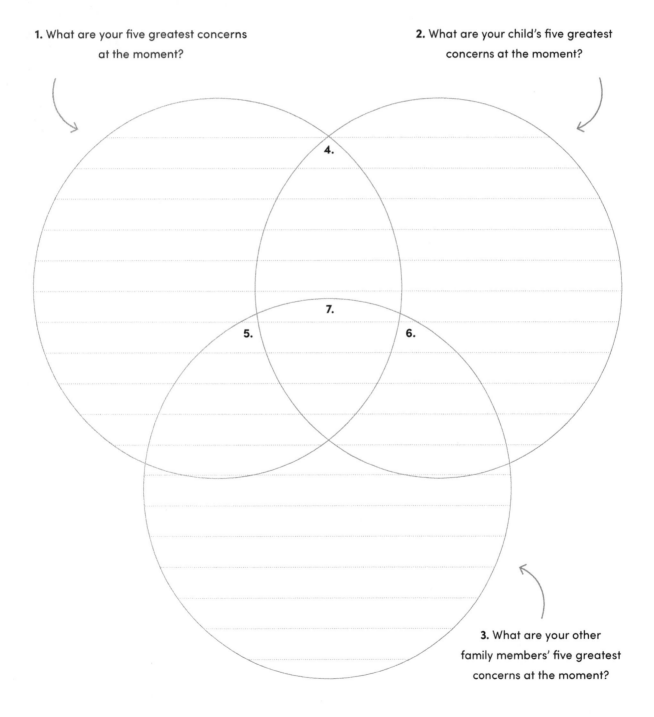

1. What are your five greatest concerns at the moment?

2. What are your child's five greatest concerns at the moment?

4.

7.

5.

6.

3. What are your other family members' five greatest concerns at the moment?

GRAPHICS GALORE

T-Chart

Write down what you now *know* about the transitioning process, then list what you want to *know* about the transition process. Continue filling in the chart as you *learn* the answers to the wants in relation to the transition process.

Know	Want	Learn

DESERVING DE-STRESSING DELIGHT

Meditation

Relaxing your mind and body at a time of stress can be very helpful in providing clarity and calmness. Many people find meditation in any form to be extremely comforting to quiet some of their concerns and fears in relation to the transition. These are a few ways others found solace and tranquility. Some days walking in an active or loud area for a period of time can awaken the sensory sights and sounds around you to assist with blocking out all the noise in your head, enabling you to just be an observer of your environment. Horns beeping, doors slamming, and people talking can become music to your ears and surprisingly soothing.

> ANECDOTAL AFFIRMATION
> *Being scared*
> *Is not knowing*
> *The answers*
> *To all of my questions.*

In contrast, others may adore the beauty and solitude of the beach. For many people, hearing the ocean and looking at the sunset can offer a feeling of peace as they sort things out. Sometimes you may need a place to cry alone and may not even realize how cathartic it can be to listen to the water and appreciate nature. For some, hiking and walking in the woods or taking a stroll on the first snowy day brought them much tranquility. Still others have shared that they found peace and comfort attending support groups, religious services, or speaking with a spiritual mentor quite comforting. If you want a more structured approach to practice stillness, you can attend a meditation class.

Listening to a guided audiotape of peaceful music or participating in a gentle yoga class can also feel relaxing. These experiences may allow you to be passive as you receive the directed suggestions. It could be soothing to close your eyes and embrace the gentleness of the harmonious sounds. If walking or being guided by an outside entity do not seem to be what you need, you may seek out an activity that is both repetitive and mindless, such as doing a jigsaw puzzle or a word search, or simply coloring or sketching. Most de-stressing for some is taking a mini-nap. You could set an alarm for five or ten minutes and close your eyes as you sit in a chair or lie on a bed. Often, repeating a mantra or imagining yourself in a specific place that you love and just letting yourself breathe will reduce tension. When the time is up, you can feel renewed and ready to face the world of the unfamiliar!

Journal your reaction to this Deserving De-Stressing Delight.

. . . .

. . . .

. . . .

GRAPHICS GALORE

Timeline

Many parents wish they had kept a log of all the critical happenings that occurred throughout the transition process, but did not. This tool can help you keep a record of these moments as time goes by. Complete the timeline as you find out different and relevant pieces of information about the transition. You may need or choose to use this information to discuss these events with a therapist, for medical needs, or for your own point of reference. Examples to record: when you may have realized that transitioning was possibly necessary; when you might have been told of the need for social or medical changes; when your child began using a different bathroom; when your child began to wear clothing of their affirmed gender; when you chose to discuss the transition with a specific person.

Date:	What happened?	People involved?
Date:	What happened?	People involved?
Date:	What happened?	People involved?
Date:	What happened?	People involved?
Date:	What happened?	People involved?
Date:	What happened?	People involved?

GRAPHICS GALORE

Box

The uncertainties of what it means to raise a trans child can be abundant and endless for some parents, especially when it is all so new. List any uncertainties that are overwhelming your mind. Writing them down can help you release some anxiety and gain some power over your life. Some parents may choose to share these thoughts with their child, other family members, or someone else. That choice is yours! (You may prefer to focus more on celebratory thoughts and/or feelings, too.)

1	2	3	4	5
6	7	8	9	10
11	12	13	14	15
16	17	18	19	20
21	22	23	24	25
26	27	28	29	30

EMPATHY-EMBRACING EXERCISE

Realizing that every experience you have in life has the potential to prepare you for the next challenge or venture that presents itself to you is empowering. Knowing you have survived and made it through a difficult or overwhelming situation fosters positive hope.

Have you experienced anything else in your life, other than the transition, that has been unexpected and confusing in any way? If so, what has it been and how did you cope, address, or handle this information?

ANECDOTAL AFFIRMATION

What scares me most?
What worries me most?
How can I take care of we?
How can I take care of me?

GRAPHICS GALORE

Bar Graph

To what degree do these concerns and related topics matter to you? Based on a scale from 1 to 10, with 1 being the lowest and 10 being the highest, color or shade in your response. This visual will illustrate where your greatest concerns lie and can be used as a tool to help you communicate your thoughts with your child and/or other family members, therapist, spiritual mentor, or for your own personal understanding. The bar graph results can vary as your child's transition progresses and/or your thoughts may shift.

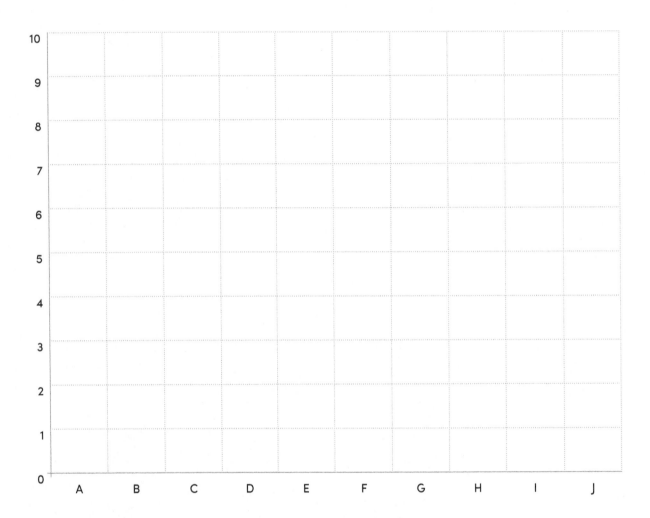

Use these ideas to fill in the bar graph or feel free to create your own!

A. Your child's safety/presence at school.

B. Your child's safety/presence in public.

C. Your family's safety/presence in public when with your child.

D. Your child's social transition.

E. Your child's medical transition.

F. Your child's physical/mental health.

G. Your financial costs and/or medical insurance in relation to the transition.

H. Your relationship with your child.

I. Your relationship with others in relation to the transition.

J. Your child's fertility preservation options.

GRAPHICS GALORE

Pie Graph

To what degree are these concerns and related topics important to you? Decide how significant these issues are to you in relation to each other. Place the number that corresponds with a suggested topic within as many slices of the pie that convey how each one matters to you. Only one number should be placed in each slice. You do not need to use all the issues, but do fill in all the slices. Feel free to create your own topics and assign them their own number.

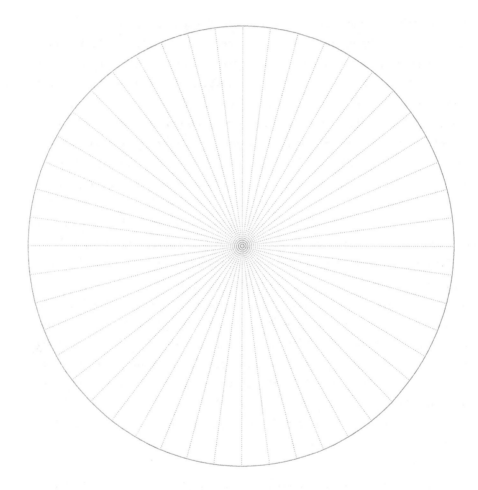

1. Your child's safety/presence at school.

2. Your child's safety/presence in public.

3. Your family's safety/presence in public when with your child.

4. Your child's social transition.

5. Your child's medical transition.

6. Your child's physical/mental health.

7. Your financial costs and/or medical insurance in relation to the transition.

8. Your relationship with your child.

9. Your relationship with others in relation to the transition.

10. Your child's fertility preservation options.

SAMPLER SHARES

All names have been changed to ensure anonymity in this section. The first initial designates an individual and the second initial identifies the relationship to the child, i.e. P = their parent, G = their grandparent, and S = their sibling.

Now that you think about it, can you recall any situation, event, activity, or moment that might have indicated that your child would need to transition?

AP: There was not just one moment but a series of moments that finally led us to realize that my child's gender identity was non-typical and needed to be explored. My daughter was around six years old when we noticed an affinity to Daphne on *Scooby Doo* that went past the norm. Assigned male at birth, she insisted on wearing everything purple to resemble Daphne and would put towels on her head to create long hair. Sometime around seven years old, we realized this was more than a phase of curiosity, but a deeper desire to not look like a boy. The day was Easter Sunday. As a family, we were getting dressed for our annual family gathering. We always got dressed up in our best. That day, my daughter refused to get dressed and she cried and carried on about looking ugly. Then I made the mistake of telling her that all the boys are going to look the same way. This is when she declared, "I don't want to look like the other boys." I already knew I had a fashion trendsetter, but this I didn't understand. Shortly after Easter, we attended our Spring Walk Through at school. We live down the block so it was a short walk to the school. At first, we sat around with all the other parents and listened to the teacher tell us about the projects the kids had been doing throughout the year. After some light snacks, we roamed the hall displays to see our kids' projects. We got to the self-portraits and much to our surprise we couldn't find her picture anywhere! We stood there looking for what felt like an eternity until my neighbor came upon us and pointed out my child's self-portrait. It was a picture of a beautiful little girl with long blonde hair, earrings, and lipstick! This is how she identified! Yay? Nay? We didn't know what to make of it. I know that we walked home a totally different family that night. *PARENT/CHILD: AMAB (Uses she/her/hers pronouns)*

BG: I didn't really think about it until he was about two. Everywhere we went, he wanted to wear glittery things, dresses, play dress-up in high heels and gowns, and so on. We'd offer to play and buy him a variety of toys, games, past-times that were gender neutral or typically male, but he'd shy away from those and beg for typically female ones. Of course, being a doting grandparent, I'd indulge but admittedly somewhat reluctantly. By age three, he'd beg to go into the dolls/girls' aisles of toy stores and just hang out there, playing "pretend" in his own personal heaven—usually beside his ideal doll palace. I thank God that now most stores maintain the aisles in a gender-neutral fashion or by age. These tendencies and preferences only grew exponentially over time, despite anyone's due-diligence efforts to offer other options. I have always believed that it is our responsibility as grandparents and parents to expose our children to many options in life, not just toys and clothes but also cultures, foods, religions, and even political points of view in order to prevent narrow-mindedness and to nurture true tolerance. I did the same with my own children. Yet to my shame, I felt no guilt offering typically male items to my daughter; however, I did feel a bit of embarrassment with my grandson's obsession with "female" items. I believe that may be due to American society's conditioning at this point that it's socially acceptable for girls to be/do/like anything they want, but the same still cannot be said for boys. It is taking far longer for our society to "catch up" with regard to boys being more "feminine." To more precisely answer the question, though, my grandchild didn't specifically state that he hated boys or wished he were a girl until about age five. He still uses he/him/his pronouns and I am not sure if this will change for him in the future. *GRANDPARENT/CHILD: AMAB (Uses he/him/his pronouns)*

GP: When my child turned three, I shared with my pediatrician that I was noticing more and more that he wanted to play with girls' stuff and didn't like it when he had a haircut. My daughter would say, "Girls don't cut their hair like this!" The doctor told me kids go through this phase and it would pass. When she turned four, we went back for a physical and the doctor asked how the gender issue was going and I told her it was progressing. The doctor thought it was worth discussing this with a psychologist. *PARENT/CHILD: AMAB (Uses she/her/hers pronouns)*

Are there any concerns going through your mind about the possibility or perhaps reality that your child (or family member) may transition, and if so, what are they?

HP: After my son came out to me on a ride back from visiting his sibling at college, I spent a lot of time just listening. My biggest initial concern was that he would have a much harder life than I would want for anyone. I worried about him being bullied, living in an area that wouldn't accept him in the future, and my biggest concern was what to do first. How could I support him as a parent, trying to not make it only about my feelings? I concluded that I could do this by being present for him as a person and not just as my child. *PARENT/CHILD: AFAB (Uses he/him/his pronouns)*

BG: To be 100 percent honest, everything frightens me about this while he's still a child. Unfortunately, it's mostly societal norms and others' reactions that I'm most concerned about, not our family's. I am so very grateful for the familial support, because we've all witnessed the naturalness of his development, and there's no arguing that that's simply who he is—and has always been. But society can be so cruel and intolerant. So, so very many believe that gender can be "shaped," and simply don't understand the magnitude of the implications of that on a growing child trying to make friends and be accepted for who he is. Despite so many efforts and legislation to protect LGBTQ rights and to prevent and stop bullying, I am so worried that the ones who overtly and covertly shame him will have a far greater, insidious impact on how he accepts himself. My prayer is that it doesn't lead to self-loathing, deep anger, and the potential of ultimately turning his back on society or himself in the most dark and dangerous of ways, as it has with others before him. While I want to cherish his childhood, and, like his parents, help arm him with enough self-love to combat this, a part of me can't wait until he's over all these hurdles and is a stronger and more positive adult. *GRANDPARENT/CHILD: AMAB (Uses he/him/his pronouns)*

CP: Honestly everything scared me. I was afraid of what medically transitioning meant for his health down the road. I was afraid of letting him out of my sight in public. I was afraid of his future. I was afraid of how people would react to and treat him. I was afraid of telling my family—I didn't know how they would react, I didn't know if they would accept my child as my son. Fortunately, in time, they all accepted him for who he is and love him just as much as they did before he began his transition. *PARENT/CHILD: AFAB (Uses he/him/his pronouns)*

COMMUNICATION CORNER

When you speak spontaneously out of anger or fear about the unknown, without thinking it through, you can sometimes regret the way you phrased your words or the tone you used to express your feelings. Rehearsing what you want to ask or discuss with your child, and other family members, can help you before you actually communicate your thoughts. This gives you a moment to reflect and pause before you converse about emotional topics. You may choose to practice asking these questions with a trusted friend, family member, spiritual mentor, or therapist first. Explain your thoughts and feelings about these statements to one another verbally or in writing. It is important to note that some families elected to only address one question or two, while others preferred to answer them all. In order to recall the questions you answered, simply highlight and/or circle the ones you addressed as a family, yet acknowledge that you may return to discuss the others in the future. Decide what feels best for two or more family members and begin the conversation. Do you, your child, and other family members answer these questions in the same way or differently? Discuss your responses to understand how all of you view the answers to the questions and make time to celebrate all you learn from being willing to communicate with each other.

> ANECDOTAL AFFIRMATION
>
> *We may not Know why, But we know Change is Going to happen!*

1. What do you think you will each need most from the other throughout the transition process?

   . . . .

   . . . .

2. How do you think the transition will affect each of your lives?

   . . . .

   . . . .

3. How do you each think the transition will affect your relationships with other family members?

   . . . .

   . . . .

4. How do you each think the transition will affect your relationships with friends?

   ....

   ....

5. How do you each think the transition will affect life at school and your role in relation to it?

   ....

   ....

6. How do you think the transition will affect your relationship with each other?

   ....

   ....

7. How do you think you will be able to keep everyone safe in public throughout the transition?

   ....

   ....

8. What changes, if any, do you believe you will need to be a part of your child's social transition?

   ....

   ....

9. What changes, if any, do you believe you will need to be a part of your child's medical transition?

   ....

   ....

10. Who are you comfortable and not comfortable discussing the transition with at this point?

   ....

   ....

Chapter 3

WHO ARE YOU?

VITAL VIGNETTE

Naming your child is one of the happiest and most exciting times of your life as a parent or future parent. Parents can spend an incredible amount of time selecting the perfect name for their anticipated child. There are parents who elect to continue a specific family

*Loss of
Pronouns,
Names,
Birthing,
Pictures,
Memories,
Loss of...*

name that has been passed down through generations. Also, names are considered based on tradition, culture, in honor of a relative or friend who is deceased, or in respect of a person who is living. When choosing a name, some parents consult baby-naming books which define what the name means in different cultures and ethnic groups, take informal polls, or excitedly recall the name they dreamed about when they were a child. Others have researched the names that are trending to either embrace them or opt for one that is more unusual. Some folks have made a conscious decision to see what their baby looks like at birth and then select a name which appears to suit the infant. Others are certain that they want to avoid a particular name, because it reminds them of something or someone they prefer not to associate with their child. Regardless of the reasoning or thought process, picking a child's name is often extremely vital, precious, and very emotional for a parent. With this knowledge, having your child express that they are changing their birth name, due to affirming, can cause anguish and sadness for a parent. In contrast, maintaining a name or pronoun given at birth, for a child who needs to live in their affirmed gender or reclaim their gender in a way that expresses who they are, can also be heartbreaking and painful, too.

It may seem insignificant to some, but a person's name is essentially intertwined with their identity. Perhaps this is why a large majority of transgender, non-binary, and gender questioning adults and children feel strongly about changing or adjusting the name they were assigned at birth. Each individual has their personal reasons and usually selects the name change, when desired, with extreme care. This selecting of a new name is not necessarily done as part of a team, and sometimes parents can be unaware that the name change will be requested or part of their child's transition. The surprise and unexpectedness of the need for a name change can be deeply saddening and very confusing for parents. However, some parents may view this as an opportunity to support their child's wishes and are quite encouraging with this aspect of the transition. Regardless, as with the rest of the process, whenever possible, this too could be something that your child considers including their parents in, as part of their transition process.

Even when parents are part of this aspect of the process and are digesting possible legal logistics, much needs to be ironed out involving the name change, such as the specifics of timing in relation to whom is told, when, and how. To add further adjustments, parents can be faced with the reality that their child desires to be addressed by a pronoun never used before. For some parents, this may seem like an extremely reasonable request, but to other parents this appeal can be overwhelming, confusing, and destabilizing. It may be understandable that your child wants their pronoun to match their affirmed gender; however, the acceptance and learning curve for this can be quite difficult for parents and could take a while to grasp. Even the most embracing parents may require time to adjust to the request of referring to their child using the new personal pronoun and a new name. The possible name and pronoun changing process truly requires much communication, soul-searching, and perhaps outside assistance to help each person process their own feelings and needs, as they address this critical topic in an appropriate and thoughtful manner.

Many family members, friends, and those connected with your child's school may also require a period of time to adjust to using the new name and any pronoun changes that your child wishes. Some people will consciously or unconsciously rebel against the name or pronoun changes. Any errors, whether intentional or accidental, can cause much public embarrassment and confusion to everyone involved. This adjustment is something that parents and others may need to figure out for themselves, and if time is necessary to process these changes, it must be granted. Although many children are usually and understandably elated about the name or pronoun change, there can be some sense of loss felt by parents. This grief needs to be acknowledged and spoken about, for it should not be overlooked. For some, it is an erasing of something that has been a major part of the child's history, and although this aspect may be the reason for much personal celebration when it occurs for those in transition, there can simultaneously be strong feelings of mourning for parents. All of those affected by these changes have the right to have their emotions recognized, without the judgment or criticism of any party involved.

In addition to no longer using their child's name or pronoun, parents are often asked to remove all photos and memorabilia connected to the life their child lived prior to the transition. These requests, though critical to their child, may cause major sadness, loss, anger, and resentment for parents who treasure the past history and memories of their life together.

Where is the space, time, and place for parents who are in desperate need for time to adjust to the transition? The pain parents and others can experience is real and it must be discussed and valued. This chapter focuses on creating that space and place for parents to process and acknowledge this possible loss and pain through writing and sharing their thoughts and, for some, grief.

One of the greatest challenges for parents during this time is coming to terms with the fact that your child may be experiencing their own sense of loss and confusion. Often, they will be needing your support and understanding, while you can be the most vulnerable and find it hard to be emotionally available for your child. You may not even know exactly how to aid them during this time. As extremely challenging as this can be, your child will need to be your priority—on many a day you may be their only lifeline or main source of help. This is one of the times where it cannot be stressed enough that seeking individual therapy, family therapy, or outside assistance is strongly recommended. Having therapy is a critical part of the picture and is for everyone's benefit, and there should be no shame attached.

Negotiating when, with whom, and under what circumstances the past history can be discussed is sometimes extremely time-consuming and exhausting. These very sensitive conversations may require an enormous amount of patience and compromise throughout the transition. These dialogues may even continue long after the transition is no longer a major focus of the family's daily life. Unanticipated circumstances involving reunions with old acquaintances or relatives can require a rehashing of history or past memories, which may once again require an explanation of the changing of pronouns and name. The loss may be triggered during very subtle or matter-of-fact tasks such as seeing the old name when opening daily mail, sorting through legal documents, looking through family photo albums, or simply viewing their name assigned at birth on an old holiday item. It is recommended that each one of these possible scenarios be addressed and thought through as much as possible. If your child requests to use new pronouns and a new name or to eliminate artifacts that make them feel very uncomfortable, it must be understood that it can all feel too much for you at first. To have these changes become more automatic for parents, time and communication may be the best healers and the kindest methods for the desired outcome sought by your child. Above all else, having patience and understanding can be key, as you navigate your own journey!

GRAPHICS GALORE

Splash

What are the pronouns or possible names your child is considering using now that they are contemplating transitioning? By creatively splashing words and short phrases, quickly attempt to express your answers randomly with as many responses as possible scattered on the paper.

GRAPHICS GALORE

Venn Diagram

What artifacts are displayed in your living environment that may need to be removed as the transition moves forward for your child?

1. What artifacts and/or photos are you willing to remove?

2. What artifacts and/or photos is your child requesting to be removed?

4.

7.

5.

6.

3. What artifacts and/or photos are the family members willing to remove?

REFLECTIVE RESPONSES

1. What is your child's identity now (name, pronoun, and gender)? What are your feelings about this?

   . . . .

   . . . .

   . . . .

2. In what ways will you play a role, when and if your child elects to select a name or pronoun that is different from the one assigned at birth?

   . . . .

   . . . .

   . . . .

3. How will you and your child each prefer to have them introduced now and when will this change begin?

   . . . .

   . . . .

   . . . .

4. Will there be different criteria for both you and your child, when your child is being introduced to different people?

   . . . .

   . . . .

   . . . .

5. What names and pronouns will be used for your child in school? At home? In public?

   . . . .

   . . . .

   . . . .

6. Did any person's reaction in relation to using a different name or different pronoun for your child surprise you? If yes, who surprised you and how?

. . . .

. . . .

. . . .

7. As you look around your home, what are the artifacts that you are not willing to remove yet?

. . . .

. . . .

. . . .

8. Which of these removals or decisions will be made by you, your child, and together?

. . . .

. . . .

. . . .

9. What will be the time frame for each one of these decisions and removals?

. . . .

. . . .

. . . .

10. How will you refer to, state, or use the new name, pronoun, or gender when you discuss memories and the past with each other or with other people?

. . . .

. . . .

. . . .

GRAPHICS GALORE

Web

What artifact does your child want removed that you do not want taken down or put out of view?

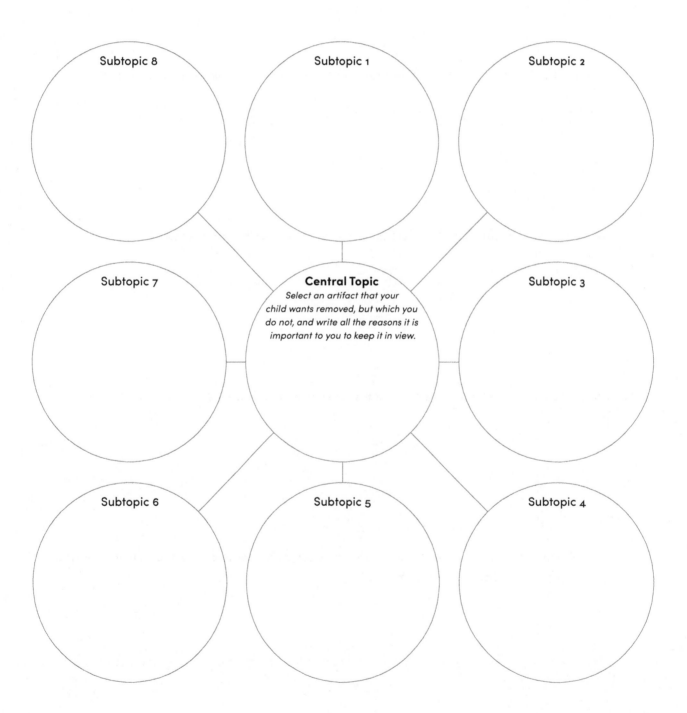

Subtopic 8

Subtopic 1

Subtopic 2

Subtopic 7

Central Topic
Select an artifact that your child wants removed, but which you do not, and write all the reasons it is important to you to keep it in view.

Subtopic 3

Subtopic 6

Subtopic 5

Subtopic 4

GRAPHICS GALORE

T-Chart

What do you view as positives, negatives, or neutral about your child changing the name and/or pronoun they were assigned at birth?

+ (Positives)	– (Negatives)	= (Neutral)

DESERVING DE-STRESSING DELIGHT

ANECDOTAL AFFIRMATION

Ask questions,
Get answers,
Keep asking,
More questions!

Creating

When and if things around you feel as if they are falling apart, build or make something that gives you a sense of strength and purpose. Nothing you create needs to be earth-shattering, but each endeavor may help remind you that you have value and importance. If you love craft activities, you can create collages of words and pictures to express how you are feeling, knit or crochet scarves and hats, embroider or create needlepoint images, and even sketch. Some people have shared that they took photographs of anything that appealed to them or designed jewelry as a tool to cope with their grief and as a way to record their past. Other parents physically built a treehouse in their backyard, painted a wall mural, or carved a bed for the family pet. One parent learned how to sculpt bushes for their garden. Find whatever it is that feels creative to you and provides an outlet that validates your worthiness. Creating is something that can nurture and honor your talents, while increasing your self-esteem and confidence level.

Journal your reaction to this Deserving De-Stressing Delight.

....

....

....

....

....

....

....

....

....

....

GRAPHICS GALORE

Timeline

Record when and with whom you and/or your child will begin using your child's new name and/or pronoun and the person's reaction, once this occurs.

With whom?	Anticipated date to discuss it with the person:	Their reaction:

GRAPHICS GALORE

Box

List all of the artifacts requested to be removed from view and check off if and when each one is taken away or down. Just because an artifact is listed, it does not mean it must be removed. This is simply a place to record those artifacts that are being considered for removal and their location at this moment.

1	2	3
4	5	6
7	8	9
10	11	12
13	14	15
16	17	18

EMPATHY-EMBRACING EXERCISE

Part of a parent's journey may involve adjusting to using a new name or pronoun. This question is designed to demonstrate that this is part of what many people have done in other instances. The greatest learning tools for grasping the change in name and pronoun are patience with yourself, willingness, time, and much practice.

Do you know anyone from your past who has asked you to call them by a different name, pronoun, or honorific, perhaps due to marriage or for other reasons? How long did it take you to adjust to this new name, pronoun, or honorific, and how did you learn to adjust to the change?

ANECDOTAL AFFIRMATION
Picking a pronoun,
Choosing a name,
Redesigning our home,
No one is to blame!

GRAPHICS GALORE

Bar Graph

To what degree do these concerns and related topics matter to you? Based on a scale from 1 to 10, with 1 being the lowest and 10 being the highest, color or shade in your response. This visual will illustrate where your greatest concerns lie and can be used as a tool to help you communicate your thoughts with your child and/or other family members, therapist, spiritual mentor, or for your own personal understanding. The bar graph results can vary as your child's transition progresses, and your thoughts may shift.

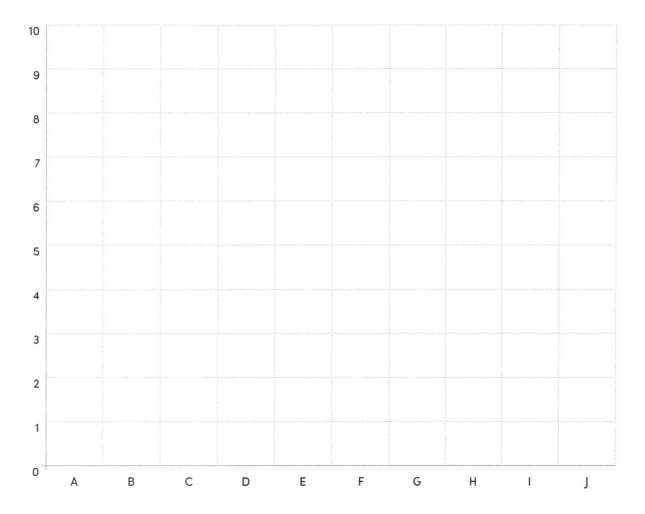

Use these ideas to fill in the bar graph or feel free to create your own!

A. The changing of your child's name and/or pronoun assigned at birth.

B. People misgendering your child.

C. Removal of your child's pre-transition photos.

D. Removal of the family's pre-transition photos.

E. Removal of your child's pre-transition photos with family.

F. Removal of your child's pre-transition photos with friends.

G. Removal of your child's special events pre-transition photos.

H. Not saying your child's name/pronoun assigned at birth in public.

I. Not saying your child's name/pronoun assigned at birth at home.

J. Not posting documents, awards, or licenses that contain your child's written name/pronoun assigned at birth anywhere.

GRAPHICS GALORE

Pie Graph

To what degree are these concerns and related topics important to you? Decide how significant these issues are to you in relation to each other. Place the number that corresponds with a suggested topic within as many slices of the pie that convey how each one matters to you. Only one number should be placed in each slice. You do not need to use all the issues, but do fill in all the slices. Feel free to create your own topics and assign them their own number.

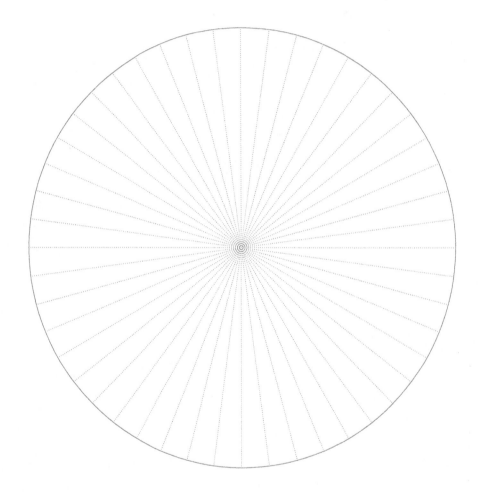

1. The changing of your child's name and/or pronoun assigned at birth.

2. People misgendering your child.

3. Removal of your child's pre-transition photos.

4. Removal of the family's pre-transition photos.

5. Removal of your child's pre-transition photos with family.

6. Removal of your child's pre-transition photos with friends.

7. Removal of your child's special events pre-transition photos.

8. Not saying your child's name/pronoun assigned at birth in public.

9. Not saying your child's name/pronoun assigned at birth at home.

10. Not posting documents, awards, or licenses that contain your child's written name/pronoun assigned at birth anywhere.

SAMPLER SHARES

All names have been changed to ensure anonymity in this section. The first initial designates an individual and the second initial identifies the relationship to the child, i.e. P = their parent, G = their grandparent, and S = their sibling.

Did any person's reaction in relation to using a different name and/or different pronoun for your child surprise you? If yes, who surprised you and how?

EP: Yes, I find the older generation (60+) has been more accepting. When I mention they go by he and him, they just reply, "Oh," and whisper, "I might forget but I'll try to remember." They don't ask a lot of questions or seem judgmental. Also, most doctors' offices are understanding. They will use my son's gender affirming name. *PARENT/CHILD: AFAB (Uses he/him/his pronouns)*

HP: There were several hurdles that we had to overcome as a family: choosing a new name, using a particular pronoun, and difficulty in always remembering. In addition, correcting family members when we talked about it and being able to tell that they were not accepting of my son or my wishes. My sibling told me directly that calling him by a different name was not going to happen. This was particularly hard as my son and sibling's child were very close. I have learned from other life-altering events that certain people do not want to be accepting of anything that is outside the norm. My parents have made it difficult to maintain a closeness with my son. He can feel that they support him in certain ways, but do not believe that it's real. The biggest support base has come from my friends, long-term clients, and people in the community. *PARENT/CHILD: AFAB (Uses he/him/his pronouns)*

CP: My son was AFAB and presented as such until he was 17. For 17 years, he went by his deadname and female pronouns, so we were pretty understanding when people would make mistakes. For a long time, his dad and I would make mistakes too, and when that happened we would just go back, change it, and move on. It took time for his name and correct pronouns to become solidified in our brains and on our tongues. *PARENT/CHILD: AFAB (Uses he/him/his pronouns)*

As you look around your home, what are the artifacts that you are not willing to remove yet?

DP: I want to emphasize that I asked my son a lot of questions and I have learned that different people in the community feel differently. For instance, my son (AFAB) does not mind that I still have photos of him up in the house from when he was female. I have heard of others who will not allow their parents to do that. When I refer to him in the past I have said "when Frank was a little girl…" When I first said this to some good friends we all looked at each other for a minute, then burst out laughing. When I told Frank, he also laughed and then said it is ok for me to say that because he was a little girl. It is important to ask your trans child how they would like to be addressed and then respect their response. *PARENT/CHILD: AFAB (Uses he/him/his pronouns)*

HP: Removing things from our home that were a resemblance of who my son no longer wanted to be took time. I willingly took down photos in the house and made a concerted effort to take down all of my past photos on social media. It was more difficult when my son took it on himself to take my phone and started removing "my" photos. This was the moment of a mom who wasn't ready to let go and I had already made a conscious effort to visually remove things that upset him. We had a long talk about me needing to process things in my own way and that I loved him as "my child." Luckily, my son is logical and has an innate understanding of seeing someone's true emotion. Over time, he slowly removed things from his bedroom and chose to keep a bin of belongings in his closet that are part of his early childhood. The most interesting part to me is that pictures of him as a baby or preschooler are ok, those are happy times in his memory. *PARENT/CHILD: AFAB (Uses he/him/his pronouns)*

COMMUNICATION CORNER

When you speak spontaneously out of anger or fear about the unknown, without thinking it through, you can sometimes regret the way you phrased your words or the tone you used to express your feelings. Rehearsing what you want to ask or discuss with your child, and other family members, can help you before you actually communicate your thoughts. This gives you a moment to reflect and pause before you converse about emotional topics. You may choose to practice asking these questions with a trusted friend, family member, spiritual mentor, or therapist first. Explain your thoughts and feelings about these statements to one another verbally or in writing. It is important to note that some families elected to only address one question or two, while others preferred to answer them all. In order to recall the questions you answered, simply highlight and/or circle the ones you addressed as a family, yet acknowledge that you may return to discuss the others in the future. Decide what feels best for two or more family members and begin the conversation. Do you, your child, and other family members answer these questions in the same way or differently? Discuss your responses to understand how all of you view the answers to the questions and make time to celebrate all you learn from being willing to communicate with each other.

> ANECDOTAL AFFIRMATION
> *I am important!*
> *I am not invisible!*
> *My needs matter!*

1. Why do you prefer a particular artifact and/or photo to be removed, and by when?

....

....

2. Why are you requesting for a particular artifact and/or photo not to be removed?

....

....

3. If any artifacts and/or photos are removed, where will they be stored and by whom?

....

....

4. Which artifacts and/or photos, if any, will be disposed of, and by whom?

. . . .

. . . .

5. Which artifacts and/or photos that are removed (if any) will not be replaced?

. . . .

. . . .

6. Which artifacts and/or photos that are removed (if any) will be replaced and by whom?

. . . .

. . . .

7. How would you like to handle misgendered moments?

. . . .

. . . .

8. How will your child's possible new name and/or pronoun be selected and who will be involved with this process?

. . . .

. . . .

9. If they are being changed, what full name and/or pronouns would your child like to be addressed with now?

. . . .

. . . .

10. What will you say when the changing of pronoun/name is explained to others?

. . . .

. . . .

Chapter 4

GRIEF MAY APPLY

VITAL VIGNETTE

> ANECDOTAL AFFIRMATION
> *Grief,*
> *So many stages,*
> *All at once!*

It is extremely difficult to explain how grief and loss may play a major role for some parents who are told their child is trans. The reverse also holds true. For some parents, learning this information can be a time of celebration with few or no feelings of loss or grief.

This chapter focuses on those who have experienced grief. From the outside looking in, this pain, loss, and grief may seem unjustified or baffling because their child is still alive and can often be in their life on a daily basis. It is true that parents can still talk to their child, eat with them, and do many or most of the things together that they did prior to knowing their child was considering transitioning. Yet in reality, so much is changing. Daily life may never be exactly the same again, and it may continue to change for a length of time even though it might not appear so different to others.

Many parents have shared that the transition feels like an erasing, fading, or passing of the relationship they have with their child. Some parents have described it as a seemingly invisible loss, while others have expressed that they feel lost and unsure of what to do to feel secure. Who can parents turn to if they need to discuss this grief and feeling of loss? Where is the space to share the loss of a child when the child is still there? How do the parents convey, without sounding harsh or unsupportive, what it feels like to not recognize the child they knew or hoped would have a different future?

Your child may be considering or in the process of changing their name, pronoun, gender expression, and/or gender marker. Their gender can now be affirmed through medical, social, and/or legal means. As part of their transition, your child may need to partake in a medical transition that includes surgery, now or in the future. Should this be part of their path, your child's body parts can be altered.

In addition, if gender-affirming therapy is part of a medical transition, their hair, scent, voice, and the visual shape of their body may be altered. Your child may elect to socially transition and begin to dress in a way that is unfamiliar to you, as well as make a myriad of other choices that may help them feel at peace with themselves. For parents, any aspects of a social and/or medical transition may be contributing to a sense of loss and leave you feeling somewhat disoriented, even if you are supportive. Yet for others, it can be a time that evokes relief and much happiness knowing that your child's body is finally aligned with their affirmed gender.

It needs to be acknowledged that the child deserves to embrace any and every aspect of the transition, in order to be true to themselves. The challenge comes into play if these critical necessities for the child affect the social, emotional, or personal life of the parents. For some parents, there can be a painful and deep mourning period filled with all or some of the stages that Kübler-Ross and Kessler explain in their book *On Grief and Grieving* (2005): denial, anger, bargaining, depression, and acceptance. Some parents speak of experiencing grief similar to these five stages.

Denial can be explained as a stage of disbelief, shock, or feeling that the situation is temporary and that perhaps you misunderstood. For example, you know your child has told you that they will never wear a type of clothing again, but when you are in a store, you see this particular clothing item they used to wear and so you purchase it hoping that your child will change their mind and will elect to wear it again in the future.

Anger can be directed towards the child in transition for changing your world. It can be focused on those who are celebrating or questioning any aspects of the transition, especially friends and family. It can be expressed as anger towards yourself, by feeling you are to blame for causing the transition to happen. In addition, you may feel anger at yourself for not being able to be as supportive as you wish you could be at this time.

Bargaining is a type of mental or even verbal deal-making. Perhaps you think you can propose that your child only use their gender-affirming pronouns and/or name at home, but not in public. Maybe you can offer to welcome a social transition, but only if they promise not to ask to discuss any medical changes, now or in the future. This stage is filled with the "what ifs" or "if onlys" where agreements are conditional—thoughts or requests such as the opposite of what is stated above: "What if I use your gender-affirming name in public, but at home I use your name and pronoun assigned at birth?"

Depression can be the stage of much sadness, isolation, exhaustion, and an abundance of tears. It may feel as if this stage will never end! Kübler-Ross and Kessler clarify that it does end for most people, but if depression is part of your journey, it can be viewed as part of the grieving process. It should be recognized that situational depression, not clinical depression, can be an appropriate and necessary response to grief.

Acceptance does not mean that you need to be happy or joyful about the outcome of the transition. It simply means that you know the transition has happened or is going to happen. Then you react or respond by realizing that your child is trans and that the transition may include aspects that you cannot alter. This stage can also incorporate a heartfelt and celebratory experience filled with elation and happiness.

These stages do not necessarily occur in the same order for all parents or they may not all be part of the parents' mourning process. Some of these stages can be felt simultaneously or be present in waves or cycles. The thoughts parents may experience can become something they never expected, and this could feel shameful. The things parents may desire to say out of anger or denial to their child may feel embarrassing or surprising.

Some parents shared that sometimes they do not even recognize themselves during this time of mourning or grieving. The pain and loss expressed by many parents during this grieving period need to be validated, honored, and allowed, without judgment from their child, family members, friends, or others who may truly have no idea how parents can feel.

It should be acknowledged that some children may elect to always live stealth, meaning never disclosing that they are transgender. However, there are children who request that their parents keep the knowledge of their transition to themselves and do not share this information until they are comfortable enough to tell others, but will not necessarily prefer to live stealth. Most importantly, parents must trust their own feelings and consider seeking professional help or assistance from others, especially if they feel they are unable to function or keep the transition to themselves, even if they have agreed to respect their child's wishes to live stealth.

Sometimes parents will ask their child to wait to let others know, simply to help the process run smoothly and not because the parents are only considering their own needs and feelings of loss. For example, in some instances, all may agree it would be more beneficial for the child to begin their social transition at the start of the following school year, rather than do it in the current year, should the current school only have a month or two until it ends. This critical aspect of the transition can demand much discussion and much self-reflection. The needs of everyone must be conveyed to each other and respected with a healthy compromise for the sake of all the individuals involved in the family. If you are unsure whether what you are experiencing is appropriate and part of the grieving process, a trained therapist may be your greatest resource.

It cannot be stressed enough how therapy, in both a family setting and individual setting, can be of major assistance throughout the entire process of the transition. In addition, forming a support team of people who will be available all day, every day could bring much comfort and relief to parents when they need to talk, grieve, or sort things out with others. Attending conferences that address the needs and questions parents may internalize can also prove to be an outstanding resource that will offer another level of support for families. For some parents, speaking with a spiritual mentor has been an option that helped bring them comfort. If parents are experiencing emotional pain or grief, there are ways to assist in easing these feelings. No one ever needs to suffer alone. The loneliness, fear, confusion, and isolation can be devastating for those parents who may be overwhelmed or perplexed.

The choices and decisions parents may seek during this time can be quite personal and private, and should be on a timeline that suits their needs. Your perspective of what seems like positive aspects versus negative aspects of the transition may evolve over time. At first, you may view the various changes as either good or bad, but as you begin to accept the transition, you may be able to think of the changes as what has remained and what has changed as a result of this process. This shift in thinking can help you embrace the transition and arrive at a place of peace within yourself, but this may take a great deal of time. This possibility may become important for you in order to acknowledge the transition as positive versus negative during your stages of anger. However, in acceptance, you may no longer see the transition as such a polarizing experience, if you had felt this way in the past.

What matters most is that parents understand that they are safe to express all they are feeling, that space is created for varying perspectives throughout the transition, and that there are professional ways to get the help they deserve.

Time can serve as a factor that may help with the adjustment period as parents become used to so much newness. Communication and support may also be used as tools to assist in easing the grief for some parents. Discussing issues and fears with an understanding family member, knowledgeable therapist, support group, spiritual mentor, trusted friend, or supportive person who has traveled a similar path, as well as exploring what the process could entail in the future, may prove to be extremely beneficial. Perhaps even including your child, when appropriate, in conversations of the next steps could alleviate some level of the loss, pain, and grief. Accepting that these five stages may be rather insignificant to some, yet crucial to the health of other parents, provides space for all those who love a trans and/or non-binary child!

GRAPHICS GALORE

Splash

Can you express all the words associated with loss or grief? By creatively splashing words and short phrases, quickly attempt to express your answers randomly with as many responses as possible scattered on the paper.

GRAPHICS GALORE

Web

Select one or more of the five stages of grief: denial, anger, bargaining, depression, acceptance. Then use the outer circles to express each thought that comes to mind in relation to that stage.

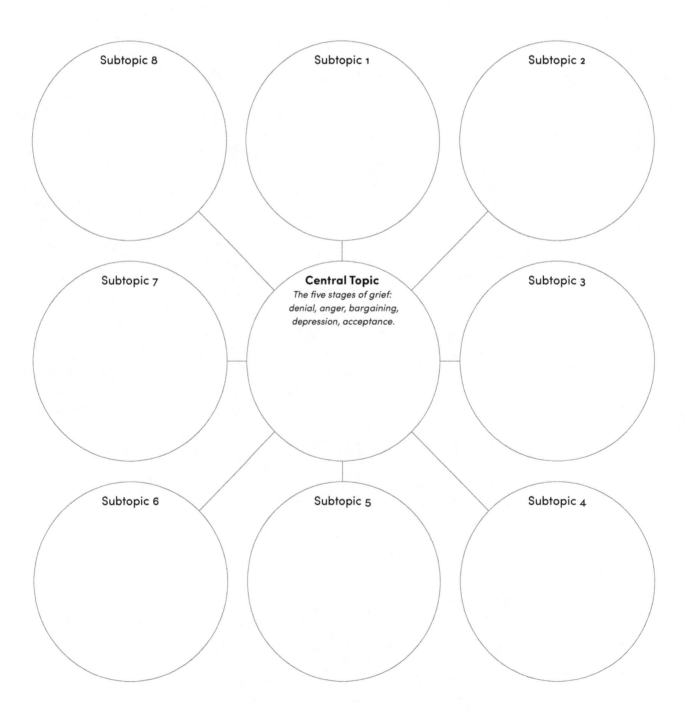

REFLECTIVE RESPONSES

1. In what ways, if any, did you experience denial in relation to your child's need to transition?

   ....

   ....

   ....

2. In what ways, if any, did you experience anger in relation to your child's need to transition?

   ....

   ....

   ....

3. In what ways, if any, did you experience bargaining in relation to your child's need to transition?

   ....

   ....

   ....

4. In what ways, if any, did you experience depression in relation to your child's need to transition?

   ....

   ....

   ....

5. In what ways, if any, did you experience acceptance in relation to your child's need to transition?

   ....

   ....

   ....

6. Explain why, if this applies, knowing that your child is trans fosters any feelings of grief, loss, or may feel like a type of death to you? (The five stages of grief: denial, anger, bargaining, depression, and acceptance.)

....

....

....

7. What aspects, if any, make you smile or want to celebrate when you think of the transition?

....

....

....

8. What do you think you may miss the most if your child transitions?

....

....

....

9. What do you wish could remain the same if your child transitions?

....

....

....

10. With whom, if anyone, will you share your concerns should you feel scared that your child will die from surgery, hormones, or the violence of others?

....

....

....

11. How will you discuss regretful, verbalized statements you may have thought or said to your child during moments of extreme grief?

....

....

....

12. How will you discuss regretful, verbalized statements your child or other family members may have said to you during moments of extreme grief?

....

....

....

13. What can you do to help your child sort out their need to transition while you may be grieving, mourning, or in any emotional pain?

....

....

....

14. How will you feel if others judge you, during the stages of grief, should you find it difficult to support your child's transition?

....

....

....

15. How will you feel if others judge you, during the stages of grief, should you support your child's transition?

....

....

....

GRAPHICS GALORE

Venn Diagram

Does anything about the transition make you feel any sense of loss? You may want to ask your child to complete this graphic organizer with you or you can simply fill it in for them, based on the knowledge you already have.

1. Does anything about the transition make you feel any sense of loss?

2. Does anything about the transition make your child feel any sense of loss?

4.

7.

5.

6.

3. Does anything about the transition make other family members feel any sense of loss?

GRAPHICS GALORE

Timeline

Do you feel it is important to record and notice if there is any pattern or whether you tend to revert to a particular stage more often than another? This is simply to assist you in being more self-aware. Fill in the timeline daily, weekly, or monthly using the five stages of grief: denial, anger, bargaining, depression, or acceptance.

Date: _____ | I experienced _____when...

Date: _____ | I experienced _____when...

Date: _____ | I experienced _____when...

Date: _____ | I experienced _____when...

Date: _____ | I experienced _____when...

Date: _____ | I experienced _____when...

Date: _____ | I experienced _____when...

DESERVING DE-STRESSING DELIGHT

Something Novel

Trying something that is risky, new, or unlike you may not sound de-stressing, but in the end, it can become comforting when you are able to achieve things you thought you might not be capable of accomplishing. If you can overcome these fears or doubts, it may be enough to show you that you can approach and possibly embrace the unknowns and concerns of the transition.

It can be taking part in a physical activity, gathering information about starting your own business, applying for a new job, or filling out the application form for college. Some people may have no idea even where to begin. Dream big and make a wish list that stems from your heart! Write down a few desires and then select one item you feel comfortable doing first. It may be as simple as dyeing your hair different colors or making a difficult phone call. Regardless of the venture, attempt it. Perhaps the confidence and self-pride you may gain will be exactly what you need to embrace the challenges and celebrations of the transition or gender questioning. Learning something new can keep your mind sharp and busy. Try to think of a class, hobby, sport, or activity that has always interested you. Some parents may have always wanted to learn a new language, take dance lessons, or sign up for a photography course. Deep within you, you know something that has always been tucked away in the back of your mind and this is the time to dust off those cobwebs and get started. It is suggested that you base this choice on your time availability, budget constraints, and where the learning will take place in proximity to your home or work.

When the transition requires much of the focus, discovering all the ins and outs of the process can feel like a full-time job and this may continue for some time. However, it must be understood that, for some parents, understanding the transition does not require coping skills or core strength. Although taking a risk or trying something new may be valuable in itself, for these parents, working out ambivalences or self-doubt in relation to the transition may not be a part of their journey. For those who know this is their story, this suggestion may only be helpful as an opportunity to remember the novel things they want to try. Yet for those who are experiencing self-doubt and feeling invisible, in respect to the transition, embarking on a new venture can be empowering. Once the dust settles and you have overcome that learning curve, it is time to de-stress and focus that energy on beginning something new that is of total interest to you to pursue!

Journal your reaction to this Deserving De-Stressing Delight.

> ANECDOTAL AFFIRMATION
> *Pain, pain,*
> *Go away,*
> *Never come back*
> *Another day!*

GRAPHICS GALORE

Box

Can you think of something that made you smile or celebrate today? Sometimes focusing on gratitude, while experiencing loss, reminds us that both can co-exist!

1. I laughed at...	**2.** I saw beauty in...
3. Someone helped me to...	**4.** I helped someone to...
5. I learned...	**6.** I treated myself to...

GRAPHICS GALORE

T-Chart

Can you acknowledge how you feel today? Be gentle with yourself and be honest with your thoughts. This space focuses on acceptance. Each parent will approach this in a different way. For some, seeing the positive will be an easy task, but finding the negative may be more difficult. Yet for others, the reverse may be true. Envisioning negative aspects of the transition may be more in the forefront, and imagining positive statements may feel impossible at this time. For some aspects, you may not even have a strong feeling either way and this is equally as important to know about yourself. This is all part of the acceptance stage. You do not need to adhere to a timeline; it varies for everyone. Fill in whatever comes to mind and do not judge your level of acceptance. It can all take time!

Positive (+) aspects	Negative (−) aspects	Neutral (=) aspects

EMPATHY-EMBRACING EXERCISE

For some parents, the transition can be compared to mourning throughout different stages of the process. Remember that as heartbreaking as other losses or grieving periods have been in your life, you have overcome your pain and continued living. It must be acknowledged that some parents will not experience any feelings of grief or loss in relation to the transition. This question is *intentionally* raised to help remind you that if you are mourning or feel a sense of loss connected to any aspect of the transition, it may not last forever.

Have you ever experienced an unexpected loss or grieved the passing of someone close to you? Who was it and how did you deal with the loss and/or grief?

ANECDOTAL AFFIRMATION

I miss
My son!
I miss
My daughter!
I miss...

GRAPHICS GALORE

Bar Graph

To what degree do these concerns and related topics matter to you? Based on a scale from 1 to 10, with 1 being the lowest and 10 being the highest, color or shade in your response. This visual will illustrate where your greatest concerns lie and can be used as a tool to help you communicate your thoughts with your child and/or other family members, therapist, spiritual mentor, or for your own personal understanding. The bar graph results can vary as your child's transition progresses and your thoughts may shift.

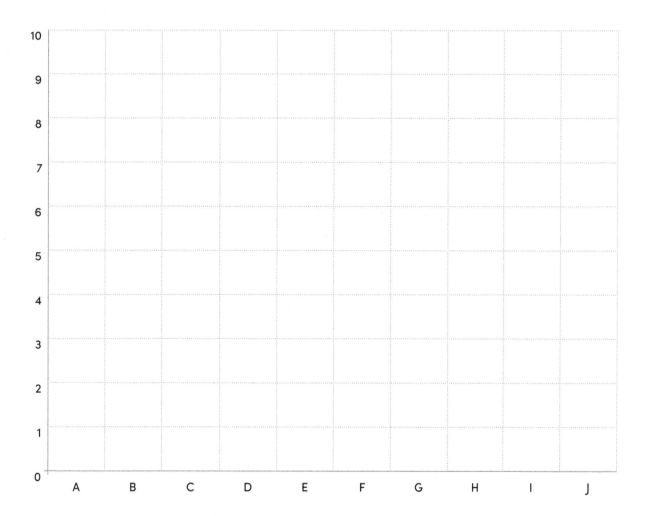

Use these ideas to fill in the bar graph or feel free to create your own!

A. Denial/Disbelief

B. Confusion/Perplexity

C. Anger/Rage

D. Loneliness/Isolation

E. Grief/Loss

F. Depression/Sadness

G. Fear/Anxiety

H. Numbness/Hopelessness

I. Relief/Serenity

J. Joyfulness/Happiness

GRAPHICS GALORE

Pie Graph

To what degree are these concerns and related topics important to you? Decide how significant these issues are to you in relation to each other. Place the number that corresponds with a suggested topic within as many slices of the pie that convey how each one matters to you. Only one number should be placed in each slice. You do not need to use all the issues, but do fill in all the slices. Feel free to create your own topics and assign them their own number.

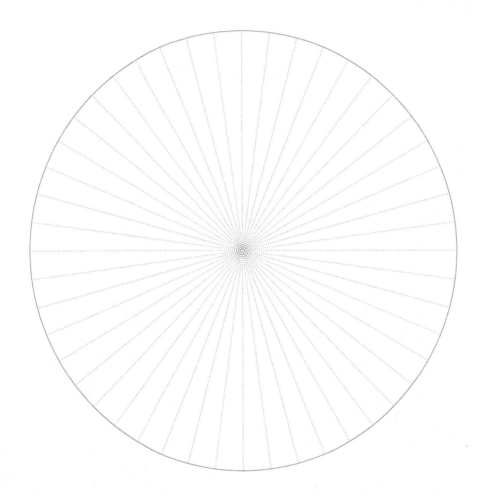

1. Denial/Disbelief
2. Confusion/Perplexity
3. Anger/Rage
4. Loneliness/Isolation
5. Grief/Loss

6. Depression/Sadness
7. Fear/Anxiety
8. Numbness/Hopelessness
9. Relief/Serenity
10. Joyfulness/Happiness

SAMPLER SHARES

All names have been changed to ensure anonymity in this section. The first initial designates an individual and the second initial identifies the relationship to the child, i.e. P = their parent, G = their grandparent, and S = their sibling.

Explain why, if this applies, knowing your child is trans fosters any feelings of grief, loss, or may feel like a type of death to you? (The five stages of grief: denial, anger, bargaining, depression, and acceptance.)

DP: I definitely have mourned the loss of a daughter. My initial thoughts when she told me she was considering transitioning to a man was that I had no idea what that meant. What would be involved? How would it change her? What would her life be like? Once we began to do research and I started to understand how her looks would change, what would happen to her menstrual cycle, that is when I really started to understand that I would no longer have my little girl. Since she had originally come out as a gay female, I still had expectations that she might carry a child—changing to a man would completely change my expectations. The good news for me as time went on was that my son was exactly like my daughter in that his personality, his taste in food, what movies and TV shows he liked remained the same. I guess I was not sure what I expected, so I was pleasantly surprised by that. But as time has gone on (he started the transition over two years ago), I miss my daughter. It has been just the two of us for a long time and it is different to be a mother and son instead of a mother to a daughter. It is not "bad," just different. *PARENT/CHILD: AFAB (Uses he/him/his pronouns)*[1]

HP: Initially, I felt that there was still hope that my son would change his mind and perhaps he was just more of a tomboy. As time went on, it became more apparent that how he felt was not going to change and I began to feel depressed over knowing that I had to accept what he wanted in order to move forward. There were many times that I felt a mix of sadness and anger, upset that this was happening to me, and I could not control the situation. In regard to my children, I always felt that I could do something to change a situation but, this time, the choice wasn't mine. Accepting my son as transgender came in time, keeping in mind that he was my child, someone I would love, no matter what. It became very clear that it was more important to have him with me and support his feelings and wishes. *PARENT/CHILD: AFAB (Uses he/him/his pronouns)*

IS: Knowing my sibling is transgender did not foster anything but acceptance inside me. Although, it did leave me wondering what built up to this decision and why? *SIBLING/ BROTHER: AFAB (Uses he/him/his pronouns)*

---

1 There may be fertility options for those in transition and discussing them with medical professionals familiar with trans fertility can be helpful.

BG: When my grandson was approximately age three and I began to realize that he might transition at some point in his life, I definitely grieved the loss of my grandson. Sometimes I still feel that grief; however, it has pretty much been replaced by an overwhelming fear. If/When he does choose to transition, will I welcome my new granddaughter with open arms and the same unconditional love I've had for my grandson? Again, I pray that he will have sufficient support from people other than his family; however, I do believe that he will at least have that family support. I have to believe that this support will sustain him through the entire process and beyond. For myself, I suppose I'll feel a great sense of relief that he'll no longer need to defend himself and his preferences, or to over-explain—or simply to hide. GRANDPARENT/CHILD: AMAB (Uses he/his/him pronouns)

COMMUNICATION CORNER

ANECDOTAL AFFIRMATION

Minute by minute,
I try to understand.
Day by day,
Acceptance comes!
Season by season,
We all celebrate!

When you speak spontaneously out of anger or fear about the unknown, without thinking it through, you can sometimes regret the way you phrased your words or the tone you used to express your feelings. Rehearsing what you want to ask or discuss with your child, and other family members, can help you before you actually communicate your thoughts. This gives you a moment to reflect and pause before you converse about emotional topics. You may choose to practice asking these questions with a trusted friend, family member, spiritual mentor, or therapist first. Explain your thoughts and feelings about these statements to one another verbally or in writing. It is important to note that some families elected to only address one question or two, while others preferred to answer them all. In order to recall the questions you answered, simply highlight and/or circle the ones you addressed as a family, yet acknowledge that you may return to discuss the others in the future. Decide what feels best for two or more family members and begin the conversation. Do you, your child, and other family members answer these questions in the same way or differently? Discuss your responses to understand how all of you view the answers to the questions and make time to celebrate all you learn from being willing to communicate with each other.

1. Can you explain your thoughts, if you feel denial/disbelief about any aspect of the transition?

....

....

2. Can you explain your thoughts, if you feel confusion/perplexity about any aspect of the transition?

....

....

3. Can you explain your thoughts, if you feel you are in anger/rage about any aspect of the transition?

....

....

4. Can you explain your thoughts, if you feel loneliness/isolation about any aspect of the transition?

. . . .

. . . .

5. Can you explain your thoughts, if you feel grief/loss about any aspect of the transition?

. . . .

. . . .

6. Can you explain your thoughts, if you feel depression/sadness about any aspect of the transition?

. . . .

. . . .

7. Can you explain your thoughts, if you feel fear/anxiety about any aspect of the transition process?

. . . .

. . . .

8. Can you explain your thoughts, if you feel numbness/hopelessness about any aspect of the transition?

. . . .

. . . .

9. Can you explain your thoughts, if you feel relief/serenity about any aspect of the transition?

. . . .

. . . .

10. Can you explain your thoughts, if you feel joyfulness/happiness about any aspect of the transition?

. . . .

. . . .

Chapter 5

IT CAN BE A FOREIGN LANGUAGE

VITAL VIGNETTE

ANECDOTAL AFFIRMATION

So many labels,
Why do
Any of
Them matter?
So many labels,
Why?
Do any of
Them matter?

The transition process involves understanding and relearning many aspects of daily life, which often starts once a child is beginning any portion of their transition and/or is questioning their gender. One aspect that may become essential for you is to focus your energy on the new vocabulary, which can humbly seem like a foreign language to you. There are commonly used words and subsets of these words that may not be extremely relevant terms when your child is transitioning and/or questioning their gender. If you attend a transgender-focused conference, some presenters or attendees may use vocabulary and terms that are unfamiliar to you. It is possible to feel you hardly have any idea what anyone is talking about and are an outsider. Many parents might find some of the vocabulary and terms offensive, but can acknowledge this may not be the case for all parents. If you grew up in an era when the word *queer* was still considered a slur, you may now need to understand that *queer* has been reclaimed by the LGBTQ+ community. In current context, some may refer to *queer* as: a sexual orientation that is not heterosexual and/or anything that is non-heteronormative. Defining *queer* is very personal to most individuals and its definition is ever evolving. The key is to understand that using the word *queer* is no longer seen as an insult, but rather as a positive identity. There are parents and family members who are at complete ease with incorporating the current vernacular into their daily vocabulary. Others will need to realize that it is important to adjust one's mindset and accept these words and phrases as simply a natural part of interacting within many transgender groups. Learning all of these words and terms may feel overwhelming. You may be wondering how you will become skilled in all of this and how you will digest it with great speed; for you now understand that doing so will enable you to connect better with your child, as well as many in the Transgender community.

In the past decade, there has been an increased discussion of transgender people in the media, and the issues and terminology may be more widely known. There may be some parents and other family members who are very familiar with the vocabulary and terms associated with transitioning—current lingo and medical terminology. Others may not be aware of and may have never used these words or terms before. For those who were or are more aware of these words and terms than others, this chapter may simply serve as a review and personal reference resource, or it can be used to share with others whom you feel may benefit from the information in this section of the workbook.

For those parents and other family members who are not familiar with the terminology, it is suggested that you gather vocabulary and terms that you do not know. Out of respect for your child, you will want to be able to comprehend and communicate with people in the Transgender community and the medical world. These activities can be the first steps in helping you see what you do not know and assisting you in the process of learning new terminology. You may quickly realize that this process can become a full-time job!

As an educator and lifelong learner, I searched for a way to assist parents to approach this learning in a way that was comfortable for them. As a result, I decided to apply all the games, methods, and skills I used in the classroom to help others grasp what they want to rapidly digest on this topic. In hopes of enabling others to learn and retain the vocabulary and terms, included in this chapter are games and exercises created for you to play. If games are not your thing or if this seems too juvenile to you, I respect that and completely grasp why you may skip portions of this chapter. For those of you who love games and learn well from them, enjoy!

Since the list is truly extensive and continuously evolving, I am incorporating blank templates and suggest that you refurbish the templates with words or terms that apply to your needs. I have included directions to help guide you in playing and using the games and exercises. You can use most of the games and exercises on your own, but some can be enjoyed with others. Using the tools together can create a celebratory environment with family members and friends who want to learn the words and vocabulary, while demonstrating their support. The games and exercises can also be of value as a conversation starter, in order to educate others and help them grasp significant vocabulary and terminology.

Through a fun and light-hearted gathering, parents, other family members, and friends can form an encouraging team and become the first line of support that a parent or couple may desperately need. It is important to be patient with yourself when learning these terms. In addition to repetition and review, many find that periodically using the vocabulary in conversation can be the best method for learning. Just like any other language, the more you use the vocabulary, the better you retain it.

Before trying to learn the vocabulary, many people may choose to review the terms first to evaluate what they already know. Once the unknown words are identified and learned, parents can personally assess which terms relate to or effectively represent their child. This identification can be powerful and enlightening. Using this knowledge often helps when parents are communicating with other family members, friends, therapists, the medical community, schools, and one another.

It is critical to note that this information is not meant to restrict, permanently label, or box anyone into something that does not feel right. Choosing language that feels right and appropriate is a private and personal choice, which can evolve and should never be used in a negative way against anyone, for any reason. The applicable vocabulary and terms must only be decided on by the individuals who choose to use them for themselves, for whatever reason they deem relevant, and for nothing more. The sole purpose of these games and exercises is to create a common language in order to communicate and educate in a gentle manner.

GRAPHICS AND GAMES GALORE

Splash

Can you jot down all of the vocabulary you can think of that is related to your child's transition process? By creatively splashing words and short phrases, quickly attempt to express your answers randomly with as many responses as possible scattered on the paper.

VOCABULARY MATCH QUESTIONNAIRE PRE-TEST

It is important to be aware of what you know and to use that knowledge as a starting point to grow. After taking the pre-test, you will know what you still need to learn. The tools in this chapter were created to help you internalize the vocabulary.

As a pre-test, match the vocabulary (the numbers) with the definitions (the letters) by drawing a line from a number to a letter to show which words or terms you already know, and those words that are new to you. Each number and letter should only be used once. What were your results? The answer keys are provided in the Answer Key section in Chapter 15. It is suggested that you check your answers after you have taken the pre-test to see how well you did. Feel free to repeat this process at a later time; you may choose to use this activity to assess your progress by using this game as a post-test.

Matching Pre-Test #1

1. agender	A. Someone who does not feel sexual attraction to other people.
2. androgynous	B. A person who is attracted to both masculine and feminine people.
3. asexual	C. A term that describes the name assigned to a person at birth, which they no longer use, as it does not align with their affirmed gender and can also be referred to as their old name.
4. bigender	D. Someone who does not identify with any gender.
5. bilateral mastectomy	E. The belief that there are only two genders: male and female.
6. binary	F. A surgical procedure that permanently changes the genitals or internal reproductive organs.
7. binding	G. Someone who possesses both masculine and feminine characteristics.
8. bisexual (bi)	H. A surgical procedure that removes breast tissue from both sides of the chest and can include the construction of a male-appearing chest.
9. bottom surgery	I. Someone whose gender assigned at birth and gender identity are aligned.
10. cisgender (cis)	J. The advantages granted by society to people whose gender aligns with the gender assigned at birth.
11. cisgender privilege	K. Someone who experiences themselves as both masculine and feminine.
12. deadname	L. A practice of using material or clothing to constrict the breasts that enables a person to flatten their chest.

Retake this pre-test as a post-test to assess your personal progress and knowledge.

Match the vocabulary (the numbers) with the definitions (the letters) by drawing a line from a number to a letter, as a pre-test, to see which words or terms you already know, and which words are new to you. Each number and letter should only be used once. What were the results? The answer keys are provided in the Answer Key section in Chapter 15. It is suggested that you check your answers when you have taken the pre-test to see how well you did. Feel free to repeat this process at a later time; you may choose to use this activity to assess your progress by using this game as a post-test.

Matching Pre-Test #2

1. dilate	A. Surgery that brings the individual's body into alignment with their gender identity.
2. drag	B. An abbreviation that describes a person who now identifies as male gendered but was assigned a female gender at birth.
3. endocrinologist	C. A gender identity and expression that encompasses a variety of aspects related to femininity and masculinity that could change over time.
4. facial feminization surgery	D. One's internal sense of being masculine-identified, feminine-identified, neither, or both.
5. FTM/F2M/MTM/ female-to-male	E. A medical doctor who specializes in glands and hormones.
6. gatekeeper	F. How a person internally experiences themselves as male, female, masculine, feminine, some combination of these, or none of them; aspects of these can be culturally defined.
7. gender	G. Enacting gender for the purpose of performance or show.
8. gender-affirming surgery (GAS)	H. A mental health or medical professional who controls access to medical treatment such as hormones and surgery.
9. gender dysphoria	I. The manner in which a person demonstrates their masculinity and/or femininity, which can include clothing, body, behavior, speech, gestures, and other forms of appearance.
10. gender expression	J. A prescribed routine post-vaginoplasty where a person inserts medical equipment into the neovagina in order to maintain the creation of the vaginal canal.
11. gender fluid	K. The uncomfortable, distressing, anxiety-provoking, and/or sometimes depressing feelings that occur in people when aspects of their body and behavior are not congruent with their gender identity.
12. gender identity	L. A variety of plastic surgery procedures to create a more feminine appearance to the features of the face.

Retake this pre-test as a post-test to assess your personal progress and knowledge.

Match the vocabulary (the numbers) with the definitions (the letters) by drawing a line from a number to a letter, as a pre-test, to see which words or terms you already know, and which words are new to you. Each number and letter should only be used once. What were the results? The answer keys are provided in the Answer Key section in Chapter 15. It is suggested that you check your answers when you have taken the pre-test to see how well you did. Feel free to repeat this process at a later time; you may choose to use this activity to assess your progress by using this game as a post-test.

Matching Pre-Test #3

1. gender marker	A. A term for people who do not meet common gender norms.
2. gender nonconforming	B. A medical term for the hormone that is released by the hypothalamus governing the production of LH (Luteinizing Hormone) and FSH (Follicle-Stimulating Hormone) by the pituitary gland, which causes the gonads to produce estrogen and testosterone.
3. genderqueer	C. A type of bottom surgery that involves the removal of testicles.
4. GnRH (Gonadotropin Releasing Hormone)	D. A type of relationship where a person is sexually and/or romantically involved with only one person at a time.
5. intersex	E. An abbreviation that describes a person who now identifies as female gendered but was assigned a male gender at birth.
6. LGBTQQIA+ (also LGBTQ and LGBTQ+)	F. An all-encompassing abbreviation which stands for lesbian, gay, bisexual, transgender, queer, questioning, intersex, allies, plus others.
7. metoidioplasty	G. A gender that is not exclusively male or exclusively female and is outside the gender binary.
8. misogyny	H. The legal designation of one's gender on official documentation or records.
9. monogamous	I. A group of medical conditions where someone can be born with ambiguous genitalia and/or internal sex organs or chromosomal differences that are not clearly male or female.
10. MTF/M2F/FTF/ male-to-female	J. A disdain, hatred, or mistrust of all people female and feminine.
11. non-binary	K. A gender-affirming bottom surgery which releases the micro phallus and can include urethra lengthening.
12. orchiectomy	L. A gender that is not exclusively masculine or exclusively feminine and is outside the gender binary.

Retake this pre-test as a post-test to assess your personal progress and knowledge.

Match the vocabulary (the numbers) with the definitions (the letters) by drawing a line from a number to a letter, as a pre-test, to see which words or terms you already know, and which words are new to you. Each number and letter should only be used once. What were the results? The answer keys are provided in the Answer Key section in Chapter 15. It is suggested that you check your answers when you have taken the pre-test to see how well you did. Feel free to repeat this process at a later time; you may choose to use this activity to assess your progress by using this game as a post-test.

Matching Pre-Test #4

1. outing	A. The ability for a person to be read as their affirmed gender by those who are unaware that the individual's identity is transgender.
2. packing	B. The practice of using or referring to a person in the way an individual desires to be addressed, when pronouns are involved.
3. pan hysterectomy	C. A term for a medicine that blocks the hormone GnRH (Gonadotropin Releasing Hormone).
4. pansexual	D. The act of a person who is attempting to figure out their own sexuality and/or gender.
5. passing	E. A surgical procedure that creates a scrotal sac and can include testicular implants.
6. phalloplasty	F. The act of disclosing someone's sexuality and/or gender identity without their knowledge or permission.
7. polyamorous	G. The use of prosthetics and/or other materials to enable an individual to possess the appearance and feeling of having a penis and testicles.
8. preferred gender pronouns	H. A type of bottom surgery that usually includes removing the uterus, ovaries, and fallopian tubes and which could involve the removal of the cervix.
9. puberty blockers	I. The pattern of thoughts, feelings, and arousal that determine sexual preferences.
10. questioning	J. A type of relationship where a person is sexually and/or romantically involved with more than one person at the same time.
11. scrotoplasty	K. Someone who is attracted to people of various genders.
12. sexuality	L. A type of bottom surgery that entails the construction of a penis and can include the construction of testicles and the implant of an erection device.

Retake this pre-test as a post-test to assess your personal progress and knowledge.

Match the vocabulary (the numbers) with the definitions (the letters) by drawing a line from a number to a letter, as a pre-test, to see which words or terms you already know, and which words are new to you. Each number and letter should only be used once. What were the results? The answer keys are provided in the Answer Key section in Chapter 15. It is suggested that you check your answers when you have taken the pre-test to see how well you did. Feel free to repeat this process at a later time; you may choose to use this activity to assess your progress by using this game as a post-test.

Matching Pre-Test #5

1. stealth	A. A word that may be used as a gender-neutral pronoun to describe a single individual.
2. Tanner stages	B. A word used for a transgender person who chooses to keep their trans status private.
3. they	C. An overarching word which can be used for people whose gender expression and/or gender identity does not align with their sex assigned at birth.
4. top surgery	D. A word coined by Julia Serano to describe a form of misogyny that is focused on trans women.
5. tracheal shave	E. The surgical construction of a vagina.
6. transgender/ trans-identified	F. A system to classify the development of puberty in children.
7. transitioning	G. A surgical procedure made to create a masculine-appearing chest or to have breast implants.
8. transmisogyny	H. An Indigenous North American identity embraced by some individuals who incorporate a variety of gender roles, identities, and expressions by embodying both masculine and feminine spirits and traits.
9. transphobia	I. The social and medical actions a person takes to explore and/or affirm their gender identity.
10. transsexual	J. Prejudice, fear, disdain, or discrimination in respect of gender nonconforming and transgender people.
11. two-spirit	K. A surgical procedure that reduces the thyroid cartilage, which makes up the Adam's apple.
12. vaginoplasty	L. A person who identifies within the gender binary (either male or female) and may have medical procedures to bring their body in line with their identity. However, not all transgender people who have medical transitions identify as transsexual.

Retake this pre-test as a post-test to assess your personal progress and knowledge.

REFLECTIVE RESPONSES

1. How do/did you prefer to learn all the vocabulary/terms related to your child's transition?

....
....
....

2. Which words/terms describe or apply to you now?

....
....
....

3. Which words/terms describe or apply to your child now?

....
....
....

4. Which words/terms describe or apply to you as a family now, and how will you decide this?

....
....
....

5. Which words/terms, if any, confuse or upset you and why?

....
....
....

6. Which words/terms, if any, do you want to share with others?

....

....

....

7. How will you decide who you will share which words and/or terms with, and when?

....

....

....

8. Are there any words/terms that will be shifting as your child's transition evolves? If so, which ones, and what is the tentative timing of the shift?

....

....

....

9. Are there any particular words and terms any family members prefer never to use in reference to your child? If so, which ones and why?

....

....

....

10. Which words and/or terms are completely new to you?

....

....

....

VOCABULARY FOR ALL GAMES

agender	dilate	gender marker	outing	stealth
androgynous	drag	gender nonconforming	packing	Tanner stages
asexual	endocrinologist	genderqueer	pan hysterectomy	they
bigender	facial feminization surgery	GnRH	pansexual	top surgery
bilateral mastectomy	FTM/F-T-M/F2M/ MTM/M-T-M	intersex	passing	tracheal shave
binary	gatekeeper	LGBTQ/LGBTQ+/ LGBTQQIA+	phalloplasty	trans-identified/ transgender
binding	gender	metoidioplasty	polyamorous	transitioning
bisexual	gender-affirming surgery	misogyny	preferred gender pronouns	transmisogyny
bottom surgery	gender dysphoria	monogamous	puberty blockers	transphobia
cisgender	gender expression	MTF/M-T-F/M2F/ FTF/F-T-F	questioning	transsexual
cisgender privilege	gender fluid	non-binary	scrotoplasty	two-spirit
deadname	gender identity	orchiectomy	sexuality	vaginoplasty

How many of the words above can you find in the Word Search on the next page?

Once found, circle or highlight them! (Can you also find the bonus words: families, parents, and queer?)

Word Search

```
S R E K C O L B Y T R E B U P X F A M I L I E S R
N Y D I L A T E Q N G T A S E G A T S R E N N A T
S T H E Y D G N I M R O F N O C N O N R E D N E G
M T M S U O N Y G O R D N A G A T E K E E P E R S
S G E N D E R M A R K E R S S U O P E H R N G I Y
N K W T I T W O S P I R I T G N I T U O Y S A C N
U G A R D V T T R A C H E A L S H A V E R B D I Y
O M P A X C R C Q T B G L T O P S U R G E R Y S G
N E A N G J A E F S U O R O M A Y L O P G G P G O
O T N S N R N T R E B I N D I N G R L H R A Y E S
R O H I I Y S S E X S G N M X S V X A A U I T N I
P I Y D N T M A D U Y Q H T A E U N U L S R I D M
R D S E O S I M N A D U E F H X G T X L M O T E V
E I T N I A S L E L K E L M E U B R E O O H N R A
D O E T T L O A G I O E Q S R A I A S P T P E P G
N P R I I P G R S T U R A V X L G P A L T S D R I
E L E F S O Y E N Y I N T E R S E X R A O Y I I N
G A C I N T N T A Y A O Z B R Z N C O S B D R V O
D S T E A O Y A R S T N E R A P D V S T W R E I P
E T O D R R M L T N P F H T L A E T S Y A E D L L
R Y M O T C E I H C R O B I N A R Y D I O D N E A
R G Y C I S P B K G L R E D N E G A R Q E N E G S
E Y R E G R U S G N I M R I F F A R E D N E G E T
F A C I A L F E M I N I Z A T I O N S U R G E R Y
E F T M S U O M A G O N O M F N O E M A N D A E D
R R E E U Q R E D N E G Y T C I S G E N D E R Z W
P A S S I N G R E D N E G D I U L F R E D N E G O
G N I K C A P G E N D E R E X P R E S S I O N Z G
P L A U X E S S N A R T A S D F Y R A N I B N O N
E J B I S E X U A L T S I G O L O N I R C O D N E
Z G N I N O I T S E U Q X T R A N S P H O B I A Z
```

The answer key for the Word Search is in the Answer Key section in Chapter 15. Good luck and have fun!

DESERVING DE-STRESSING DELIGHT

A Date with Yourself

Make a date with yourself, which can lovingly be called "Getting to Know Yourself." Making a date with yourself can be quite a liberating and exhilarating experience but can also feel strange and scary. Taking time to reflect and feel rejuvenated from all the decisions that require your energy, can be draining. If you are the type of person who craves the company of others, it might surprise you if you suddenly have the yearning to spend periods of time by yourself. Perhaps this will possibly be due to your desire to explore your individual journey, knowing your child seems to be aware of what they want and need, while you may be unsure of what you want and need alongside their evolving transition.

> ANECDOTAL AFFIRMATION
>
> *Options galore,*
> *Sometimes*
> *Too abundant!*

Friends and family may often express their opinions of what they would do if this was their own journey. They can all be well intentioned, but in the end, it will be you who will have to explore all of your options. Out of this unknowing, perhaps you will decide that you want to make dates with yourself and try to figure out what is right for you. Make a list of the things you enjoy and then attempt to do one or two of them. You may like to write in solitude or prefer to reflect as you experience an event or activity. Little by little, hopefully, you will be able to look within yourself to find the answers and results that work for you.

Some people have elected to take mini-vacations alone, while others told those in their lives that they were away on vacation, but in actuality stayed home and did not respond to outside communication. Those with financial obstacles searched for free events happening in their areas. One person shared that they went alone for a quiet bike ride by a lake for several hours and then stopped to paint with watercolors to capture what they had seen. All of these self-dates are offered only as examples of how beautiful the experience can be to explore your own truth through "Getting to Know Yourself" dates. Find what you love to do and then discover those hidden spaces and bravely unwrap them. As you date yourself from time to time, you can find exactly what you seek. The answers will come because they are inside you right now!

Journal your reaction to this Deserving De-Stressing Delight.

. . . .

. . . .

. . . .

. . . .

> **ANECDOTAL AFFIRMATION**
>
> *I want to hit rewind,*
> *Will cope with pause,*
> *Yet, you still*
> *Want to push*
> *FORWARD!*

GRAPHICS AND GAMES GALORE

ABC Game

Using the vocabulary listed in the chart on page 104, select 12 of the vocabulary words and then write each one of them on a separate index card. Mix the vocabulary word cards up and then place them in alphabetical order from left to right in a straight line. This will help you become more familiar with the vocabulary words.

Mix-n-Match Game

Print a copy of all vocabulary words and definition cards on pages 109–116, then cut up and glue/tape all of the words and the definitions from the vocabulary cards onto index cards. Next, select the 12 words and their matching meanings from any one of the Pre-Tests and use the index cards they are on to play the Mix-n-Match Game.

Randomly place the 12 vocabulary word cards face down, on the left side of a flat surface, in a vertical line from top to bottom. Then player one randomly places the 12 vocabulary definition cards face down, on the right side of the same flat surface, in a 3x4 configuration that is visually three rows of four cards. Now, player one turns over the top card from the vertical line of vocabulary word cards and reads it aloud. Next, the same player turns over any one of the vocabulary definition cards from the 3x4 configuration and reads it aloud. If they match, then player one keeps the matching pair and turns over the next vocabulary word card from the top of the vertical line and goes again by repeating the same directions. If they do not match, player one turns the vocabulary definition card back over, but keeps the vocabulary word card face up on top of the vertical line. The next player turns a new vocabulary definition card over and reads both the vocabulary word card and new vocabulary definition card aloud. If they match, then player two keeps the matching pair and turns over the next vocabulary word card from the top of the vertical line and goes again by repeating the same directions. If the cards do not match, player two turns the vocabulary definition card back over, but keeps the vocabulary word card face up on the vertical line. This process continues for all players, as long as necessary, until all pairs are matched. The player with the most pairs wins the game. An alternative is to play this game with the vocabulary definition cards forming the vertical line, from top to bottom, on the left side of a flat surface and the vocabulary word cards forming the 3x4 configuration on the right side of the same flat surface. You may elect to play with only the vocabulary words and/or only the definitions you do not know, in order to master them and/or use any combination of words and definitions provided on pages 109–116.

Solo Mix-n-Match Game

If playing alone, line any 12 vocabulary words face up on a flat surface and hold their matching definition cards in your hand. Turn over one index definition card at a time and place it under the corresponding vocabulary word until all words have a match. If you prefer to create your own Mix-n-Match cards, do so, and then add them to the ones you previously used. Feel free to make as many copies as you need to help you learn the vocabulary words and matching definitions.

Game Cards

agender	Someone who does not identify with any gender.	androgynous	Someone who possesses both masculine and feminine characteristics.
asexual	Someone who does not feel sexual attraction to other people.	bigender	Someone who experiences themselves as both masculine and feminine.
bilateral mastectomy	A surgical procedure that removes breast tissue from both sides of the chest and can include the construction of a male-appearing chest.	binary	The belief that there are only two genders: male and female.
binding	A practice of using material or clothing to constrict the breasts that enables a person to flatten their chest.	bisexual (bi)	A person who is attracted to both masculine and feminine people.

THE REFLECTIVE WORKBOOK FOR PARENTS AND FAMILIES OF TRANSGENDER AND NON-BINARY CHILDREN

bottom surgery	A surgical procedure that permanently changes the genitals or internal reproductive organs.	cisgender (cis)	Someone whose gender assigned at birth and gender identity are aligned.
cisgender privilege	The advantages granted by society to people whose gender aligns with the gender assigned at birth.	deadname	A term that describes the name assigned to a person at birth, which they no longer use, for it does not align with their affirmed gender and can also be referred to as their old name.
dilate	A prescribed routine post-vaginoplasty where a person inserts medical equipment into the neovagina in order to maintain the creation of the vaginal canal.	drag	Enacting gender for the purpose of performance and/or show.
endocrinologist	A medical doctor who specializes in glands and hormones.	facial feminization surgery	A variety of plastic surgery procedures to create a more feminine appearance to the features of the face.

FTM (used in games) F-T-M Female-To-Male F2M MTM (used in games) M-T-M	An abbreviation that describes a person who now identifies as male gendered but was assigned a female gender at birth.	gatekeeper	A mental health or medical professional who controls access to medical treatment such as hormones and surgery.
gender	How a person internally experiences themselves as male, female, masculine, feminine, some combination of these, or none of them; aspects of these can be culturally defined.	gender-affirming surgery (GAS)	Surgery that brings the individual's body into alignment with their gender identity.
gender dysphoria	The uncomfortable, distressing, anxiety-provoking, and/or sometimes depressing feelings that occur in people when aspects of their body and behavior are not congruent with their gender identity.	gender expression	The manner in which a person demonstrates their masculinity and/or femininity, which can include clothing, body, behavior, speech, gestures, and other forms of appearance.
gender fluid	A gender identity and expression that encompasses a variety of aspects related to femininity and masculinity that could change over time.	gender identity	One's internal sense of being masculine-identified, feminine-identified, neither, or both.

gender marker	The legal designation of one's gender on official documentation or records.	gender nonconforming	A term for people who do not meet common gender norms.
genderqueer	A gender that is not exclusively masculine or exclusively feminine and is outside the gender binary.	GnRH (Gonadotropin Releasing Hormone)	A medical term for the hormone that is released by the hypothalamus governing the production of LH and FSH by the pituitary gland, which causes the gonads to produce estrogen and testosterone.
intersex	A group of medical conditions where someone can be born with ambiguous genitalia and/or internal sex organs or chromosomal differences that are not clearly male or female.	LGBTQ (used in games) LGBTQ+ LGBTQQIA+	An all-encompassing abbreviation which stands for lesbian, gay, bisexual, transgender, queer, questioning, intersex, allies, plus others.
metoidioplasty	A gender-affirming bottom surgery which releases the micro phallus and can include urethra lengthening.	misogyny	A disdain, hatred, or mistrust of all people female and feminine.

monogamous	A type of relationship where a person is sexually and/or romantically involved with only one person at a time.	MTF (used in games) M-T-F Male-To-Female M2F FTF (used in games) F-T-F	An abbreviation that describes a person who now identifies as female gendered but was assigned a male gender at birth.
non-binary	A gender that is not exclusively male or exclusively female and is outside the gender binary.	orchiectomy	A type of bottom surgery that involves the removal of testicles.
outing	The act of disclosing someone's sexuality and/or gender identity without their knowledge or permission.	packing	The use of prosthetics and other materials to enable an individual to possess the appearance and feeling of having a penis and testicles.
pan hysterectomy	A type of bottom surgery that usually includes removing the uterus, ovaries, and fallopian tubes and which could involve the removal of the cervix.	pansexual	Someone who is attracted to people of various genders.

passing	The ability for a person to be read as their affirmed gender by those who are unaware that the individual's identity is transgender.	phalloplasty	A type of bottom surgery that entails the construction of a penis and can include the construction of testicles and the implant of an erection device.
polyamorous	A type of relationship where a person is sexually and/or romantically involved with more than one person at the same time.	preferred gender pronouns (PGP)	The practice of using or referring to a person in the way an individual desires to be addressed, when pronouns are involved.
puberty blockers	A term for a medicine that blocks the hormone GnRH (Gonadotropin Releasing Hormone).	questioning	The act of a person who is attempting to figure out their own sexuality and/or gender.
queer	A word that refers to a sexual orientation that is not heterosexual and/or anything that is non-heteronormative.	scrotoplasty	A surgical procedure that creates a scrotal sac and can include testicular implants.

sexuality	The pattern of thoughts, feelings, and arousal that determine sexual preferences.	stealth	A word used for a transgender person who chooses to keep their trans status private.
Tanner stages	A system to classify the development of puberty in children.	they	A word that may be used as a gender-neutral pronoun to describe a single individual.
top surgery	A surgical procedure made to create a masculine-appearing chest or to have breast implants.	tracheal shave	A surgical procedure that reduces the thyroid cartilage, which makes up the Adam's apple.
transgender/ trans-identified	An overarching word, which can be used for people whose gender expression and/or gender identity does not align with their sex assigned at birth.	transitioning	The social and/or medical actions a person takes to explore and/or affirm their gender identity.

transmisogyny	A word coined by Julia Serano to describe a form of misogyny that is focused on trans women.	transphobia	Prejudice, fear, disdain, or discrimination in respect to gender nonconforming and transgender people.
transsexual	A person who identifies within the gender binary (either male or female) and may have medical procedures to bring their body in line with their identity. However, not all transgender people who have medical transitions identify as transsexual.	two-spirit	An Indigenous North American identity embraced by some individuals who incorporate a variety of gender roles, identities, and expressions by embodying both masculine and feminine spirits and traits.
vaginoplasty	The surgical construction of a vagina.		

Blank Cards

Create your own game cards to add to the ones above. Feel free to make as many copies as you need to help you learn the vocabulary and definitions.

GRAPHICS AND GAMES GALORE

Crossword Puzzle

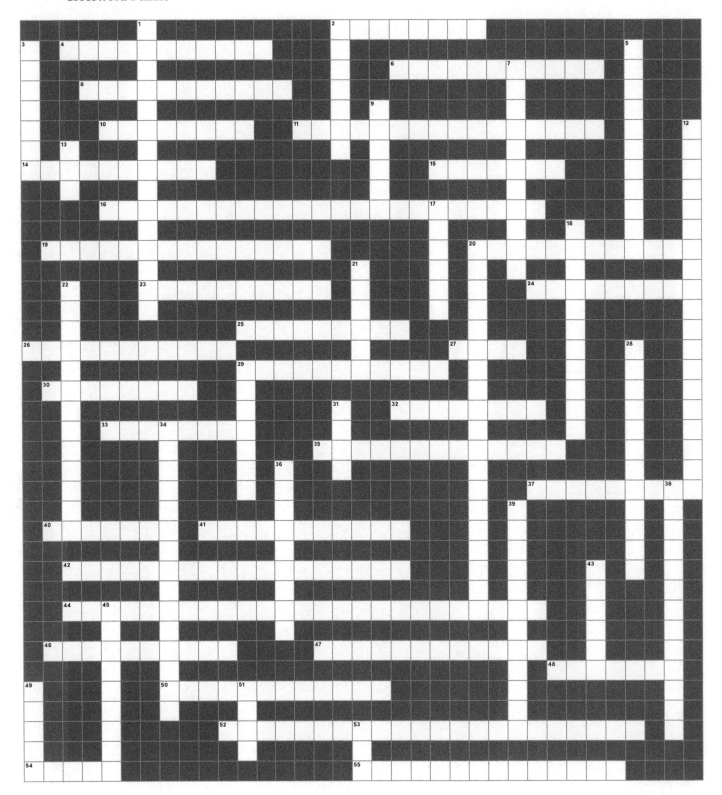

How to Do the Crossword Puzzle

Read the clues that correspond with the "across" and "down" numbers and fill in the puzzle with the answers. All the answers are words from the vocabulary chart on page 104. The answer key is provided in the Answer Key section in Chapter 15. These words from the vocabulary chart are *not* in the crossword puzzle: bottom surgery, gender dysphoria, gender identity, and trans-identified; however, this Bonus Word is included: *queer*.

Crossword Puzzle Clues

ACROSS

2 An 8-letter word that means someone who experiences themselves as both masculine and feminine.

4 An 11-letter word that means a type of relationship where a person is sexually and/or romantically involved with more than one person at the same time.

6 An 11-letter word that means a gender that is not exclusively masculine or exclusively feminine and is outside the gender binary.

8 An 11-letter word that means a type of bottom surgery that involves the removal of testicles.

10 An 8-letter word that means a person who is attracted to both masculine and feminine people.

11 A 16-letter term that means the manner in which a person demonstrates their masculinity and/or femininity and which can include clothing, body, behavior, speech, gestures, and other forms of appearance.

14 A 10-letter word that means a mental health or medical professional who controls access to medical treatment such as hormones and surgery.

15 A 7-letter word that means the ability for a person to be read as their affirmed gender by those who are unaware that the individual's identity is transgender.

16 A 23-letter term that means the practice of others using or referring to a person in the way an individual desires to be addressed, when pronouns are involved.

19 A 15-letter term that means a medicine that blocks the hormone GnRH (Gonadotropin Releasing Hormone).

20 A 12-letter term that means the legal designation of one's gender on official documentation or records.

23 A 10-letter word that means a type of relationship where a person is sexually and/or romantically involved with only one person at a time.

24 A 9-letter word that means someone who is attracted to people of various genders.

25 A 9-letter word that means a gender that is not exclusively male or exclusively female and is outside the gender binary.

26 An 11-letter term that means a gender identity and expression that encompasses a variety of aspects related to femininity and masculinity that could change over time.

27 A 4-letter word that means enacting gender for the purpose of performance and show.

29 An 11-letter word that means someone who possesses both masculine and feminine characteristics.

30 An 8-letter word that means a disdain, hatred, or mistrust of all female and feminine people.

32 An 8-letter word that means a term that describes the name assigned to a person at birth, which they no longer use, for it does not align with their affirmed gender and can also be referred to as their old name.

33 An 8-letter word that means a group of medical conditions where someone can be born with ambiguous genitalia and/or internal sex organs or chromosomal differences that are not clearly male or female.

35 A 13-letter word Julia Serano coined to describe a form of misogyny that is focused towards trans women.

37 A 9-letter word that means the pattern of thoughts, feelings, and arousal that determines sexual preferences.

40 A 7-letter word that means someone who does not identify with any gender.

41 An 11-letter word that means a person who identifies within the gender binary (either male or female) and may have medical procedures to bring their body in line with their identity. However, not all transgender people who have medical transitions identify as transsexual.

42 An 18-letter term that means the advantages granted by society to people whose gender aligns with the one assigned at birth.

44 A 25-letter term that means a variety of plastic surgery procedures made to create a more feminine appearance to the features of the face.

46 A 10-letter term that means a surgical procedure made to create a masculine-appearing chest or to have breast implants.

47 A 12-letter word that means a type of bottom surgery that entails the construction of a penis and can include the construction of testicles and the implant of an erection device.

48 A 7-letter word that is used for a transgender person who chooses to keep their trans status private.

50 A 12-letter word that means a surgical procedure that creates a scrotal sac and can include testicular implants.

52 A 22-letter term that means surgery that brings the individual's body into alignment with their gender identity.

54 A 5-letter word that refers to a sexual orientation that is not heterosexual and/or anything that is non-heteronormative.

55 A 14-letter word that means a gender-affirming bottom surgery which releases the micro phallus and can include lengthening of the urethra.

DOWN

1 A 15-letter term that means a type of bottom surgery that usually includes removing the uterus, ovaries, and fallopian tubes and which could involve the removal of the cervix.

2 A 7-letter word that means a practice of using material or clothing to constrict the breasts that enables a person to flatten their chest.

3 A 7-letter word that means the use of prosthetics and/or other materials to enable an individual to possess the appearance and feeling of having a penis and testicles.

5 An 11-letter overarching word which can be used for people whose gender expression and/or gender identity does not align with their sex assigned at birth.

7 An 11-letter word that means the act of a person who is attempting to figure out their own sexuality and/or gender.

9 A 6-letter word that means how a person internally experiences themselves as male, female, masculine, feminine, some combination of these, or none of them; aspects of these can be culturally defined.

12 A 19-letter term that means a surgical procedure that removes breast tissue from both sides of the chest and can include the construction of a male-appearing chest.

13 A 3-letter abbreviation that describes a person who now identifies as female gendered but was assigned a male gender at birth.

17 A 6-letter word that descrbie the act of disclosing someone's sexuality and/or gender identity without their knowledge or permission.

18 An 11-letter word that means prejudice, fear, disdain, or discrimination in respect of gender nonconforming and transgender people.

20 A 19-letter term that means people who do not meet common gender norms.

21 A 6-letter word that means the belief that there are only two genders: male and female.

22 A 13-letter word that means the social and/or medical actions a person takes to explore and/or affirm their gender identity.

28 A 12-letter word that means the surgical construction of a vagina.

29 A 7-letter word that means someone who does not feel sexual attraction to other people.

31 A 4-letter acronym which stands for Gonadotropin Releasing Hormone and means a medical term for the hormone that is released by the hypothalamus governing the production of LH (Luteinizing Hormone) and FSH (Follicle-Stimulating Hormone) by the pituitary gland, which causes the gonads to produce estrogen and testosterone.

34 A 15-letter word that means a medical doctor who specializes in glands and hormones.

36 A 9-letter word that means an Indigenous North American identity embraced by some individuals who incorporate a variety of gender roles, identities, and expressions by embodying both masculine and feminine spirits and traits.

38 A 13-letter term that means a surgical procedure that reduces the thyroid cartilage, which makes up the Adam's apple.

39 A 12-letter term that means a system to clarify the development of puberty in children.

43 A 6-letter word that means a prescribed routine post-vaginoplasty where a person inserts medical equipment into the neovagina in order to maintain the creation of the vaginal canal.

45 A 9-letter word that means someone whose gender assigned at birth and gender identity are aligned.

49 A 5-letter abbreviation which stands for lesbian, gay, bisexual, transgender, and queer.

51 A 4-letter word that may also be used as a gender-neutral pronoun to describe a single individual.

53 A 3-letter abbreviation that describes a person who now identifies as male gendered but was assigned a female gender at birth.

GRAPHICS AND GAMES GALORE

Three-in-a-Row

All players write nine of the vocabulary word cards, from the Mix-n-Match game, directly onto the empty spaces of a blank Three-in-a-Row board. One player reads the vocabulary definition cards aloud. If a player's Three-in-a-Row board has the vocabulary word that matches the vocabulary definition which was just read, the player puts a coin or placeholder onto the corresponding vocabulary word on their Three-in-a-Row board. Once a player's Three-in-a-Row board contains three placeholders in a row, they are the winner and verbally states: "Three-in-a-Row!" The player who reads the vocabulary definitions may opt to have their own Three-in-a-Row board too. Should all or some of the players prefer to each take turns reading the vocabulary definitions aloud, this option may also work well. An alternative is to have a player verbally state the vocabulary word and then players mark the matching vocabulary word on their Three-in-a-Row board. Another version is to have a player read the vocabulary words and the players mark the corresponding vocabulary definitions on their Three-in-a-Row board. It should be noted that each player will need to have written the vocabulary definitions onto the nine blank spaces of a blank Three-in-a-Row board, prior to playing this version of the game.

Supplies: Each player begins with a Three-in-a-Row board and nine coins or other placeholders. You may copy the Three-in-a-Row board from the workbook for the sole purpose of playing this game.

Suggestion: Feel free to make 6–10 copies of the Three-in-a-Row board below!

Board for Three-in-a-Row

SAMPLER SHARES

All names have been changed to ensure anonymity in this section. The first initial designates an individual and the second initial identifies the relationship to the child, i.e. P = their parent, G = their grandparent, and S = their sibling.

How do/did you prefer to learn all the vocabulary/terms related to your child's transition?

DP: Most of what I learned, I learned from my transgender son. When I was not sure, I asked him. I did a bit of research online and I also attended a support group. The support group was extremely helpful in that it was attended by family members of the LGBTQ+ community, as well as young trans people. Other parents, spouses, children, and friends of LGBTQ+ people attended as well. *PARENT/CHILD: AFAB (Uses he/him/his pronouns)*

HP: Listening is key to understanding and asking a lot of questions. I asked my son to explain the differences and it became even more clear to me in listening to him that he had been doing his own research for some time. There was a lot that I learned from his counselor and group meetings that we attended. Not to mention that once you have a child who is transgender, you will begin to hear and see a lot on the television and Internet. *PARENT/CHILD: AFAB (Uses he/him/his pronouns)*

FP: I attended a training with some co-workers about the needs of the population we serve that are a part of the LGBTQ+ community and discovered that there is so much more work to be done. A co-worker was puzzled by the fact that they had a term (cisgender) for people who identify with the gender that they were assigned at birth. Knowing that I have a transgender son, my co-worker asked, "Why do we need a label? Isn't that just 'normal'?" Of course, I remained professional and asked him whether he was implying that anything other than cisgender was abnormal. He said no, but his previous statement told me otherwise... *PARENT/CHILD: AFAB (Uses he/him/his pronouns)*

KP: Naturally, I was aware of the term non-binary and the use of the pronouns, "they/them/their" prior to my child's coming out, however, they had done a lot of research and shared the importance of using the information with me. Although it is sometimes difficult for me to get used to, I am trying to remember to do so regularly. *PARENT/CHILD: AFAB (Uses they/them/their pronouns)*

COMMUNICATION CORNER

ANECDOTAL AFFIRMATION

Honor
Your transition,
As your
Child
Transitions!

Which game/s, if any, would you like to invite your child, other family members, and/or friends to play with or without you and which game/s would you prefer to play alone?

1. If you played the Pre-Test Vocabulary Match #1 game and/or as a Post-Test, what did you learn?

. . . .

. . . .

. . . .

2. If you played the Pre-Test Vocabulary Match #2 game and/or as a Post-Test, what did you learn?

. . . .

. . . .

3. If you played the Pre-Test Vocabulary Match #3 game and/or as a Post-Test, what did you learn?

. . . .

. . . .

4. If you played the Pre-Test Vocabulary Match #4 game and/or as a Post-Test, what did you learn?

. . . .

. . . .

5. If you played the Pre-Test Vocabulary Match #5 game and/or as a Post-Test, what did you learn?

. . . .

. . . .

6. If you completed the Word Search, what did you learn?

. . . .

. . . .

7. If you played the ABC game, what did you learn?

. . . .

. . . .

8. If you played the Mix-n-Match and/or Solo games, what did you learn?

. . . .

. . . .

9. If you played the Three-in-a-Row game, what did you learn?

. . . .

. . . .

10. If you completed the Crossword Puzzle, what did you learn?

. . . .

. . . .

Chapter 6

SOCIAL AND MEDICAL OPTIONS: SORTING IT OUT!

VITAL VIGNETTE

The choices connected to social and medical options are as varied as the children questioning what is correct for them. Will your child need to transition socially and/or medically?

If so, how and to what extent will you and other adults be involved? For some parents and other family members, the answers to these questions will be obvious, straight forward, and very easy to support without much, if any, hesitation or doubt. For others, even if they are advocates, the road there may not be as immediate, if ever. Whether this is all extremely new to a family member or not, the decisions that you may be asked to make can be frightening and the reasons for this can vary.

Socially and/or medically transitioning can look very different in every circumstance. For some parents and other family members, your first experience of knowing someone who is transitioning and/or questioning their gender occurs when your child self-identifies on the transgender spectrum. For many, this can be an area with which you are unfamiliar, have questions to ask, or are not sure where to turn in order to obtain this knowledge.

One fundamental distinction that must be understood by all parents and other family members is that gender and sexuality are different from one another, but they are interrelated. Gender is how a person internally experiences themselves as male, female, masculine, feminine, some combination of these, or none of them; aspects of these can be culturally defined. Sexuality is the pattern of thoughts, feelings, and arousal that determine sexual preferences. For the purposes of this workbook, whenever sexuality is mentioned, it is specifically referring to sexual orientation that is described as: to whom a person is attracted and/or with whom they want to have sex.

As a parent or other family member, gaining this insight, should it not be previously known, will help you become better informed in terms of Transgender and Gender Non-Binary (TGNB) children. As this and other information is being learned, it is also essential for you to be aware that special needs children and/or those on the autism spectrum can also identify on the transgender spectrum and/or be questioning their gender.

Moreover, if or when your child transitions and/or is questioning their gender, two major aspects will be introduced: socially transitioning and/or medically transitioning. If your child is under legal age, parents or others legally responsible for your child's welfare will be involved with both the process and decision making in relation to the outcome. In many instances, a key difference between socially transitioning and medically transitioning is that most social interventions can easily be implemented or reversed on their own. Whereas, a large majority of medical interventions would require trained and highly skilled professional assistance in making any changes.

To help untangle misinformation, most young children who identify on the transgender spectrum and/or are questioning their gender begin their process by socially transitioning. Socially transitioning can be in an abundance of forms and in most cases these changes are not invasive. If this aspect is part of your child's journey, there is no specific order in which any of the social interventions need to occur. Each child, ideally with the involvement of an adult legally responsible for their care, will determine for themselves which, if any options, feel correct for them. Since a large number of children may be discovering what feels right for them, these factors may be adjusted throughout the transition process. It is critical that parents and other family members acknowledge this process by providing flexibility as their child travels this path.

For some children, changing their pronouns to align with their affirmed gender can be an extremely vital part of their social transition. This is also true for their name. Whether this is done legally or not, having parents and other family members support these two simple modifications can have an enormous, positive, and emotional effect on your child's daily life.

Dressing and/or wearing their hair in a manner that aligns with your child's affirmed gender can be a physical type of adjustment that helps them feel at ease with their body and it is also quite helpful in reducing their gender dysphoria. Gender dysphoria is the uncomfortable, distressing, anxiety-provoking, and/or sometimes depressing feelings that occur in people when aspects of their body and behavior are not congruent with their gender identity. By dressing and/or styling their hair in a way that empowers them to accurately express their affirmed gender, it can also offer visual cues which enables your child to be seen properly and, in many instances, may prevent them from being gendered incorrectly. For those children who identify as non-binary, their affirmed gender may not align with the binary options often imposed on children in Western culture. As a result, though a non-binary child may dress and/or style their hair in a manner that is being true to and representative of themselves, it is imperative that those who interact with your child make every attempt to correctly use the pronouns and/or name that affirms their gender, for if this does not occur, it can be emotionally humiliating to them.

Furthermore, where your child and/or family lives, may affect the choices you ponder in reference to the social aspects of the transition. Your child and family's safety must always be taken into consideration. That being said, for some children, purchasing their clothes online may be their preference and/or the best option; while for others, they may want to try on new clothes in a physical store. Sometimes, family members will offer to visit a store ahead of time, to explore whether the store has private dressing rooms or to simply observe the pulse of a venue's culture. When using a hair salon, some families will opt to use a stylist that they already know is an ally. Other times, children may want to go to a particular salon, which they never used in the past. For some salons, this can be a non-issue; yet for others, the potential exists for encountering an uncomfortable and/or volatile situation, if that salon is not an ally of the LGBTQ+ community. Being cognizant of this, a parent shared that they found it advantageous to inquire about a salon's specific policies and to explain what they were looking for ahead of time. This practice can be used to examine a myriad of venues your child may desire to use in the future.

Socially transitioning can also include other attributes which signal visual cues to allow your child to be read in a way that aligns with their affirmed gender and/or combats some aspects of gender dysphoria they may be experiencing. For some children, wearing makeup or not wearing makeup, can also be a non-invasive technique to implement, and can easily be adjusted over time. There may be children who will find comfort in flattening their chest through binding, creating a flattened appearance of genitals by tucking, or constructing the visual presence of genitals by packing. In addition, some will have the need to non-surgically enhance their chest through padding, as well as padding or dressing in a manner that contours the shape of their hip area. Doing so can provide emotional relief when medical interventions are currently not an option during the transition process. Whether identifying within the binary or as non-binary, these modifications may not be visibly obvious to parents and other family members, nevertheless, they can be occurring.

Other ways your child can socially transition is by altering their voice, mannerisms, and movements. A person's voice is often a vital component that influences others to categorize someone's gender and if improperly perceived, it can create an array of misunderstandings. Being aware of this, your child may investigate ways to project their voice in a manner that aligns with their affirmed gender in hopes of having others, whether in person or on the phone, recognize them according to the gender they self-identify. One way your child can learn to alter their voice is by consulting the expertise of a trans-competent, speech and language pathologist. Should this option not be accessible, those seeking this type of intervention may opt to use vocal exercises demonstrated by some online videos. There may be other means in which your child can appropriately obtain methods to alter the pitch and/or sound of their voice without the interventions being permanent.

People will often assess your child's gender through their physical movements such as walking, dancing, sitting, laying, standing, or posing, as well as by their mannerisms and gestures. Your child may be at ease with their current physical movements, mannerisms, and gestures, knowing that they convey and match their affirmed gender. If this is not the case, they can now be consciously learning and working towards adjusting these to align with the way they feel their gender should be viewed.

Transitioning may impact dating for both trans youth and trans adults. Dating for TGNB and/or gender questioning youth and adults, just as for cisgender individuals, can be fairly complex. This may be especially valid for some youth and adults who identify as TGNB and/or questioning their gender, yet, this may not be true for all. It is important for parents and other family members to understand that your child's sexual orientation can be fluid and if this occurs, their choices must be respected.

In addition, medically transitioning is commonly what most individuals assume transitioning means and for many, depending on their age, finances, laws, guidelines, and personal needs, this can be part of the process. Some parents and other family members may not be aware that there are strict guidelines involving medical interventions for children and young adults. These Standards of Care (SOC), provided by the World Professional Association for Transgender Health (WPATH), are created with the utmost caution and sound medical judgment available to guide all medical and mental health professionals as to how to follow proper protocol when serving all those who identify as transgender. WPATH has specific guidelines that apply to all minors and can be accessed through their website, which is contained in the resource section of this workbook. Most medical interventions are not recommended nor permitted for minors regarding any type of gender-affirming related surgery. This is typically not a part of a minor's medical transition.

Taking puberty blockers or gender-affirming hormones may be or become part of your child's medical transition, should your child state they need this intervention. If either one of these interventions play a role in their medical transition, your child's physical development and hormone levels will be determining considerations when consulting with medical providers. Medical professionals, knowledgeable about these factors, will need to monitor Tanner stages and consult with you or those who are legally responsible for your child's medical decisions, before deciding whether puberty blockers or gender-affirming hormones are appropriate to be used as part of their medical transition. Should a procedure and/or hormone treatment be an option for a minor, based on their individual circumstances and their obtained data, important conversations will need to occur in reference to any risk factors and/or side effects. Detailed planning must be put in place according to WPATH guidelines, for each step has to be explained to you and your child alike, prior to consent. Quite often a qualified mental health professional is part of the team along with medical professionals to determine if a medical intervention is both warranted and appropriate for a minor according to SOC protocol. Being armed with the knowledge of understanding the differences between socially and medically transitioning can dispel many of the misconceptions held by parents and other family members. While many TGNB children and/or those questioning their gender may socially transition in a variety of ways as minors, far fewer seem to do so medically. Nevertheless, should these minors partake in medically transitioning, it is primarily hormone related.

Transitioning without any medical interventions is a real possibility and one that many children may begin or end with, but since this is something that could play an important role in your child's life, critical conversations are essential. For many, adding puberty blockers or gender-affirming hormones to the equation are other layers that can have an impact on the dynamics of the family. The physical changes that can occur are varied. Some parents, aware of the options or not, may find these viable alterations hard to absorb as they learn some gender-affirming hormones can affect their child's genitals, skin texture, vocal pitch, personal scent, the gain or loss of hair in different locations, and mood. When studying puberty blockers or gender-affirming hormones, it is significant to understand the role Tanner stages play in the medical transition process and how they will be addressed and supervised. Knowing the recommended guidelines for various ages and/or stages and how to manage them throughout medical interventions, as well as, what future fertility options there might be, are major considerations that may need to be discussed in a highly responsible and well-informed manner.

During the interview process with experienced medical professionals in this field, and/or in facilities in which they work, it is suggested that you and/or a person to whom you granted consent to advocate for your child, prepare questions prior to meeting with medical professionals and also decide who will record the answers. It is key that everyone involved with this aspect of the process be determined ahead of time and that they will review the questions prior to any medical appointments.

With the prospect of surgery, it can become too much to absorb, especially if communication is a struggle. Nevertheless, for many parents, being included in all aspects of the social and/or medical transition can be a lifesaver and a way to bond with your child. Acknowledging the value of parents' voices in decision making and listening to their concerns are critical forms of respect and cannot be overstated. Gathering information from reliable sources, acquiring the advice of experienced medical professionals in this field, and speaking with others who have gone through the medical process, can be of tremendous help for the entire family.

Once aware of the needs of your child, parents may request a period of time, before anything medical, or even social begins, to figure out what they are comfortable being present for and what they are not. Parents may also reserve the right to change their mind, as some things have to be experienced before one can know exactly how they will feel about changes in their life. However, parents must comprehend how the impact of their choices can affect their child's emotional and physical well-being, now and in the future.

For some parents, their understanding and involvement are extensive. For others, much or a portion of the transition may be overwhelming and not participating in certain aspects may be the decision that works best for them. There is no exact way to navigate the transition, and no family member should be judged on how they need to process the transition for themselves. Parents must give themselves permission to set boundaries and allow themselves time to sort out what is and is not comfortable for them. It is as important to know what you can handle, as it is to know what you cannot handle. Simultaneously, parents must always respect what their child needs to feel whole.

It is necessary to recognize that if a parent cannot accept their child's needs, it is suggested that they contemplate allowing a mutually agreed upon adult to be their child's advocate. In this situation, parents may be required to sign legal documentation granting permission for this person to act on their child's behalf. It is highly recommended and extremely critical that parents of minors seek counsel who have specific and expert knowledge of the laws and policies in order to address legal matters. The guidance you receive from these legal professionals must be considered before making any decisions and whenever possible, you should request that their advice not only be stated verbally, but also in writing.

Though some parents will be 100% on board; others can ask for additional time to consider their child's needs, even if it is not on the exact timeline of their child. The more transparent and informed a family is, the better they will be able to discuss and communicate what each person wants, needs, and is able to contribute. Being prepared is also fundamental since surgeries may have complications, hormone levels need monitoring, and finances can be greatly drained. Having multiple plans in place for many potential situations can help in moments of urgency, and having the parents and other family members be part of this planning can prove to be invaluable.

Researching the amount of experience a medical professional and/or mental health provider has in regard to the transition process, in order to determine if they have the skills and experience necessary to fully address your child's specific needs, is imperative. The WPATH SOC have a checklist of how to determine a provider's competency. It is recommended that professionals explain how they will convey relevant information to you and your child, if interventions are necessary. If inquiring about medical procedures, you may elect to ask to view photos of past surgeries and/or a list of people who are willing to speak with you about having used the medical professional's services for the same type of procedures and/or interventions you may be seeking for your child.

Armed with this information, families can then decide what, in each and every situation, will enable their child and family to choose what is best for them as they explore this journey. Every single determination made in sorting out medical and/or social options is extremely vital and should never be taken lightly. There can be real risks, emotional roller coasters, fearful unknowns, and extremely difficult decisions that can make you feel as if you are drowning. Equally notable, there can also be ample moments of celebration for what has changed, excitement sparked by seeing your child dressed in their affirmed gender, and a sense that your child will be able to live in the body that helps them feel whole. Working together, communicating regularly with your child and family members, as well as with respected professionals in the field of transgender health, and creating supportive teams throughout this process, are the best assurances for success in navigating varying stages of the transition. Above all else, being true to yourself is important, but honoring and listening to your child's needs are absolutely crucial!

GRAPHICS GALORE

Splash

Can you record the social and medical interventions that you believe your child may consider based on the knowledge you have now? By creatively splashing words and short phrases, quickly attempt to express your answers randomly with as many responses as possible scattered on the paper.

GRAPHICS GALORE

T-Chart

How has my knowledge of social and medical options changed throughout the transition?

These are social and medical options I know about in relation to the transition process:	These are social and medical options I want to know about in relation to the transition process:	These are social and medical options I learned about in relation to the transition process:

REFLECTIVE RESPONSES

1. In what ways, if any, are you comfortable or uncomfortable with helping your child, if they decide to socially and/or medically transition, now or in the future?

    . . . .

    . . . .

    . . . .

2. What role does your child expect or want you to play throughout any portion of their social and/or medical transition, now or in the future?

    . . . .

    . . . .

    . . . .

3. What do you think you will do if you do not feel comfortable with the social and/or medical interventions, now or in the future?

    . . . .

    . . . .

    . . . .

4. How did/does it feel to address and/or introduce your child to others using their affirmed name and/or pronouns?

    . . . .

    . . . .

    . . . .

5. How did/does it feel to experience your child at home as they are living in their affirmed gender, as a result of socially transitioning?

. . . .

. . . .

. . . .

6. How did/does it feel to experience your child with family and/or friends as they are living in their affirmed gender, as a result of socially transitioning?

. . . .

. . . .

. . . .

7. How did/does it feel to experience your child when attending school functions, clothes shopping, or in other public activities as they are living in their affirmed gender, as a result of socially transitioning?

. . . .

. . . .

. . . .

8. Which doctor appointments will you, and/or another designated representative, go to with your child?

. . . .

. . . .

. . . .

9. How do you feel about not going to any of the medical appointments, now or in the future?

. . . .

. . . .

. . . .

10. What questions do you, your child, and/or another person want to ask the doctors, now or in the future?

....

....

....

11. How do you plan to find out what you will need to know in order to help with the medical post-operative caretaking, now or in the future?

....

....

....

12. What type of information will you need to give the medical providers, now or in the future?

....

....

....

13. Who will be your support team, if there is a the surgical portion of the transition, and what does that look like for you, now or in the future? (That is, who will relieve you, so you can sleep or eat during the post-surgery period?)

....

....

....

14. What are the potential medical complications of interventions your child is considering and what are the visual, behavioral, and physical signs you may notice, now or in the future?

. . . .

. . . .

. . . .

15. How will you find out if your medical insurance will pay for the medicine, puberty blockers, gender-affirming hormones, and surgery, now or in the future?

. . . .

. . . .

. . . .

GRAPHICS GALORE

Web

What type of social and/or medical interventions do you feel are options for your child at this point? (Feel free to incorporate responses from the Splash or not.) If you find it easier, create two different webs, one titled "Social Interventions" and the other titled "Medical Interventions." You may elect to revisit your responses as your child ages or their needs progress.

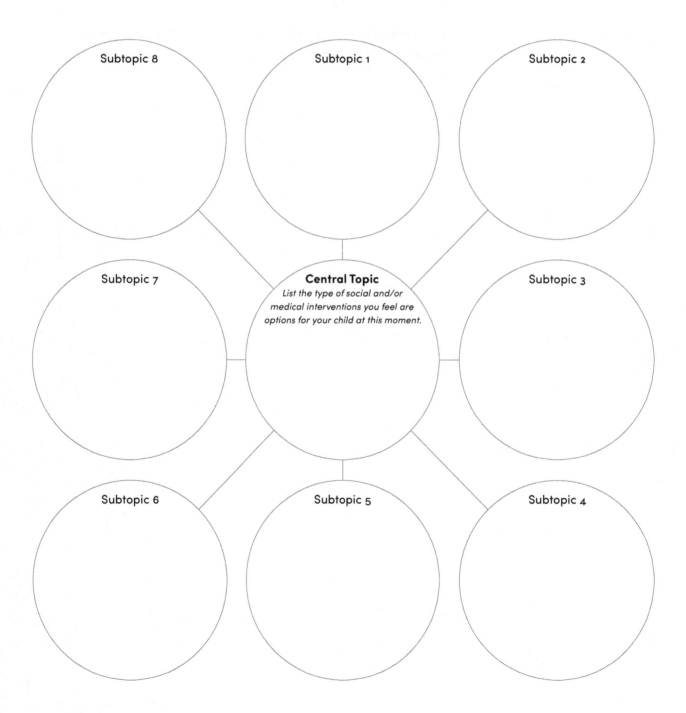

GRAPHICS GALORE

Venn Diagram

Which social and/or medical interventions do you feel or know...

1. ...you are comfortable with your child pursuing, now or in the future?

2. ...your child is comfortable with pursuing, now or in the future?

4.

7.

5.

6.

3. ...other family members are comfortable with undertaking, now or in the future?

DESERVING DE-STRESSING DELIGHT

Time with Your Child and Other Family Members

Often, your child and other family members can spend a great deal of time on transition-related goals. Hours can quickly turn into days of going to appointments, filling out forms, changing marker, discussing—and sometimes fighting—over options, explaining details to others, and researching next steps. While all of this is happening, everyone can grow further and further apart and lose sight of how the family once interacted.

It is critical to nurture the family relationships throughout the transition. One healthy way to address this is to schedule time with each other, where the process is not the major focus during a family outing, activity, or event. Some days, this will be extremely difficult to do, but those are probably the days when these relationships will need it the most. Plan how structured time can be scheduled. Some families elect one evening a week to do something they all enjoy as a unit, while other families alternate having one family member plan the time together. This planned time together is only for the family members who have taken an active role in the transition of the child. It can also be one-to-one scheduled time with a particular family member, if that is preferred, or whatever way best suits the needs of the individuals. You may want to discuss these ideas when negotiating the ground rules in relation to the family time.

Questions you may ask one another are:

- What type of things do you still like to do together?
- What topics are off the table?
- Which family members will be included?
- Who will plan this time?
- What will be the budget?
- How often will this occur?
- How will this be scheduled?

Whether all family members participate in the family time or completely support your child's transition may not be known yet. It is suggested that you continue communicating openly with each other and intentionally create the space to experience family time with one another. Even as the changes unfold, try not to allow the transition to be the only topic of conversation among all of you. The key is to make family time happen and for all of you to be committed to the ground rules you will create together as a team.

Journal your reaction to this Deserving De-Stressing Delight.

. . . .

. . . .

ANECDOTAL AFFIRMATION

Include me,
Talk to me,
I am here,
And will
Always be!

GRAPHICS GALORE

Box

What social interventions have you, your child, and/or another family member researched?

Type of intervention?	Date it was researched:	Who researched it?	Important information to record?
Type of intervention?	Date it was researched:	Who researched it?	Important information to record?
Type of intervention?	Date it was researched:	Who researched it?	Important information to record?
Type of intervention?	Date it was researched:	Who researched it?	Important information to record?

GRAPHICS GALORE

Timeline

Record information pertaining to any medically scheduled procedures your child needs to pursue, now or in the future. Some parents wish they had kept a log of all the critical happenings that occurred throughout the transition process. Feel free to adjust the timeline as you find out different, relevant information about the transition. You may choose to use this timeline to discuss these events with a therapist, or for your own reference, or to record for medical needs.

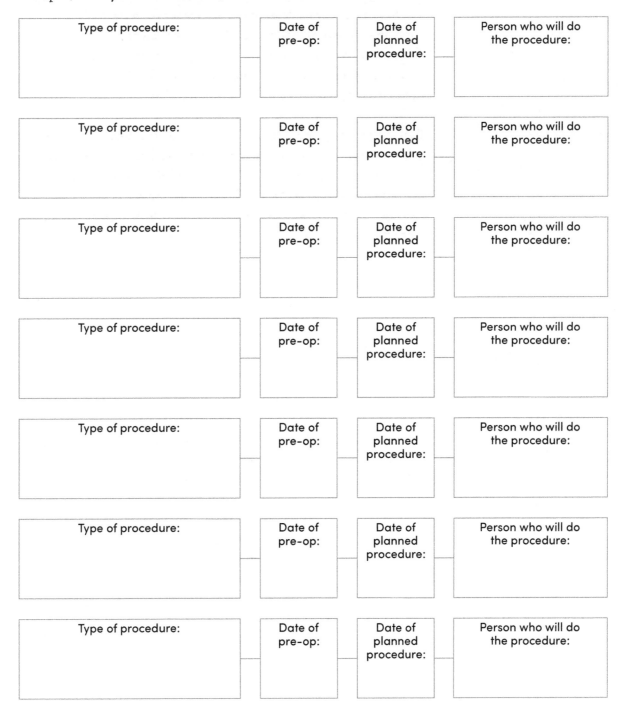

Type of procedure:	Date of pre-op:	Date of planned procedure:	Person who will do the procedure:
Type of procedure:	Date of pre-op:	Date of planned procedure:	Person who will do the procedure:
Type of procedure:	Date of pre-op:	Date of planned procedure:	Person who will do the procedure:
Type of procedure:	Date of pre-op:	Date of planned procedure:	Person who will do the procedure:
Type of procedure:	Date of pre-op:	Date of planned procedure:	Person who will do the procedure:
Type of procedure:	Date of pre-op:	Date of planned procedure:	Person who will do the procedure:
Type of procedure:	Date of pre-op:	Date of planned procedure:	Person who will do the procedure:

EMPATHY-EMBRACING EXERCISE

Gender dysphoria can motivate your child to seriously consider socially and/or medically transitioning. If your child is feeling extremely uncomfortable with aspects of their body in relation to their gender assigned at birth, those feelings can negatively impact their socialization, the activities they partake in, and their emotional state of mind. It can also affect their sex life in the future, and current experiences.

By incorporating this exercise, family members have an opportunity to reflect on what makes them feel uncomfortable with their own body and have at least some level of understanding of the struggle their child often faces on a daily basis. While acknowledging it is not the same experience as to what the child may encounter, it is important for family members to try to understand the critical role gender dysphoria may play in a child's transition process.

Does any part of your body impede you from participating socially, affect you emotionally, or prevent you from any daily activities? If yes or no, why do you think you feel this way? How does this make you feel? Is there any part of your body that you dislike or would prefer not to have sexually touched? If yes or no, why do you think you feel this way? How does this make you feel?

> ANECDOTAL AFFIRMATION
>
> *My senses*
> *Are overwhelmed,*
> *Shock has set in,*
> *Fear is loud,*
> *Concerns abundant.*
> *How did I not know?*
> *Now I do!*
> *What next?*

GRAPHICS GALORE

Bar Graph

To what degree do these concerns and related topics matter to you? Based on a scale from 1 to 10, with 1 being the lowest and 10 being the highest, color or shade in your response. This visual will illustrate where your greatest concerns lie and can be used as a tool to help you communicate your thoughts with your child and/or other family members, therapist, spiritual mentor, or for your own personal understanding. The bar graph results can vary as your child's transition progresses and your thoughts may shift.

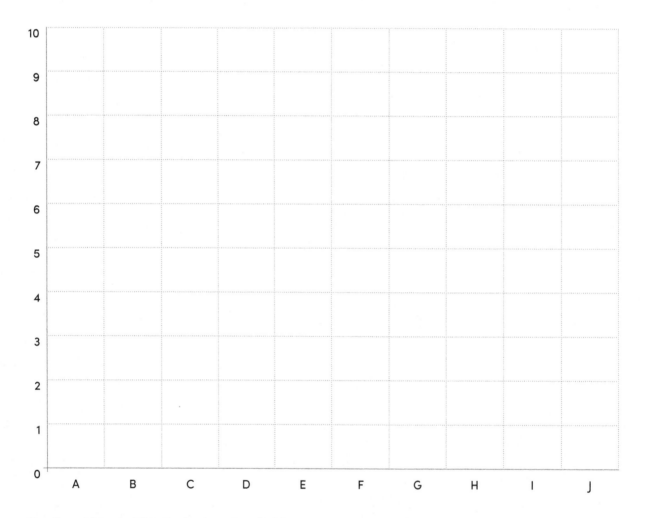

Use these ideas to fill in the bar graph or feel free to create your own!

A. Comfort with your child having bottom surgery.

B. Comfort with your child having top surgery.

C. Comfort with your child taking puberty blockers.

D. Comfort with your child taking gender-affirming hormones.

E. Comfort with your child altering their hairstyle and/or facial hair.

F. Comfort with your child's vocal range changing or not.

G. Comfort with your child dressing in a way (and using accessories) that is more aligned with their affirmed gender.

H. Comfort with your child's facial structure looking differently, in the future, due to medical interventions.

I. Comfort with your child adding or stopping the use of makeup.

J. Comfort with your child presenting more or less feminine or masculine.

GRAPHICS GALORE

Pie Graph

To what degree are these concerns and related topics important to you? Decide how significant these issues are to you in relation to each other. Place the number that corresponds with a suggested topic within as many slices of the pie that convey how each one matters to you. Only one number should be placed in each slice. You do not need to use all the issues, but do fill in all the slices. Feel free to create your own topics and assign them their own number.

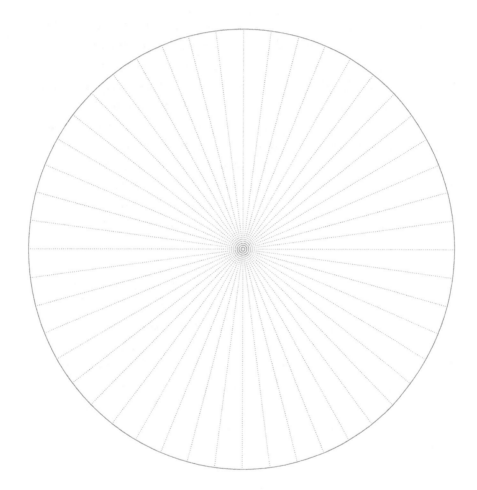

1. Comfort with your child having bottom surgery.

2. Comfort with your child having top surgery.

3. Comfort with your child taking puberty blockers.

4. Comfort with your child taking gender-affirming hormones.

5. Comfort with your child altering their hairstyle and/or facial hair.

6. Comfort with your child's vocal range changing or not.

7. Comfort with your child dressing in a way (and using accessories) that is more aligned with their affirmed gender.

8. Comfort with your child's facial structure looking differently, in the future, due to medical interventions.

9. Comfort with your child adding or stopping the use of makeup.

10. Comfort with your child presenting more or less feminine or masculine.

SAMPLER SHARES

All names have been changed to ensure anonymity in this section. The first initial designates an individual and the second initial identifies the relationship to the child, i.e. P = their parent, G = their grandparent, and S = their sibling.

In what ways, if any, are you comfortable or uncomfortable with helping your child, if they decide to socially transition and/or medically transition, now or in the future?

CP: My son came out to us at 17 and he turned 18 nine months later. It doesn't seem like such a huge deal now. He could have waited the nine months to begin his transition on his own without his dad and me, but that's not what he did. His social transition started almost immediately; we went clothes shopping, emptied his closet of dresses, got a haircut, informed the school. Within a couple weeks we had an appointment to start the process of medical transition. Within a couple of months, we had a legal name change. We did as much as we could before he started his senior year of high school so that he could graduate as the person he was always meant to be. I sat and cried with him when we were told that his gender confirmation surgery would be delayed from June to October which would be at the very beginning of his first semester of his freshman year of college, and I told him that I would still be there with him every step of the way. *PARENT/CHILD: AFAB (Uses he/him/his pronouns)*

GP: There was a conference coming up and we shared with our therapist that I felt like taking girls' clothing to the conference and letting my child choose if she wanted to wear them there. Of course, my daughter loved the idea. We were at the conference for a few days and my daughter was very happy being herself and free of judgments. When we came back home she didn't want to take the nail polish off. We passed by a carnival close to home and she wanted to go but refused to wear boys' clothing. So, we didn't go. After that, it was very clear to me that our journey had begun. My daughter went for an evaluation at a university that has a gender center, and that gave me the confidence to let my child socially transition. It was one of the hardest decisions I ever made, but yet the best one. *PARENT/CHILD: AMAB (Uses he/him/his pronouns)*

EP: I am currently taking my son to a hospital, close to where we live, to talk to their gender clinic to discuss the best route to start hormones. Our family doctor is very concerned about prescribing certain birth control pills that can cause clotting and then after six months starting testosterone, which can also cause clotting. Her concerns were exactly mine when she said, "Yes, the people at the hospital clinic are helpful now, but what if he has a stroke? Who will be there for him then? It won't be them...it will be you." I want my son to live a happy and fulfilled life and he knows I won't move forward with any treatment to alter his hormones until we have the most accurate and complete advice. I'm praying for a way forward and hoping the answer will be clear. I'm also concerned and question that if he starts to change with the testosterone while he's a minor, at 16 years old, will he be able to afford to keep it up once he is an adult and on his own? He knows this concern and is working hard in school to keep his grades up in order to move on with his education and ultimately be able to get a very good job that has insurance. I'm proud of him for showing an understanding of these very adult issues and being patient with the process, as well as working hard in the meantime until we move forward. *PARENT/ CHILD: AFAB (Uses he/him/his pronouns)*

COMMUNICATION CORNER

When you speak spontaneously out of anger or fear about the unknown, without thinking it through, you can sometimes regret the way you phrased your words or the tone you used to express your feelings. Rehearsing what you want to ask or discuss with your child, and other family members, can help you before you actually communicate your thoughts. This gives you a moment to reflect and pause before you converse about emotional topics. You may choose to practice asking these questions with a trusted friend, family member, spiritual mentor, or therapist first.

Explain your thoughts and feelings about these statements to one another verbally or in writing. It is important to note that some families elected to only address one question or two, while others preferred to answer them all. In order to recall the questions you answered, simply highlight and/or circle the ones you addressed as a family, yet acknowledge that you may return to discuss the others in the future. Decide what feels best for two or more family members and begin the conversation. Do you, your child, and other family members answer these questions in the same way or differently? Discuss your responses to understand how all of you view the answers to the questions and make time to celebrate all you learn from being willing to communicate with each other.

1. Does your child plan on having bottom surgery, now or in the future? If so, in what time frame and what type?

    . . . .

    . . . .

2. Does your child plan on having top surgery, now or in the future? If so, in what time frame and what type?

    . . . .

    . . . .

3. Does your child plan on beginning puberty blockers or gender-affirming hormones, now or in the future? If so, in what time frame and what type?

    . . . .

    . . . .

4. Does your child want and/or need to change their facial structure, now or in the future? If so, in what time frame and how?

. . . .

. . . .

5. Does your child plan on having vocal training, now or in the future? If so, in what time frame and what type?

. . . .

. . . .

6. Does your child plan on changing their hairstyle and/or facial hair, now or in the future? If so, in what time frame and to what style?

. . . .

. . . .

7. Does your child plan on presenting more or less feminine or masculine, now or in the future? If so, in what time frame and how?

. . . .

. . . .

8. Does your child plan on using or not using makeup, now or in the future? If so, in what time frame and how?

. . . .

. . . .

9. Does your child plan on dressing in a way (and using accessories) that is more aligned with their affirmed gender, now or in the future? If so, in what time frame and how?

. . . .

. . . .

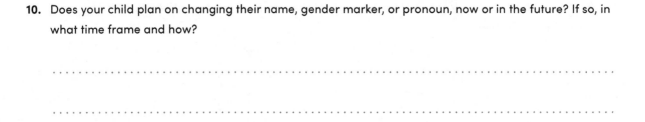
10. Does your child plan on changing their name, gender marker, or pronoun, now or in the future? If so, in what time frame and how?

. . . .

. . . .

Chapter 7

FRIENDS AND FAMILY: WILL THEY STAY, OR WILL THEY GO?

VITAL VIGNETTE

Discussing the transition with family and friends can be one of the most nerve-racking and confrontational parts of the process itself. It can also be a time when family and friends can easily embrace and celebrate the gender questioning and/or transition. None of us lives in a bubble and, therefore, the love, support, and opinions of others can play a vital role in how the process unravels. As you approach coming out to family and friends, pre-planning and discussing the way you and your child elect to share any part of the transition, questioning, or changes can be critical. That being said, these conversations can also make things much more complicated and frustrating. Though some friends and family members may attempt to shame you for advocating for your child's needs, even blaming you for not stopping them from transitioning, others will stand side by side with you and align with your decision to be there for your child, as you all travel this road together.

> ANECDOTAL AFFIRMATION
>
> *Who will be there when I am sad?*
> *Who will be there when I am scared?*
> *Who will be there when I am mad?*
> *Will you be someone who cared?*

All families and friends have their own history and dynamics, which can vary dramatically. Some may carry more baggage, unknowns, and complexities than others. While some may offer unconditional love regardless of the circumstances, others may not. There are those who offer advice, and incorporate religious beliefs and cultural norms into the conversation. They may find it difficult to separate how the information you are explaining will affect their own personal lives. In some cases, it can be a combination of all of these. As hard as it may be, the focus must address the needs of both you and your child. At times, the support team comprised of your family and friends may be a major safe haven for you and your child, for in most instances you and your child will be their priority. Your welfare will be first and foremost with them, and your well-being the prize.

This is a time where you truly want to evaluate the relationships you have fostered. You will have to search for what you value, whom you trust, and why they matter to you. Deciding when, where, why, and with whom to discuss specific topics or feelings will become essential decisions you will need to determine for yourself, as well as for your child and other family members.

Processing what is best for you, as you soul-search and engage in much self-reflection, all takes time. You will want to assess each relationship in a way that you may never have done so before. It is a job that can only be done by you and you alone. Start with one person on your list of family and friends, then build a team from there. Make the time to figure out what you value in a situation of need or crisis. You will have to find a balance that feels right, safe, and comfortable for you. Begin with one person, by trusting your instinct. Above all else, search for that place within you that has the loudest voice leading you to that one person or two who will have your back and best interests at heart. Some have found that privately answering the questions below (Reflective Responses) was key for them to navigate the next steps of creating their support network. You, and perhaps your closest family members, will need to make time to decide who will be a part of your separate support teams and who will be on the team for all of you as a family. It is also important to communicate who is off limits for each of you to share with, and what, if anything, is off limits to discuss with anyone. Once these discussions take place, verbally or written, you and your family, with your child's needs and preferences in mind, will have to determine what you can and cannot agree to at this time. It is strongly suggested that you do not make any final decisions out of anger or fear. It may all feel urgent and not fast enough or it may feel as if things are speeding out of control and you do not know how much longer you can last without speaking with a family member or friend. The order in which you share what is going on, and with whom, may require an abundance of energy and much care from all of you. Remember, it is completely acceptable to embrace the positive care of family and friends, as their support may play a key role in the lives of both you and your child!

GRAPHICS GALORE

Splash

Can you list all of your closest friends and family members? By creatively splashing words and short phrases, quickly attempt to express your answers randomly with as many responses as possible scattered on the paper.

GRAPHICS GALORE

Venn Diagram

Select and record 15–20 of your closest friends or family members. You can then elect to have your child and/or another family member fill out their section or you may choose to do it alone.

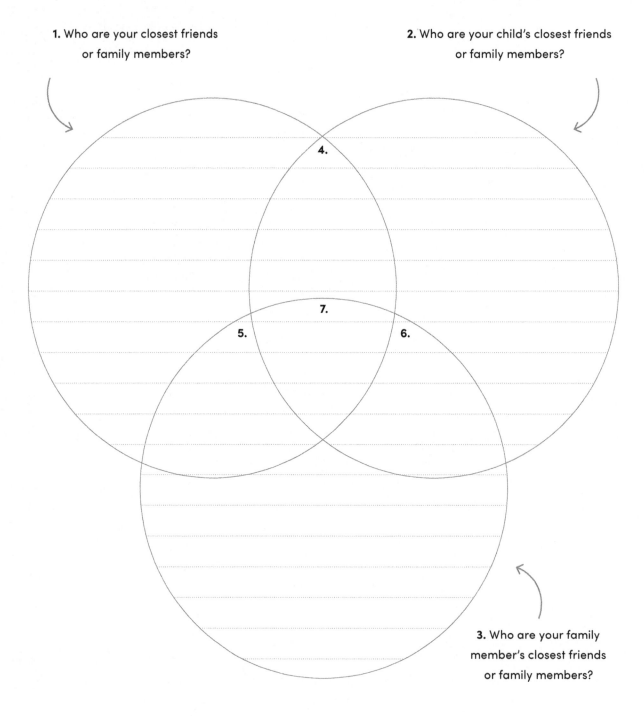

1. Who are your closest friends or family members?

2. Who are your child's closest friends or family members?

3. Who are your family member's closest friends or family members?

REFLECTIVE RESPONSES

1. Which family members and friends will you, your child, and/or other family members tell about your child's transition alone?

   . . . .

   . . . .

   . . . .

2. Which family members and friends will you, your child, and/or other family members tell about your child's transition together?

   . . . .

   . . . .

   . . . .

3. What, where, and how will you, your child, and/or close family members tell other family members and friends about your child's transition?

   . . . .

   . . . .

   . . . .

4. Will your other children, nephews, nieces, or grandchildren need to know about your child's transition? Why or why not?

   . . . .

   . . . .

   . . . .

5. How do you believe your child's transition will/did impact your relationship with your child, spouse, and/ or all other family members?

....

....

....

6. When, and if necessary, will you and/or another close family member set up the appointments with other family members and friends to discuss your child's need to transition?

....

....

....

7. How will you each answer the appropriate and inappropriate questions of others?

....

....

....

8. Do you want friends or family members on any of your lists to support you during any social and/or medical interventions? How will they know?

....

....

....

9. Are there people who you absolutely do not want to know about your child's transition? Does this mean that you cannot tell certain people, because of concerns that those unwanted people would find out? Who and why?

....

....

....

10. If your lists are different, how will you navigate honoring all of your preferences, when you share the information about your child's transition with family and friends?

. . . .

. . . .

. . . .

11. What concerns do you, your child, and/or close family members feel you should share with your other family members and friends?

. . . .

. . . .

. . . .

12. What concerns do you, your child, and/or close family members feel you should not share with your other family members and friends?

. . . .

. . . .

. . . .

13. Do you know anyone else who has gone through having their child transition, with whom you feel safe to discuss your own journey during this time?

. . . .

. . . .

. . . .

14. Do you prefer to reach out to someone in person, on the phone, by email, or another way?

. . . .

. . . .

. . . .

15. What do you believe is at risk if you tell others about your child's transition?

. . . .

. . . .

. . . .

16. Who do you fear will leave or keep their distance for a while, if you tell them about your child's transition?

. . . .

. . . .

. . . .

17. What ground rules will be agreed on between you, your child, and/or close family members before, during, or after discussing your child's transition with a third party? Who will determine and explain the ground rules?

. . . .

. . . .

. . . .

18. Will you have a follow-up meeting with your child and/or other family members after you meet with a particular person to discuss what transpired? With which person or people? When and where? Will they do the same with you?

. . . .

. . . .

. . . .

19. Who will be creating and negotiating the ground rules throughout the process in relation to family and friends? What will you, your child, and/or other close family members say and not say?

. . . .

. . . .

. . . .

20. Do you feel the dynamics will be different when engaging with each of your friends, families, and other family members, now that your child is transitioning? How and why, or why not?

. . . .

. . . .

. . . .

GRAPHICS GALORE

Web

Can you list all of the various groups of important living family members and friends you can think of at this moment? (For example: grandparents, siblings, tennis group, book club, college friends, etc.)

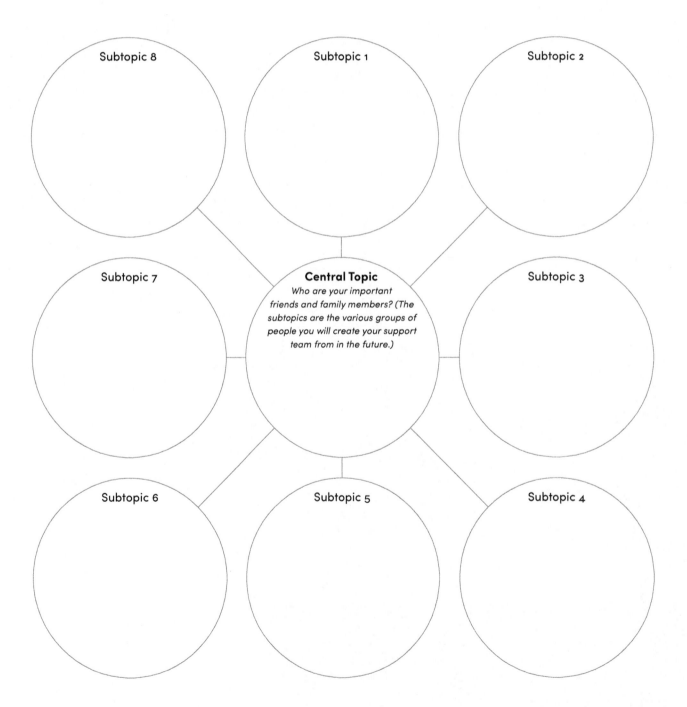

GRAPHICS GALORE

Box

Can you list all of the people in each of these categories: immediate family members, all cousins, aunts and uncles, childhood friends, college friends, inner circle friends, medical support staff? (Use these or feel free to use your own grouping ideas! You could base them on your Web categories listed above.)

Immediate family members:	All cousins:	Aunts and uncles:
Childhood friends:	**College friends:**	**Inner circle friends:**
Medical support staff:	**Your ideas…:**	

DESERVING DE-STRESSING DELIGHT

Time with Friends and Family

When parents need support, they often turn to close friends and trusted family members. Arranging a date with friends or family can help you feel less isolated and remind you that you do not have to be alone throughout the process. This holds true even once the focus on the transition becomes part of the past. Laughing, sharing, and experiencing moments with those who know you well and love you unconditionally can be the best medicine of all. Perhaps you will want to ask them not to discuss the transition sometimes and request that you simply talk about other topics. Yet, other times, it may be exactly what you will prefer to focus on. Most supportive people will respect your lead, but the responsibility to communicate your desires is yours. Be direct and let them know. If they are not made aware of your needs, they will be unable to help you as well as they could. Plan activities and celebrations that make you look forward to spending time with them and value what they have to offer in the form of friendship and care. You deserve it!

> ANECDOTAL AFFIRMATION
>
> *I reject*
> *The blame game,*
> *And know,*
> *I feel no shame!*

Journal your reaction to this Deserving De-Stressing Delight.

....

....

....

....

....

....

....

....

....

GRAPHICS GALORE

T-Chart

Who do you want to tell about your child's transition? You may elect to consider listing individuals from the following categories, but not limited to, immediate family members, aunts, uncles, cousins, childhood friends, college friends, inner circle friends, support groups, religious affiliations.

As the transition begins...	During the transition...	After the transition is no longer the major focus...

GRAPHICS GALORE

Timeline

Who will you tell about your child's transition? Who will tell them? When and where? What will you tell them? (Your response may vary for different people.)

Who will you tell?	Who will tell them?	When will you tell them?	Where will you tell them?	What will you tell them?

EMPATHY-EMBRACING EXERCISE

For many transgender, non-binary, and gender questioning children, the fear of losing the love and support of family and friends can prevent them from disclosing their affirmed gender.

Was there ever a time in your life that you feared losing the love and support of family and friends if you disclosed something personal about yourself? If so, what was it and did you disclose it? If not, why? If yes, what was the outcome?

ANECDOTAL AFFIRMATION

Will people talk about me?
Will people laugh at me?
Will people pity me?
Will people leave me?
Will people care about me?
Will people judge me?
Will people fear me?
Will people love me?
People, support me!

GRAPHICS GALORE

Bar Graph

To what degree do these concerns and related topics matter to you? Based on a scale from 1 to 10, with 1 being the lowest and 10 being the highest, color or shade in your response. This visual will illustrate where your greatest concerns lie and can be used as a tool to help you communicate your thoughts with your child and/or other family members, therapist, spiritual mentor, or for your own personal understanding. The bar graph results can vary as your child's transition progresses and your thoughts may shift.

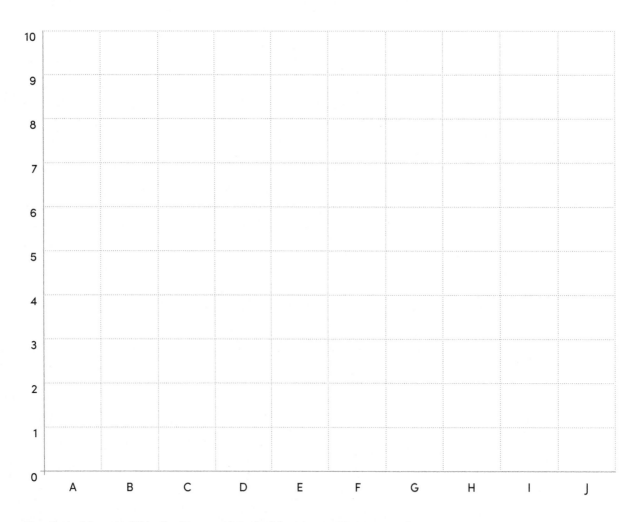

Use these ideas to fill in the bar graph or feel free to create your own!

A. Telling your family about your child's transition alone.

B. Telling your family about your child's transition with your child there.

C. Having your child tell their family about their transition alone.

D. Having your child tell their family about their transition with you.

E. Having only one of you tell the siblings about your child's transition alone.

F. Having both of you tell the siblings about your child's transition.

G. Telling your friends about your child's transition alone.

H. Telling your friends about your child's transition with your child there.

I. Having your child tell their friends about their transition alone.

J. Having your child tell their friends about their transition with you.

GRAPHICS GALORE

Pie Graph

To what degree are these concerns and related topics important to you? Decide how significant these issues are to you in relation to each other. Place the number that corresponds with a suggested topic within as many slices of the pie that convey how each one matters to you. Only one number should be placed in each slice. You do not need to use all the issues, but do fill in all the slices. Feel free to create your own topics and assign them their own number.

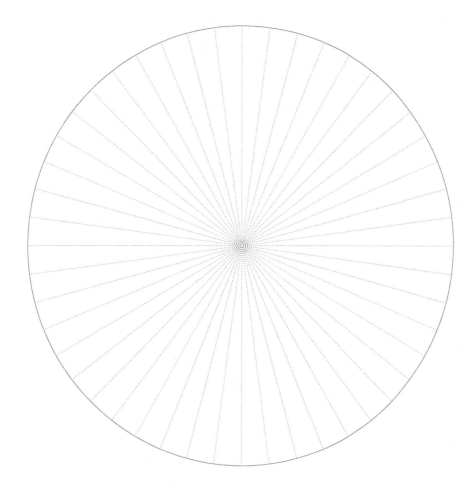

1. Telling your family about your child's transition alone.

2. Telling your family about your child's transition with your child there.

3. Having your child tell their family about their transition alone.

4. Having your child tell their family about their transition with you.

5. Having only one of you tell the siblings about your child's transition alone.

6. Having both of you tell the siblings about your child's transition.

7. Telling your friends about your child's transition alone.

8. Telling your friends about your child's transition with your child there.

9. Having your child tell their friends about their transition alone.

10. Having your child tell their friends about their transition with you.

SAMPLER SHARES

All names have been changed to ensure anonymity in this section. The first initial designates an individual and the second initial identifies the relationship to the child, i.e. P = their parent, G = their grandparent, and S = their sibling.

How do you believe your child's transition will/did impact your relationship with your child, spouse, and/or all other family members?

IS: At first my sibling's transition hindered our relationship. I believe he felt uncomfortable around me and uncomfortable in his own skin. I thought there was some dysphoria, and I had no choice but to accept it because I realized there wasn't much I could do. Besides the dysphoria, there were days where he wouldn't hug me or talk to me, and I hadn't fully comprehended this. It was all new to me. Recently, we regained portions of our relationship. *SIBLING/BROTHER: AFAB (Uses he/him/his pronouns)*

CP: My husband and I had been married for close to 20 years when my son (assigned female at birth) came out to us. I had wrongly assumed that I knew all about the man, that he was who he was and knew what he knew, and that is who he would always be. I was wrong, but happily wrong. It was like meeting him all over again, meeting this person who I didn't know was inside there. My husband accepted our child as his son as easily and readily as I did. He asked lots of questions, such as when did you know, what do you need from us, and was so very willing to learn all he could. Watching him interact with our son was almost like watching him interact with a child for the first time. Watching them become so much closer, as well as watching my son finally become genuinely happy, made me happier in my relationship with both him and my husband. My spouse and I became closer. I got to see a side of him that I didn't know was there. I always knew that my husband wasn't a bigot, but I was enamored all over again at how ready he was to stand up and protect his son in a way that I hadn't seen before. We became closer over the need to learn new things, new terms, opening ourselves up to ideas and possibilities. We became closer talking about shared fears and hopes, shared excitement at hearing our son's voice change, excitement at seeing the first few strands of facial hair. We felt like "new" parents all over again. My relationship with my daughter changed too, she was now *the* daughter. She began joking about how dad will walk her down the aisle when she gets married, but that when her brother gets married, I'll be able to dance with my son. She brought into focus all the future changes that we hadn't even thought of yet. She has become one of her brother's fiercest advocates. She has always been quick witted and sharp tongued, but now she uses it to shut down bigoted comments. Watching their relationship change has made me really understand what unconditional love really is. My relationship with my son has changed as well. There was this "feeling out" phase. Before the transition, I would have no problem walking into the bathroom while he was in the shower. Now, I hesitated the first time, and wondered would the mom of a cis teen boy do this? It was situations like this that prompted us to have conversations around appropriate and inappropriate behavior and what he was comfortable and uncomfortable with. Did he want me to say my son, or my child? These conversations made us closer and helped us to understand each other in ways that we never had before. *PARENT/CHILD: AFAB (Uses he/him/his pronouns)*

HP: I have become more comfortable over time in answering questions from family and friends. It has become apparent that there are some people who will never be able to understand or accept the changes of my child. In those cases, I make individual decisions to ignore their comments or ignorance. Regarding those who I know are loving and supportive, it is enjoyable to share what I have learned and get their additional support. I know that there will always be those people in the family who will embrace the decisions made along the way and others who will never fully believe or understand the process. *PARENT/CHILD: AFAB (Uses he/him/his pronouns)*

FP: Seven years ago, I was at the end of my rope trying to lift up my trans son as he slowly transitioned in a small community that was not embracing of trans people at all. I felt as if it was the two of us against the world. Our bond strengthened and flourished into a beautiful mother–son relationship. I still fondly remember the look on his face, as the hairstylist cut off his waist-length hair. It was an adjustment for me, as I no longer had a little girl that imitated me and tried to be a smaller version of me. I quickly adapted and learned that I was beyond fortunate to now have an amazing son, who is more courageous at this young age than most people will ever be. It was my relationship with my husband that I thought may not survive. My husband was so thrilled to finally have a little girl. So, when I told him that our child was only biologically a girl and that he is actually a boy, he felt a great sense of loss and blamed me for it. In his mind, this was all happening because I was encouraging it. He was non-accepting of the change, and worried about what others would think or say. When our son was bullied at the non-embracing school, he would blame our son. He would say that if our son "wants to be trans, then that is what comes with it." I knew that I was supporting, not encouraging. I knew that he was transitioning because he *is* trans, not because he wants to be trans. I also saw his struggle, and stayed up with him late at night as he cried himself to sleep due to the cruelty he was facing at school and the lack of acceptance from his dad. So, I concluded that I would have to make a very simple choice. Choose my child or my husband of over a decade. So, I approached my husband and advised him that our child was someone we should be proud of, not ashamed of. I let him know that this was also new to me and that I had my own fears about the journey of parenting a transgender son, but that it was not a choice. The question was, was he going to join us in that journey or not? Well, he decided to join us. He buys my son all of his boy clothing, and even goes with him to the male bathroom at the mall. I have come to realize that he may never fully understand, but he does accept our son for who he is. He *never* mixes up the pronouns, has signed off on the paperwork for our son to get puberty blockers and then testosterone, and has expressed that he is looking forward to teaching him how to shave once he gets his facial hair. In the end, our husband–wife bond actually grew stronger as we now face this journey as a team. *PARENT/ CHILD: AFAB (Uses he/him/his pronouns)*

COMMUNICATION CORNER

When you speak spontaneously out of anger or fear about the unknown, without thinking it through, you can sometimes regret the way you phrased your words or the tone you used to express your feelings. Rehearsing what you want to ask or discuss with your child, and other family members, can help you before you actually communicate your thoughts. This gives you a moment to reflect and pause before you converse about emotional topics. You may choose to practice asking these questions with a trusted friend, family member, spiritual mentor, or therapist first. Explain your thoughts and feelings about these statements to one another verbally or in writing. It is important to note that some families elected to only address one question or two, while others preferred to answer them all. In order to recall the questions you answered, simply highlight and/or circle the ones you addressed as a family, yet acknowledging that you may return to discuss the others in the future. Decide what feels best for two or more family members and begin the conversation. Do you, your child, and other family members answer these questions in the same way or differently? Discuss your responses to understand how all of you view the answers to the questions and make time to celebrate all you learn from being willing to communicate with each other.

> ANECDOTAL AFFIRMATION
>
> *Sometimes friends*
> *Become family.*
> *We welcome*
> *The unconditional*
> *Love!*

1. What will you say or do if a person asks what transitioning means?

    . . . .

    . . . .

2. What will you say or do if a person asks what the transition process will entail for your child?

    . . . .

    . . . .

3. What will you say or do if a person asks what is the correct pronoun/name to use for your child?

    . . . .

    . . . .

4. What will you say or do if a person asks what they can tell others about your child's transition?

· ·

· ·

5. What will you say or do if a person asks how they can help with your child's transition?

· ·

· ·

6. What will you say or do if a person asks what type of surgeries will be involved for your child, if any?

· ·

· ·

7. What will you say or do if a person asks what type of hormones will be involved for your child, if any?

· ·

· ·

8. What will you say or do if a person makes inappropriate statements about your child's transition?

· ·

· ·

9. What will you say or do if a person asks inappropriate questions about your child's transition?

· ·

· ·

10. What will you say or do to explain what are inappropriate questions about your child's transition?

· ·

· ·

Chapter 8

WORK: IN OR OUT?

VITAL VIGNETTE

In many instances, deciding whether or not to share with colleagues the very personal issue of one's own child who is in transition is a sensitive and often difficult decision. In reality, the parents, sometimes in consultation with other family members including the child who has a stake in the outcome, need to ask themselves the same question: Should we let people at work know about this very confidential information or not? There are numerous reasons that might support either stance, but it is important that parents examine their own objectives. Similar thoughts come into play when parents ponder the best and most appropriate manner in which to tell others in the workplace about their child's private path, if they conclude they will do so.

> ANECDOTAL AFFIRMATION
>
> *Why do you Need to know THAT?*

The first question you may want to pose to yourself is: Why would you need or want to disclose this knowledge at work? For some, it can simply be a personal choice or preference. For others, it may become necessary for several reasons. Is your child, who is in transition, on your medical insurance? If the answer is yes, and if your child is planning on medically transitioning by using any portion of the medical insurance to pay for it, then it may become necessary for you to consult with the human resources department and medical insurance company. It is important to ask a person who knows your rights prior to speaking to anyone in the workplace, so that you have the most accurate legal advice available to you.

It should be noted that many people may not have medical insurance through their employer and therefore cannot address their insurance needs in reference to transition-related care with the help of a human resources liaison or other representative. If you do not have this benefit, you may be able to access medical insurance provided by state or federal programs; therefore, it is important to investigate these options. In some cases, you may be able to speak with someone about these issues over the phone or via email; however, it can become necessary to discuss this topic in person. It is suggested that you investigate if there is a local NGO (Non-Governmental Organization) that could assist you with this process, especially if doing it alone feels too overwhelming or confusing.

If you are not a legal expert in this area and possibly do not know the laws in your country, city, province, state, or town, it is advisable to consult someone who knows your legal rights and the laws that may affect your employment, safety, and well-being before you take the step of inquiring. These legal rights, insurance policies, and laws can affect you and your coverage. Whether you plan to specifically disclose your child's plans to medically transition or simply inquire about policies, before you do so, consult a lawyer, agency, or someone you completely trust and know is giving you the most up-to-date advice based on facts and not opinion. Although people often have the best of intentions, unless their information is credible and accurate, it is suggested that you seek the advice of someone else with more knowledge in this area, since it can possibly affect more areas of your life than you may realize.

In addition, research the legal rights in the jurisdiction in which you work, in order to protect you at your place of employment. Then decide, as parents or as a family, whether you should reveal your child's transition plans with your employer, based on current laws and legal advice. You may also want to research insurance coverage and what the rules are for medical and family leave. Under some circumstances, unions and companies have negotiated policies already put in place for time off or leaves of absence. If you are comfortable and it is legally recommended, you can investigate these options. Asking about your options, in a protected environment, does not mean you must do what they offer or recommend. It can simply be fact-finding and nothing more. Knowledge is power, and gathering information to find out what works best for you is key, once you have the facts. If and when you feel comfortable moving forward, based on legal advice, you may opt to speak with your employer, the human resource liaison, benefits manager, or someone who can help navigate the process of using insurance, and then do so. It is suggested that you get the recommendations and agreements in writing, rather than simply hearing verbal approval over the phone or in person. In addition, every conversation, including the person's name, contact number, and any information provided, should be documented in writing by you and, if possible, by the person with whom you are corresponding at the time. There is space for recording these interactions in this chapter. You will want to record the date, time, phone number, extension, name of the person to whom you spoke (full name if possible), the person's position or title, and exactly what was discussed, including your questions and the person's reply.

If you are unclear about the response or unsure of any detail, ask for the answer to be rephrased or repeated. It is advisable to ask for a supervisor up front, and continue to follow up with the same person, if possible. This requires keeping track of names and extensions for any supervisors with whom you may speak, and inquiring when they are most often available to call back and answer your questions. Some insurance companies or doctor's offices will only speak to the person who is the primary policyholder or legally responsible for the child. It can be smoother and easier if most decisions and choices are clear before any inquiries are made or any information gathering begins.

You may be surprised to find out how many people have never heard the words "transgender" or "transitioning" when it pertains to health benefits and rights. In some instances, you could be told that there is no policy put in place with respect to this probe. In fact, if there is a policy, sometimes the person helping you is unsure of the specifics, and will have to research it and get back to you. If this happens, record this fact and ask when the follow-up call can be expected. Then make a phone or in-person appointment to continue the conversation, so you can obtain the critical information you need. Emphasize the urgency of the situation and, whenever possible, ask if there is someone with whom you can speak at that moment, who may be able to assist you better. Before you end your conversation, thank them for all their help in regard to this matter and let them know how much you appreciate all their assistance with this inquiry.

This process can be emotionally draining, so you may need to take breaks and nurture yourself as much as possible. There can be an extra layer of exhaustion for the parents, since as you are moving forward with the logistics, you may still feel internally conflicted, confused, scared, and worried. Even if none of these feelings is part of your journey, it may be emotionally necessary to implement some self-care throughout this portion of the process. Moreover, if your child's medical insurance is covered under another person other than yourself, that individual may need your assistance when obtaining the facts. The insured parent can feel unsure of what to say when interacting with a person who is unaware of the meaning of "transgender" or "transitioning." To make things easier, perhaps you can write out a short response ahead of time that reflects your voice, for the sake of efficiency and consistency, so you will know exactly how to reply should this occur. In addition, it is best not to come across as resentful or annoyed as you realize that you may need to educate others about what you believe is their responsibility to know. Once you accept this fact, that educating the public, as well as friends and family, comes with the territory of being the parents of a child who is transgender, you can come to terms with this reality.

After you obtain legal advice and acquire the facts about what is covered and what you can afford financially, you may choose to decide what you will do next.

Questions that may come to mind include:

- Do you, your child, and/or the other parent, if they are a part of the equation, believe it is best and necessary to disclose your child's gender status with a co-worker, employee, client, boss/employer?
- Do you and/or the other parent, if they are a part of the equation, want to speak with your employer/boss as a team to show unity?
- Would you prefer to go alone (and why or why not)?
- Do you want to take along a person who knows your legal rights, such as a union representative, to an in-person appointment?
- How much time will you need off from work based on the information you have obtained? Be prepared to discuss this if necessary, since it is a commonly asked question.
- What documentation will be needed to prove why you are taking time off from work?
- Will the time off affect your employment or promotions?

- Do insurance benefits have any exclusions in your policy for transgender care? If so, what are those exclusions, and where is the reference to the exclusions within the certificate of coverage?

The answers to these questions may influence how you proceed. Take the time to process the replies, either alone or with other family members.

Deciding to tell or not to tell co-workers, employees, and clients is another choice you should make in consultation with your child and/or other family members. Some people feel strongly about not outing their child without permission, while others suggest doing what you need to feel whole and at peace. However, it is strongly recommended that you discuss this with your child and/or other family members to find a solution, which meets the needs of most, if not all of you. Your decision could have consequences that may not be able to be undone. Consider this carefully and then make the choice that works for all involved.

If you are selecting the path to discuss your child's transition at work, perhaps for support or the need to be transparent, carefully choose those who you feel will keep your confidence, and respect both your needs and those of your child. As with family members and friends, who may also be co-workers, employees, clients, bosses, or employers too, start with one person and pre-plan where, what, and when you will tell them. Be prepared for any questions they may have and consider how you will address any probing or inappropriate questions. Remember that you may be asked to educate them and explain many facts and details that are extremely personal and not what you may have anticipated as part of sharing information with a co-worker, employee, client, boss, or employer. It is recommended to set boundaries in reference to questions, and emphasize the crucial role of confidentiality. Knowing the guidelines and boundaries you have agreed on with your child and/or other family members can be critical before discussing the transition and/or gender questioning with anyone in the workplace.

It is important to understand that there are many children who request to remain "stealth," and parents who simply do not feel the need to disclose their child's transition. This is something that should be measured and thoroughly communicated before you take any steps in relation to work. There are numerous considerations and each person will have to make this determination for themselves. With whom, what, where, when, why, and how you come out at work in respect to your child's transition, often based on legal advice, is a decision that requires essential planning, information gathering, soul-searching, and crucial communication with everyone involved. There are no rules and very often parents and family members struggle with how to share information about these life changes at work, while at the same time attempting to comprehend them for themselves. Remember, if you do not know the answer to a question, it is acceptable to let those in the workplace know you need to think about their inquiry before you respond!

GRAPHICS GALORE

Splash

Can you list all of your clients, employees, co-workers, bosses, and employers? By creatively splashing words and short phrases, quickly attempt to express your answers randomly with as many responses as possible scattered on the paper. Suggestions: Do not edit or leave out anyone who comes to mind. Feel free to list people from different departments or from various levels of the organization.

GRAPHICS GALORE

Box

Can you divide up, by categorizing, the clients, employees, co-workers, bosses, and employers you have listed from the Splash? (There are optional columns to include input from your child.)

Those people who you feel comfortable telling about your child's transition.	Those people who you do not feel comfortable telling about your child's transition.	Those people who you are unsure of whether you are comfortable telling them about your child's transition.
Those people who your child feels comfortable with you telling about their transition.	Those people who your child does not feel comfortable with you telling about their transition.	Those people who your child is unsure of whether they are comfortable with you telling about their transition.

REFLECTIVE RESPONSES

1. With whom will you discuss your legal rights, laws, and employment before you take any action to discuss your child's transition with anyone at work in regard to insurance, job security, and any relevant factors, in order to legally protect both you and your child?

   . . . .

   . . . .

   . . . .

2. What workplace laws and policies did you learn about in relation to your child's transition, and what have you decided to do based on these facts?

   . . . .

   . . . .

   . . . .

3. If it is legally advisable to inquire, what information did you acquire from the human resources liaison, benefits manager, and medical insurance company about the rights, policies, and financial options in relation to your child's transition, now or in the future?

   . . . .

   . . . .

   . . . .

4. Who are the clients, employees, co-workers, bosses, and employers you will elect to share information with about your child's transition, now or in the future, and why?

   . . . .

   . . . .

   . . . .

5. What will you tell clients, employees, co-workers, bosses, and employers about your child's transition, now or in the future?

....

....

....

6. What will you not tell clients, employees, co-workers, bosses, and employers about your child's transition, now or in the future?

....

....

....

7. What concerns do you have about discussing your child's transition at your respective workplace, now or in the future?

....

....

....

8. What have you and your child decided not to share about their transition with any client, employee, co-worker, boss, and employer, now or in the future?

....

....

....

9. What is the timeline or order for you to possibly discuss your child's transition with each co-worker, client, and employee, now or in the future?

....

....

....

10. What is the timeline or order for you to possibly discuss your child's transition with your boss and employer, now or in the future?

....

....

....

GRAPHICS GALORE

Web

Who are the people or the resources you will consult or have consulted to find out your legal rights, the laws, and company policies in relation to your child's transition, in order to protect your employment at your current job, now or in the future?

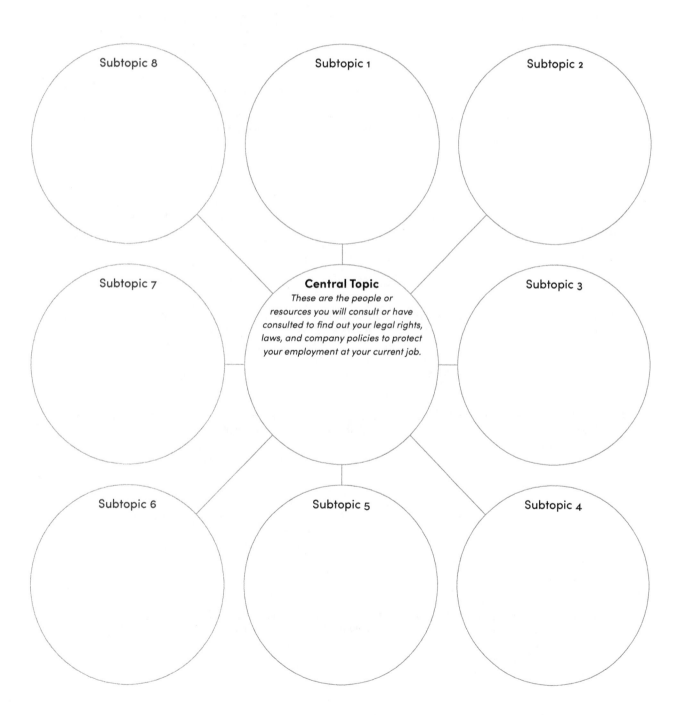

GRAPHICS GALORE

Timeline

Who will you tell about your child's transition? Why will you tell them? When and where? What will you tell them? Feel free to use the information gathered from the other graphic organizers to fill this in. (Your response may vary for different people.)

DESERVING DE-STRESSING DELIGHT

Experience a Sport

Participating in or watching others take part in a sport or physical activity can allow anger or nervous energy to disperse in a healthy way. One bonus of either joining a team sport or cheering for a team is the camaraderie. It offers you the inherent feelings of belonging and being united. The individuals with whom you engage in this activity can become yet another layer of support for you without them even knowing about your child's transition. They can play the role of a safe haven where your interactions can be entirely based on the sport and not the transition. Perhaps they will not even be people who know about or understand anything in relation to the transition. This may become one area in which you can easily separate from all the ups and downs of your child's transition and simply experience the joy of the sport or physical activity. For some people, being connected to a physical sport or activity can also provide a level of meditation that may have a calming or comforting effect on the body and mind.

> ANECDOTAL AFFIRMATION
> *Hard choices!*
> *Does anyone know*
> *How hard?*

Journal your reaction to this Deserving De-Stressing Delight.

. . . .

. . . .

. . . .

. . . .

. . . .

. . . .

. . . .

. . . .

. . . .

. . . .

GRAPHICS GALORE

T-Chart

Who are the appropriate people with whom you should consult at work, and what are the company's policies and laws in relation to the protection of employment and medical insurance coverage? (Complete this graphic organizer based on legal advice that is current and factual, any other credible sources, and research you acquire both verbally and in writing.)

Who are the appropriate personnel with whom you need to consult, in relation to your child's transition?	What are the laws in your workplace, if any, with regard to your child's transition?	What are the company's policies in your workplace, if any, with regard to your child's transition?

GRAPHICS GALORE

Venn Diagram

What are you comfortable sharing with clients, employees, co-workers, bosses, and employers in respect to discussing your child's transition?

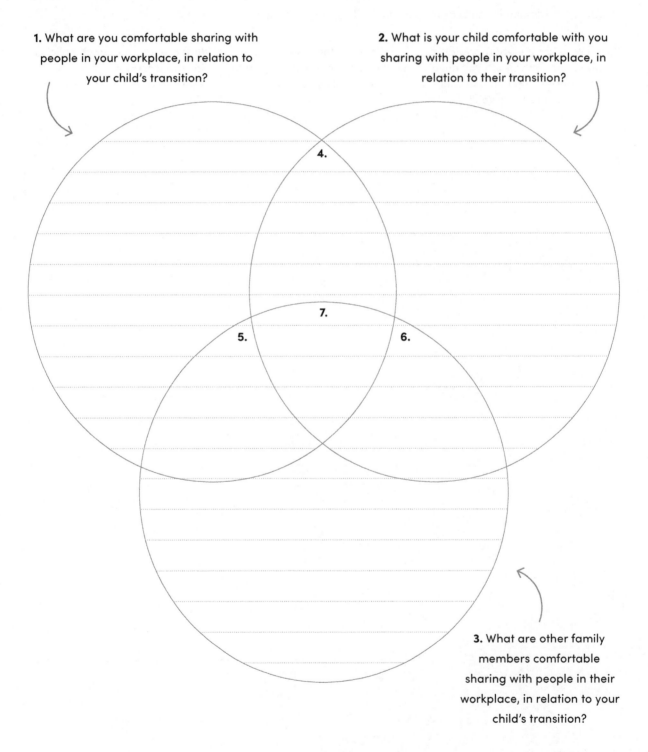

1. What are you comfortable sharing with people in your workplace, in relation to your child's transition?

2. What is your child comfortable with you sharing with people in your workplace, in relation to their transition?

3. What are other family members comfortable sharing with people in their workplace, in relation to your child's transition?

4.

5.   7.   6.

EMPATHY-EMBRACING EXERCISE

For many people who are trans, the fear of losing the respect and/or support of those in the workplace can prevent them from disclosing their affirmed gender. This also holds true for children disclosing their affirmed gender at school.

Was there ever a time in your life that you feared losing the respect and/or support of those in the workplace if you disclosed something personal about yourself? If so, what was it and did you disclose it? If not, why? If yes, what was the outcome?

> ANECDOTAL AFFIRMATION
>
> *You are rude,*
> *There are unsaid rules...*
> *Figure them out!*

GRAPHICS GALORE

Bar Graph

To what degree do these concerns and related topics matter to you? Based on a scale from 1 to 10, with 1 being the lowest and 10 being the highest, color or shade in your response. This visual will illustrate where your greatest concerns lie and can be used as a tool to help you communicate your thoughts with your child and/or other family members, therapist, spiritual mentor, or for your own personal understanding. The bar graph results can vary as your child's transition progresses and/or your thoughts may shift.

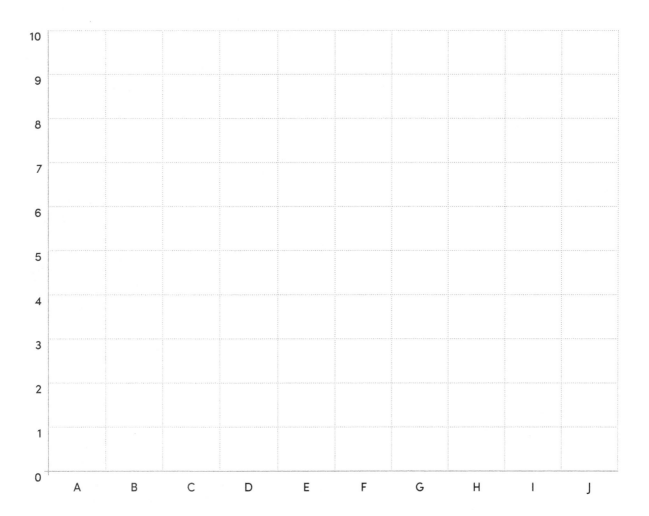

Use these ideas to fill in the bar graph or feel free to create your own!

A. Telling your clients, employees, and co-workers about your child's transition alone.

B. Telling your clients, employees, and co-workers about your child's transition with another person present.

C. Your concerns about how your clients, employees, and co-workers may react to you at the time you disclose your child's transition.

D. Your concerns about how your clients, employees, and co-workers may treat you once you disclose your child's transition.

E. Your concerns about how sharing your child's transition with people will affect your future with the employer.

F. Telling your boss/employer about your child's transition alone.

G. Telling your boss/employer about your child's transition with another person present.

H. Your concerns about how your boss/employer may react to you at the time you disclose your child's transition.

I. Your concerns of how your boss/employer may treat you once you disclose your child's transition.

J. Your concerns about being able to take time off from work when you feel it is critical to do so, without a negative outcome.

GRAPHICS GALORE

Pie Graph

To what degree are these concerns and related topics important to you? Decide how significant these issues are to you in relation to each other. Place the number that corresponds with a suggested topic within as many slices of the pie that convey how each one matters to you. Only one number should be placed in each slice. You do not need to use all the issues, but do fill in all the slices. Feel free to create your own topics and assign them their own number.

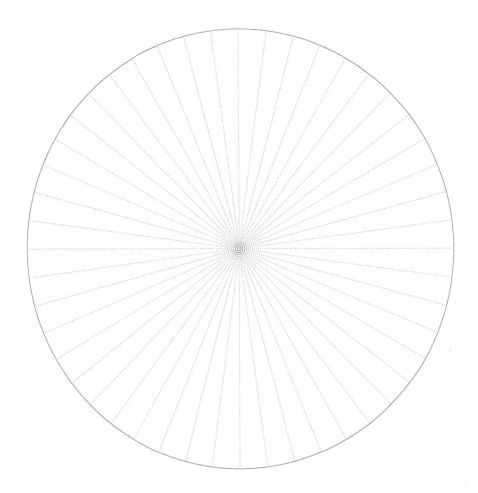

1. Telling your clients, employees, and co-workers about your child's transition alone.

2. Telling your clients, employees, and co-workers about your child's transition with another person present.

3. Your concerns about how your clients, employees, and co-workers may react at the time you disclose your child's transition.

4. Your concerns about how your clients, employees, and co-workers may treat you once you disclose your child's transition.

5. Your concerns about how sharing the transition with people will affect your future with the employer.

6. Telling your boss/employer about your child's transition alone.

7. Telling your boss/employer about your child's transition with another person present.

8. Your concerns about how your boss/employer may react to you at the time you disclose your child's transition.

9. Your concerns about how your boss/employer may treat you once you disclose your child's transition.

10. Your concerns about being able to take time off from work when you feel it is critical to do so, without a negative outcome.

SAMPLER SHARES

All names have been changed to ensure anonymity in this section. The first initial designates an individual and the second initial identifies the relationship to the child, i.e. P = their parent, G = their grandparent, and S = their sibling.

What will you tell and/or not tell clients, employees, co-workers, bosses, and/or employers about your child's transition, now or in the future?

FP: I work for the City of New York, in an environment that happens to be fairly inclusive. Prior to his transition, my son had always loved my work environment, and would often go to my job and interact with my co-workers. So, as I boasted about my courageous and just overall amazing son, my co-workers were not shy to ask a million questions about my experience. I was elated about their interest because it gave me an opportunity to use all of the information I have learned through this experience to educate others. Then some of my co-workers came out to me as members of the LGBTQ community, so I would say that it actually helped me form a community of support and acceptance within my workplace. They are intrigued by the whole process of my son's transition, and still care for my son as much as they did prior to his transition process. *PARENT/CHILD: AFAB (Uses he/him/his pronouns)*

HP: The decision in deciding who to tell was a challenge to say the least. I decided that it was necessary to tell my clients who had worked with me for years, but I told them over a period of time. Because they were clients, it was important to me that I was professional and didn't make them feel uncomfortable. I decided to tell others who had known me and my family for years. Like my clients, I told each family member and friend as time permitted and when I felt personally more comfortable in understanding everything myself. It was important to respect what my son was going through and, at first, I was too emotional. A few of my friends are of the religious belief that being transgender is not real, although, I knew that they had children with many challenges. This was when I made the decision to assess each circumstance differently. Being a fairly intuitive person, it became apparent that to talk about it to someone who was not broad minded and educated was a disservice to my son and the LGBTQ community. *PARENT/CHILD: AFAB (Uses he/him/his pronouns)*

DP: When my son first started to transition, I told the people I was working with because instead of talking about my daughter I would now be talking about my son. I was just very straightforward about it and told them that my child was transitioning and what her name would now be. As time went on, they saw him again many times. I started a new job six months ago and I just talk about my son. In general, anyone new that I meet I talk about my son and do not mention anything else. While my son believes he should have the same rights as every other male, he is not the type of person to be very outspoken. Therefore, I respect his desire to just be a man and I do not talk about it much. That being said, I have had many people refer others to me who are struggling regarding their children's gender and sexual identity choices. I talk openly and freely with them and my son knows that. I guess what I am trying to say is that I am proud of my son and he is proud of himself. He just wants to be himself and I respect that. He is grateful that I support him. *PARENT/CHILD: AFAB (Uses he/him/his pronouns)*

EP: I have worked at the same place for over 13 years and now I just say "the kids" instead of "the girls." There are a few co-workers that I'm close with that know, but just like anything else in life, you don't share all your personal news with everyone, just those who care. *PARENT/CHILD: AFAB (Uses he/him/his pronouns)*

COMMUNICATION CORNER

When you speak spontaneously out of anger or fear about the unknown, without thinking it through, you can sometimes regret the way you phrased your words or the tone you used to express your feelings. Rehearsing what you want to ask or discuss with your child, and other family members, can help you before you actually communicate your thoughts. This gives you a moment to reflect and pause before you converse about emotional topics. You may choose to practice asking these questions with a trusted friend, family member, spiritual mentor, or therapist first. Explain your thoughts and feelings about these statements to one another verbally or in writing. It is important to note that some families elected to only address one question or two, while others preferred to answer them all. In order to recall the questions you answered, simply highlight and/or circle the ones you addressed as a family, yet acknowledge that you may return to discuss the others in the future. Decide what feels best for two or more family members and begin the conversation. Do you, your child, and other family members answer these questions in the same way or differently? Discuss your responses to understand how all of you view the answers to the questions and make time to celebrate all you learn from being willing to communicate with each other.

> ANECDOTAL AFFIRMATION
>
> *Each challenge*
> *Is met with bravery,*
> *Each obstacle*
> *Is met by courage,*
> *Each battle*
> *Is met with*
> *Inner strength.*

1. What will you say or do if a person at work asks what transitioning means?

. . . .

. . . .

2. What will you say or do if a person at work asks what the transition will entail for your child?

. . . .

. . . .

3. What will you say or do if a person at work asks what is the correct pronoun/name to use for your child and why either one needs to change?

. . . .

. . . .

4. What will you say or do if a person at work asks what they can tell others about your child's transition?

....

....

5. What will you say or do if a person at work asks how they can help with your child's transition?

....

....

6. What will you say or do if a person at work asks what type of surgeries will be involved, if any?

....

....

7. What will you say or do if a person at work asks what type of hormones will be involved, if any?

....

....

8. What will you say or do if a person at work makes inappropriate statements about your child's transition?

....

....

9. What will you say or do if a person at work asks inappropriate questions about your child's transition?

....

....

10. What will you say or do if people at work ask you to explain what are considered inappropriate questions in relation to your child's transition?

....

....

Chapter 9

INSURANCES, GENDER MARKER, AND DOCUMENTS... OH MY!

VITAL VIGNETTE

ANECDOTAL AFFIRMATION

New name,
Learn about hormones,
Research surgery options,
Change gender marker.
So much to do,
So much time!

When trying to change your child's gender marker and name, the complex web of government agencies and health insurance agencies can either be viewed as important friends or as frustrating foes—sometimes both at the same time. You will need to communicate with your child, with other family members, and with additional individuals from your support team as to what, if any, your role will be in this often complex process. A gender marker is the gender designation on all official documents, usually stating male or female. Some places have a third option, but this is rare. In most cases, parents will need to assume most of the responsibility, and they will have to determine what they will need to do to protect their child's future in connection to any current documentation. This will take time, patience, and endurance.

This chapter will assist with establishing timelines and delegating commitment. For some, these welcome changes can be done rapidly and with much ease. For others, fear and confusion can disrupt the process. Many of the issues and suggestions discussed in this chapter will involve legality and rights, which can vary from country to country, state to state, province to province, from year to year, and so on. So be vigilant. You may find yourself dealing with people and institutions that will not always have the most current information or the most dedicated personnel.

As far as banks are concerned, most are not overly concerned about a gender marker. You may need to change your child's name and gender marker on their own account and if they are listed as a beneficiary on any of your accounts and on any others. Quite often, banks will honor the documentation required to change the name and gender marker on accounts once you provide a copy of the legal name change order, which is the documentation provided by the court stating an individual has legally changed the name indicated on their birth certificate to a new name.

Sometimes all the individuals who are on the account will need to be present for changes to be made. It is suggested that you inquire about the bank's policy before you plan on making these changes, so you know their procedures ahead of time. The same holds true for any wills, trusts, and documentation of which your child may be a beneficiary of now or in the future. It is suggested that you check with an experienced lawyer who knows the laws and rights pertaining to transgender issues, or a knowledgeable professional who specializes in policies that involve beneficiary clauses before you make changes to any important documents.

Some insurance companies may require name changes and other legal changes, while for other insurance companies it may be advantageous for a child not to change anything legally on their documentation but, rather, keep the policy exactly as it is presently, in order for medications, surgeries, and other procedures to be covered (if and when medically transitioning is part of your child's journey). For example, if a child has a pre-existing condition in relationship to hormones or a specific type of cancer which is associated with their gender assigned at birth, the policy may need to retain the same gender marker on their health insurance, in order to have the treatment covered by the insurance company, should there be a need for such medical intervention in the future. These specifics and details are critical and must be researched and discussed in advance. In addition to consulting with a well-informed lawyer who is aware of current laws and practices prior to any medical and legal changes, the best action for these types of inquiries will most likely be talking to the human resources liaison of your employer, researching the insurance company's policies, and speaking to your medical provider.

In regard to name changes, it is strongly recommended that you get multiple (at least ten) certified copies of name change orders. If the name change is sealed, it is even more important to buy multiple certified copies, because it can be quite difficult or even impossible to get it unsealed and obtain more copies later. Some banks and Social Security, for example, will only accept certified copies, not just photocopies. In "friendly" states, it is possible to get a name change order sealed to help with privacy and safety. Some believe it is worth petitioning for it. This can save the trouble and expense of publishing a public notice in a newspaper, especially since many newspapers now have online archives and the name/gender change information becomes public record and may appear in online searches. Also, once your child's legal name change is complete, it can be essential to share this information with the Social Security office. If your child is receiving Social Security benefits, their name may need to be corrected in order for them to receive their benefits. Lastly, it is important to note that sometimes if a child has a criminal record, it may complicate their and your ability to legally change their name. Once more, it is strongly suggested that you consult a competent lawyer about this prior to doing anything, should this apply to your child.

There may come a time when you feel completely panicked and want to scream as a result of all the details and paperwork. If this happens, as it sometimes does, perhaps this may be an ideal time to try one of the Deserving De-Stressing Delights. You can and will be able to do all that is necessary, but you must take breaks or even long pauses should it all feel too much. Knowing this ahead of time can help, and relying on your support team will get you through it. On a positive note, once these changes in legal documentation have been completed to the best of your ability, you will probably sleep better and feel a sense of relief that will be worth the energy it may require.

The following forms and tools have been created to assist you in relation to helping legally change your child's name and gender marker and you are welcome to copy or enhance anything you desire to meet your goals. In addition, the comprehensive list of documents may be of use for parents and legal guardians who elect to begin the name and gender marker changes. It cannot be stressed enough that you should be consulting legal experts, accountants, financial institutions, and any other professional who can advise you about the laws that pertain to changing a name and gender marker, before you proceed with anything permanent or anything that can possibly affect your child or even you in a negative way. Consulting a mental health provider should be considered when discussing specifics of name and gender marker changes with your child, both for your well-being and that of your child.

In summary:

1. Always record the name of the person you spoke to, the time, date, and details of what you discussed.
2. For each formal change, find out the documentation you will need and record it.
3. Find out if you need to do it in person, or if you are able to do it by phone, fax, email, online, or snail mail; keep records of when forms are submitted and to whom.
4. Record whether your child will need to be present to change any document/s or if only you are required to be present to make these changes.
5. Based on the above (points 1–4), make a list and then create a plan for addressing each change.
6. Label physical folders for each name and gender marker change and attach the sheet from the graphic organizer in this chapter on the front or create online folders and place the form from this chapter in the online folder as an attachment. Place everything you need for this change in a physical folder or in a safe and private computer file. It is suggested that you have digital copies in a password-protected file. Make copies of forms ahead of time and review what is needed prior to beginning the process. Consider making two physical copies of everything!
7. Decide on a realistic schedule that is both practical and makes sense time-wise.
8. Schedule a weekly meeting with your child to discuss what tasks have been accomplished and what tasks still have to be completed. You may need to decide what you still need to address, if someone can assist you with your tasks, and by what date it needs to be done. Updating, reviewing, and altering original plans can be critical to reaching your goals.
9. Make notes of when you will need legal advice, a notary, or the assistance of a professional before you proceed in addressing a name or gender marker on a particular document. Some documents will require a notary, so create a list of the days, times, and the location of one who is available, and their cost.

10. Ask for help and support if it becomes too much or overwhelming. Sometimes, simply having a person sit with you when you call or fax something feels better.

11. Create boundaries for yourself, such as allocating a specific amount of time for each task or deciding to begin and end at specific times.

12. If you are unsure whether you have received the correct information, ask to speak with someone else, or call back again and ask the same questions of another person. Perhaps you can have the other parent (when applicable) or other family member or trusted friend call again, with you present, to find out if they get the same answers to the same questions.

13. You may need a witness or two when signing legal documents, so compile a list of the names of people with whom you are comfortable doing this, and then create a list of their typical dates and times of availability.

14. Take the time to celebrate what you have completed by making a date with yourself, only with your child, other family members, or friends, in order to acknowledge all you have achieved. It can re-energize you and others!

GRAPHICS GALORE

Splash

On which documents do you think your child's name (if it applies) and gender marker (if it applies) will need to be changed as a result of the transition? By creatively splashing words and short phrases, quickly attempt to express your answers randomly with as many responses as possible scattered on the paper.

GRAPHICS GALORE

Box

Which documents will need your child's gender marker and name changed on them? Highlight or circle your choices below. It is strongly suggested you discuss this with a professional who knows the legality and requirements for the town, city, state, province, and country that you and your child legally reside in! (Some of these may not apply, for they may be based on your child's age.)

Child's emergency information	Child's birth certificate	Child's social security card	Child's passport
Your emergency information	Child's school records	Child's camp information	Child's school ID
Extra-curricular activities in and out of school	Child's online accounts/ social media presence	Child's email address and information	Child's school report cards
Child's medical insurance information	Child's medical card information	Doctor's offices, including dentist	Child's pharmacy records and cards
Administration for Children's Services, if it applies	Any court cases in which your child is named, if it applies	Adoption papers, if it applies	Parole/probation officer information, if it applies
Any pension with your child as the beneficiary	Any IRAs with your child as a beneficiary	Any 403Bs with your child as a beneficiary	Any trusts with your child as a beneficiary
Any wills with your child as a beneficiary	Life insurance, with your child as a beneficiary	Long/short-term insurance, if the child is a beneficiary	Child's disability insurance, if it applies
Any child custody forms, if it applies	Child's library cards	Cell phone account and change on phone list	Cell phone voice message
School/college transcripts (if needed in the future)	All diplomas (if needed in the future)	Old/current colleges' information (if needed in the future)	Professional licenses (if needed in the future)
Male/female actuary stuff, if applicable	IRS information/taxes	Accountant records	Bank accounts and checkbooks
Grocery/chain stores	Gym memberships	Museum memberships	Business cards
Religious institutions: information	Child's bedroom signage	Weight loss program memberships	Address labels
Driver's license (if needed in the future)	Car insurance/registration (if needed in the future)	Credit cards (if needed in the future)	All utilities (if needed in the future)
Healthcare proxy (if needed in the future)	Remains form (if needed in the future)	Funeral plots/plans (if needed in the future)	Apartment maintenance (if needed in the future)
Hotel accounts (if needed in the future)	Department stores (if needed in the future)	Hair/barber/nail salons (if needed in the future)	Warranties (if needed in the future)
Additional ideas:			

REFLECTIVE RESPONSES

1. How can you help with the process of legally changing your child's name and/or their gender marker, if they request this to happen?

    . . . .

    . . . .

    . . . .

2. Which documents will be affected when changing your child's name and gender marker?

    . . . .

    . . . .

    . . . .

3. Which documents will not be affected by the changing of your child's name and gender marker on them?

    . . . .

    . . . .

    . . . .

4. What will you need to bring to each appointment and who will gather these items?

    . . . .

    . . . .

    . . . .

5. Who can be of assistance with the legal process of changing your child's name and gender marker on documents, and how can they help?

    . . . .

    . . . .

    . . . .

6. Which name and gender marker changes require specific paperwork, and who, you or someone else, will gather those materials?

   . . . .

   . . . .

   . . . .

7. What organizations and services can help support you with your questions and research?

   . . . .

   . . . .

   . . . .

8. What are the school policies, procedures, and laws to enable your child to change their gender marker and name on all school-related documents? Can any of this occur before or without it being done legally?

   . . . .

   . . . .

   . . . .

9. Do you know a lawyer or another qualified individual who can help you with all of this? If so, what is the lawyer's information? If not, what resources can help you obtain one?

   . . . .

   . . . .

   . . . .

10. What are the most important pieces of knowledge you feel helped you and may assist others as your child transitioned, in relation to changing their name and gender marker, legally or not, on insurances and on any other documentation?

   . . . .

   . . . .

   . . . .

GRAPHICS GALORE

Venn Diagram

Which documents…

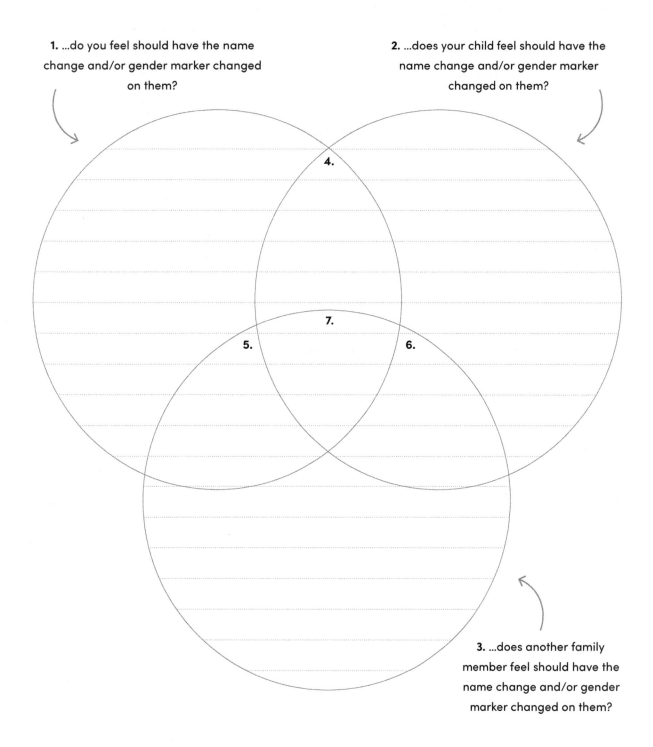

1. …do you feel should have the name change and/or gender marker changed on them?

2. …does your child feel should have the name change and/or gender marker changed on them?

4.

7.

5.   6.

3. …does another family member feel should have the name change and/or gender marker changed on them?

GRAPHICS GALORE

Web

By what means will the gender marker and name be changed on documents? It is suggested you complete six separate webs to help you by using the titles listed below as a guide and place each title (A–F) one at a time in the center on your own: A. Completed in person by you. B. Completed through email/online by you. C. Completed by phone by you. D. Completed by fax by you. E. Completed by mail by you. F. Completed by someone other than you. (List each item based on the central topic in the subtopic.)

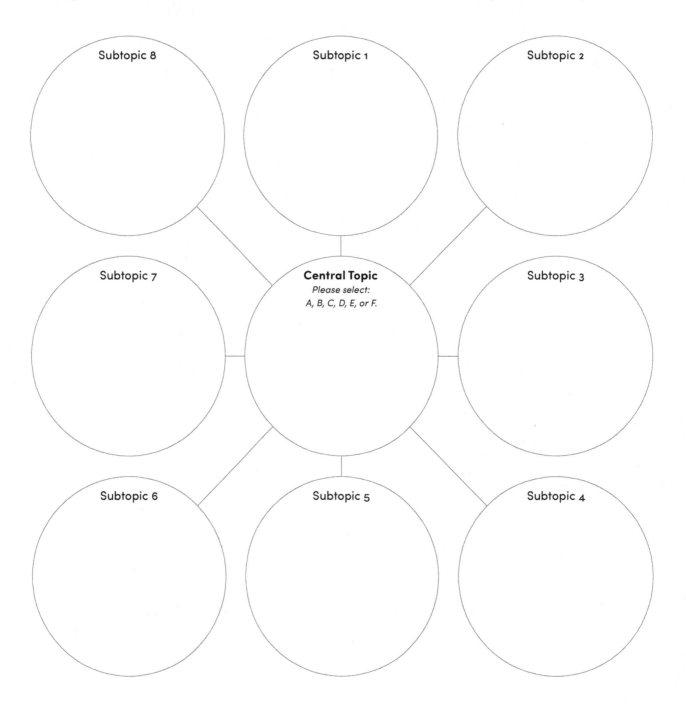

DESERVING DE-STRESSING DELIGHT

Arts Appreciation

For many parents, the arts can allow them to creatively identify with what they are experiencing. Going to a museum, theater, or concert can give them a chance to look at the transition from a different perspective. It can transport them to another place or shift their mindset. They may share these feelings either through journaling or by open discussion. Expressive arts—painting, singing, or acting—can release emotions or supply a sense of comforting joy. These types of activities can give parents the permission to feel deeply, but still allow them simply to breathe should events feel overwhelming. Whether it is through studying a piece of artwork or participating in a theatrical performance, these experiences can provide a cathartic opportunity and help one to gain insight about the transition. What can be evoked is something quite personal and unexpected, but extremely healing!

> ANECDOTAL AFFIRMATION
> *Choices...*
> *Challenging at times,*
> *Not always fair.*

Journal your reaction to this Deserving De-Stressing Delight.

....

....

....

....

....

....

....

....

....

. . . .

. . . .

. . . .

. . . .

. . . .

. . . .

. . . .

. . . .

. . . .

. . . .

. . . .

. . . .

. . . .

. . . .

. . . .

. . . .

. . . .

. . . .

GRAPHICS GALORE

Timeline

Record the best time frame for your child's gender marker and/or name to be changed on each document.

Type of document:	Start date:	Follow-up date:	Date done:

Type of document:	Start date:	Follow-up date:	Date done:

Type of document:	Start date:	Follow-up date:	Date done:

Type of document:	Start date:	Follow-up date:	Date done:

Type of document:	Start date:	Follow-up date:	Date done:

Type of document:	Start date:	Follow-up date:	Date done:

Type of document:	Start date:	Follow-up date:	Date done:

GRAPHICS GALORE

T-Chart

What are the pieces of information you may need to record in relation to changing your child's gender marker and name? This form is created to assist you! Feel free to make copies and use this form for each document that will need to have the gender marker and/or name changed on it.

What type of procedure or documentation are you preparing to discuss?		How did you communicate with the agency? Phone, mail, fax, in person, or email/online?	
How much time do you have to finish this today?		Will you need someone to be with you when you call? If so, who?	
Agency/doctor's name called?		Email of agency:	
Date of contact:		Fax number:	
Phone number: Extension:		What address is the information to be mailed to?	
Who made the call?		Whom did you speak to?	
Where will you get any forms that you will need?		What costs, if any?	

What are any deadlines?		Do you need a notary?	
Date it must/will be done by?		Will you need a witness?	
Do you need authorization from insurance or anywhere else?		Is a letter required, and if so, from whom?	
What documents do you need to complete before this document can be changed?		What will the letter need to state?	
What was said, discussed, and transpired?		Will you need a lawyer for any of these changes?	
Who will be in charge of changing the gender marker after the information is gathered?		How many copies of this updated document can you receive? What is the cost?	
Is there any old documentation that must be shown before this document can be changed?		What day will the agency or doctor be contacted again to make sure it is done and received?	
Where will this information be filed or stored?		Who will confirm that this transaction is completed?	

Record any additional information or other questions below.

....

....

....

....

....

....

....

....

....

....

....

....

....

....

....

....

....

EMPATHY-EMBRACING EXERCISE

Dealing with insurance companies can be exhausting and overwhelming—especially without the proper documentation. Try to imagine a situation where incomplete paperwork or minor errors could delay or prevent any critical surgery or medicine you may need to feel whole. That is exactly how it feels for your child when they are at the mercy of insurance companies for the financial funding of these necessary procedures or medicines.

Has there been a time in your life when you were financially dependent on an organization or a person to support something that was crucial to your health and well-being, or the betterment of your life? If so, what was it and did you disclose it? If not, why? If yes, what was the outcome?

ANECDOTAL AFFIRMATION

*So much
Paper work,
So many
Legal matters,
I just want
To sleep!*

GRAPHICS GALORE

Bar Graph

To what degree do these concerns and related topics matter to you? Based on a scale from 1 to 10, with 1 being the lowest and 10 being the highest, color or shade in your response. This visual will illustrate where your greatest concerns lie and can be used as a tool to help you communicate your thoughts with your child and/or other family members, therapist, spiritual mentor, or for your own personal understanding. The bar graph results can vary as your child's transition progresses and your thoughts may shift.

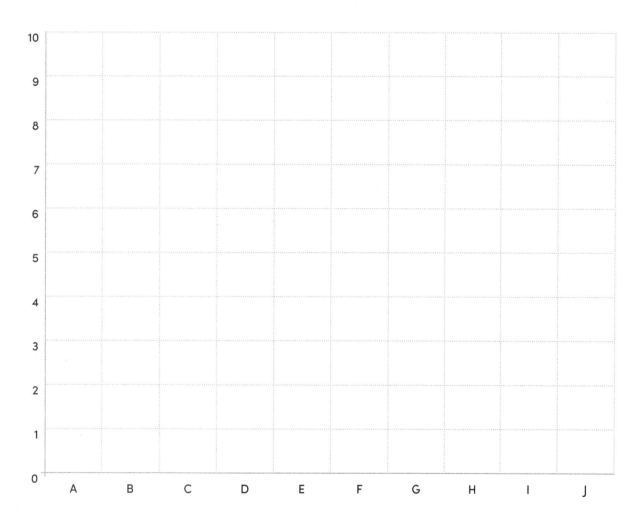

Use these ideas to fill in the bar graph or feel free to create your own!

A. Legally/officially changing your child's name/pronoun assigned at birth.

B. Legally/officially changing your child's name/gender marker on their birth certificate.

C. Legally/officially changing your child's name/gender marker on their passport.

D. Legally/officially changing your child's name/gender marker on social security card/country documents.

E. Legally/officially changing your child's name/gender marker on all medical/hospital records.

F. Legally/officially changing your child's name/gender marker on all school and camp documentation/extra-curricular forms.

G. Legally/officially changing your child's name/gender marker on all insurance policies/emergency documents related to illness and/or death.

H. Legally/officially changing your child's name/gender marker on all cell phones/credit cards/memberships/online accounts.

I. Legally/officially changing your child's name/gender marker on all wills/trusts/inheritance documentation.

J. Legally/officially changing your child's name/gender marker on all documents in relation to legal custody and court documentation, if this is part of your family's needs.

GRAPHICS GALORE

Pie Graph

To what degree are these concerns and related topics important to you? Decide how significant these issues are to you in relation to each other. Place the number that corresponds with a suggested topic within as many slices of the pie that convey how each one matters to you. Only one number should be placed in each slice. You do not need to use all the issues, but do fill in all the slices. Feel free to create your own topics and assign them their own number.

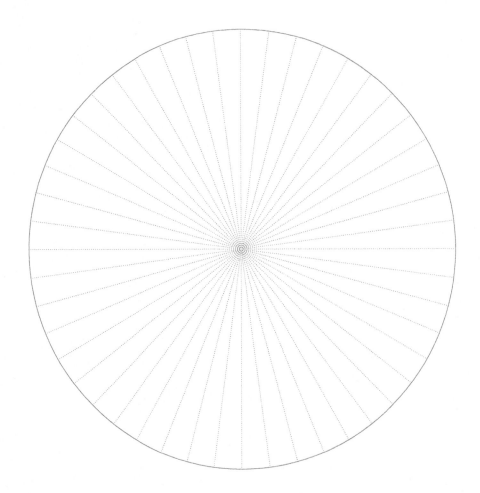

1. Legally/officially changing your child's name/pronoun assigned at birth.

2. Legally/officially changing your child's name/gender marker on their birth certificate.

3. Legally/officially changing your child's name/gender marker on their passport.

4. Legally/officially changing your child's name/gender marker on social security card/country documents.

5. Legally/officially changing your child's name/gender marker on all medical/hospital records.

6. Legally/officially changing your child's name/gender marker on all school and camp documentation/extra-curricular forms.

7. Legally/officially changing your child's name/gender marker on all insurance policies/emergency documents related to illness and/or death.

8. Legally/officially changing your child's name/gender marker on all cell phones/credit cards/memberships/online accounts.

9. Legally/officially changing your child's name/gender marker on all wills/trusts/inheritance documentation.

10. Legally/officially changing your child's name/gender marker on all documents in relation to legal custody and court documentation, if this is part of your family's needs.

SAMPLER SHARES

All names have been changed to ensure anonymity in this section. The first initial designates an individual and the second initial identifies the relationship to the child, i.e. P = their parent, G = their grandparent, and S = their sibling.

How can you help with the process of legally changing your child's name and/or gender marker, if they request this to happen?

HP: The legal changes are timely and one of the first things that my son wanted done. Keep it in mind that we called him by at least five different names before the final name was chosen. Therefore, I would suggest to anyone that you pull patience from your toes and don't get too attached to what they choose. Letting go of his birth name was a big part of my grieving process and many tears were shed over the name that he chose and I *"did not"* like. I was happy to find a website which provided a wealth of information and gave me guidance. PARENT/CHILD: AFAB *(Uses he/him/his pronouns)*

EP: I am currently working with a local non-profit organization that has legal clinics where attorneys come and talk with parents to give legal advice revolving around transgender issues. We will be making his name change official, hopefully before his 17th birthday! PARENT/CHILD: AFAB *(Uses he/him/his pronouns)*

FP: My child originally asked to change his name to a gender neutral one, since he was aware that his father was struggling with his transition. I ran to my computer and did a thorough online search on the issue. I got all of the required documents together and proceeded to the Office of Vital Records. At the time, I was told by staff at the Office of Vital Records that the gender marker could not be changed until my son was 18 years old. I did not know any better, so I took their word for it and just changed the name. I had to go through a judge and have the order published in a local paper. There was a waiting time, but we eventually received the new birth certificate in the mail. My son later decided that he wanted a more masculine name and a gender marker change. By that time, I had learned from a major gender center that the gender marker could be changed as long as I have the required medical documentation. So, I went ahead and returned to the Office of Vital Records. This time, the judge waived the "publishing of the order" part of the process and we simply had to wait for the birth certificate to come in the mail. This was such an important change, as my son was previously humiliated whenever we went to a doctor and they would call out his original name. It just did not match at all with his masculine appearance, and the stares that came as a result were not at all something he could simply ignore. Now that anxiety is gone, and he does not have to be embarrassed by something as basic as his name. PARENT/CHILD: AFAB *(Uses he/him/his pronouns)*

COMMUNICATION CORNER

The wording shared in the Communication Corner of this chapter differs from the other chapters. Though the other chapters pose questions to discuss with others, this chapter offers statements. These statements were originally planned to be used as a helpful script if you are attempting to communicate with others on the phone when trying to change or get information on how to change your child's name and gender marker on a document. Its purpose was to be used as a "how to do" tool intended to make this task easier. If you are unsure of your safety or protections at work or any agency, it is suggested you check with an experienced legal organization or knowledgeable professional who can advise you on which information to share with the individual or company you are about to contact. However, should you decide to use the statements, this script sampler was made to assist you to navigate its use by separating each sentence into individual steps. Feel free to combine these steps to form a script or use them one at a time as provided. You may opt to explain your thoughts and feelings about these statements with other family members or someone else you trust to decide which statements, if any, will be used. Do you and the individual/s you have chosen to communicate with respond to these statements in the same way or differently? Discuss your responses to understand how you view them and make time to celebrate all you learn from being willing to communicate with others.

> ANECDOTAL AFFIRMATION
> *Your ignorance*
> *Is NOT*
> *My responsibility!*

If this conversation is occurring over the phone, you may elect to ask if it is being recorded. If the answer is yes, you may prefer to ask that it not be recorded and inform the person with whom you are speaking that the information you may be sharing is highly confidential. Some agencies allow the conversation to not be recorded, if this is your preference, but it needs to be requested by you. If you prefer the conversation to be recorded, then this may be a non-issue for you, but at least you will be able to obtain this information for yourself.

1. Initial attempt: Hello, my name is . . . . and I want to update my records/documents. You have my child listed as male/female, but my child is actually female/male and should be recorded as female/male. (Please note that some jurisdictions allow a third option other than female/male, so you may need to inquire about this, should it be your child's preference.) Also, their name may appear as . . . . , but it should actually appear as . . . . Can you help me with this? If not, would you please connect me with someone who can? (Get the name and phone number/extension for each interaction.)

2. If you are getting nowhere with this person, thank them for their time and help and...

. . . .

. . . .

3. Then state you are requesting to speak with their supervisor or the highest-ranking person available. Once you reach this person, repeat the first statement again.

    . . . .

    . . . .

4. If the supervisor or highest-ranking person is unavailable to speak with you, you can request to have that person call you back or you can ask for their direct number in order to contact them. Make sure you inquire as to when they will be able to be reached. Record that number and get the details of the person who gave you this information, so that you can state that person recommended you contact them. It may be helpful to list the name of the person and their phone number in your cell phone in case it shows up on your screen when they call you back.

    . . . .

    . . . .

5. If you are speaking with the supervisor or highest-ranking person and they are questioning how there can be such an error, simply make the point that all you need to know is how to get this changed. Ask what documentation the company/business needs to prove your child's gender. Record this information and thank them for their help. However...see step 6!

    . . . .

    . . . .

6. If the person presses you and you feel you need to explain about the transition, which is a personal choice, remind them that the information you are sharing is highly confidential. Decide how you and your child want to define the transition and how your child prefers to refer to their process, prior to making this phone call. (Some parents state that their child is transgender and/or non-binary and has legally transitioned.) State that you have all the legal documentation, if this is correct, to prove this fact and that you were advised to contact them. Ask what forms they may or may not need to change this document. Who do you send it to? What else do you need? What is the time frame in which this will be completed?

    . . . .

    . . . .

7. If they state they will need to get back to you, ask exactly when that will be; ask if they will call you back with the update or whether you need to call back. Then inquire if they need any information from you, what that is, and what is the best or most effective way to get this information to them.

. . . .

. . . .

8. Before you hang up, ask if they can complete the name/gender marker changes over the phone, with no further steps needed; ask them to email or mail you the corrected documentation as proof and thank them for their assistance.

. . . .

. . . .

9. If you feel that you are still not able to obtain the results you seek with the supervisor, you may choose to elect to contact a legal or advocacy organization that can help you with this.

. . . .

. . . .

10. Much information about changing the gender marker and name can be found online. Some key words to use: changing name and gender marker/transition/transgender/non-binary. Also, it may be important to include the country or state in which your child resides. In addition, you may elect to ask others what they did, whom they used to help them, and what steps they took to change the gender marker and name.

. . . .

. . . .

Chapter 10

PRIVILEGE: LOSS OR GAIN?

VITAL VIGNETTE

"Privilege" can be an unfamiliar concept that you might not have previously considered. Privilege is a special advantage or right granted to a particular person or group. It is something that rarely, if ever, may have crossed your mind before transitioning affected

any part of your family's life. Perhaps you have heard of privilege or the lack of it in relation to sexual orientation, class, race, religion, ethnicity, ability, age, aesthetics, size, and gender, but it is not something you probably ever expected could become another layer of the transition. How you and your child are treated now will determine the reality or perception of whether you, your child, and other family members have lost or gained privilege. A way the loss or gain of privilege can manifest is that you may no longer be viewed as you once were, in relation to respect from others. It can affect your feelings of visibility and value to those around you. Some forms of privilege implicitly confer a level of worthiness on a person by society that can be either extremely harmful or ego-boosting to individuals, depending on their situation. As a result of the transition, this ranking is often re-evaluated throughout each experience and every situation, requiring a reassessment of the role privilege plays in your life and in the lives of your family members.

The major question you may continuously ask yourself in relation to privilege is: How does or will privilege impact my life and the lives of my family members? This question is often followed by two other questions: What am I and my family losing or gaining as a result of the transition? Is there something that can be done about privilege to make my family and me feel better or more whole around this issue? Much of the loss or gain depends on how you were publicly perceived prior to the transition compared with now and in the future. In every case, the loss or gain of privilege may be subtle, ambivalent, or blatant, and only you can decide how it feels for you.

For some families, living with the fear of their child being racially profiled can cause them and their child a realistic terror. In addition, they can feel a tremendous loss of a specific freedom. The reality is that a child of color who was once read as a girl may now be stopped by the police as they walk down the street with their male friends. This is probably an action that had never happened to them prior to passing as their affirmed male gender. Your child can be profiled purely because they are now seen as a boy of color. There are trans children who were assigned male at birth, now living in their affirmed gender, who may lose the privilege of safely socializing alone under certain circumstances. They can become more vulnerable to various types of physical and sexual abuse, merely for being viewed as female. For non-binary children, the continuous questioning of their gender and misgendering by others can become exhausting and cause them safety concerns as they simply live their daily life. Furthermore, the bullying of trans children and the constant embarrassment they are forced to endure can reduce the daily privilege of existence by increasing their stress level. Those who identify as trans often learn to tolerate this burden, which cisgendered individuals will never face as they encounter society as a whole.

Although many families have expressed that they and their child are still welcome at friends and family functions or social gatherings, in exactly the same manner as they were before their child began to transition, others have not been as fortunate. Some parents have stated that they are no longer accepted at their place of worship. Others are uninvited to events with family and friends. And when included, they are met with a multitude of inappropriate questions that make the occasion practically unbearable. Sometimes these circumstances can be based on cultural or religious beliefs that have been part of their heritages and traditions. The rejection and criticism these families and children are expected to endure can be heartbreaking for all involved. Other parents have discussed that in some cases, even if friends and family members are supportive of their child's transition when their child's preferences and gestured mannerisms continue to align with their gender assigned at birth, many friends and family members begin to question the child's need to be seen in their affirmed gender. Moreover, parents are blamed, judged, and shamed for being advocates for their child. In fact, some parents have reported that there are times when friends, family members, and even school personnel have called child protective services to assess the welfare of their child, in the hope of having the child removed from their home/school. Unfortunately, many families have had to suffer much loss of social privilege and emotional agony, due to the ignorance of others. As a result, some parents and families of trans children say that it is critical for them to find organizations and support groups that lovingly embrace their presence. They describe these new social opportunities as a lifeline and have created a family circle of choice where unconditional love and acceptance are abundant.

It is commonly known that children are often invited to parties, most definitely sleepovers, according to their gender assigned at birth, especially if these gatherings are based on friendships fostered at school and club membership settings. These invitations are regularly aligned according to the child's gender, and once a child recognizes their affirmed gender, various friendships may begin to change. For some children, their friendships will remain intact. Yet for others, they can lose the privilege of being included in social circles they treasure. The parents of trans children have shared that sometimes the parents of a child having a party are no longer inviting their child to attend a celebration, which they would have been asked to do prior to the child identifying as trans. The reasons that are given for this change can be plentiful and extremely hurtful to both the trans child and their family. The parents of the celebrant may express that they are uncomfortable having their child around the trans child, that they feel the child will not fit in, or they think the child will no longer have an interest in what the other children will be doing at the party.

According to some educators and parents who offered their experiences, there are some school practices that can be based primarily on gender, such as class makeup, student classroom jobs, grouping, and seating. Something as routine as class photo day or assigning vocal parts in a chorus can become sources of much emotional pain for trans children. Rarely will teachers assign or read aloud books that include trans characters or offer examples using "they" pronouns, but rather only "he" or "she" pronouns, leaving students who use "they" for their pronoun struggling to see themselves respected and part of the school community. However, cisgendered, binary-identified students are afforded this privilege. Furthermore, there are times children have been encouraged to select specific topics and activities according to their gender, not considering the child's talents and preferences. Even being called on in class, in relation to particular subjects based on a child's perceived gender, has been described as occurring differently by students once they identify in their affirmed gender. Therefore, some children will gain privilege as a result of these practices, while others will lose privilege as well as important opportunities that would have been afforded them prior to identifying in their affirmed gender. In fact, in most grades, when any aspect of sexual health education is part of the curriculum, it is devoid of any reference to anything other than traditional gender binary and heteronormative stereotypes. Often, if there is any inclusiveness of gay and lesbian sex education, the needs of transgender and non-binary individuals are more than likely ignored and excluded.

As discussed in other chapters, bathroom privileges and locker room accessibility, which enable a child to use the facility aligned with their affirmed gender, may be removed and can be replaced with the stigma of the child being viewed as a threat to other children. This line of thinking is not only outlandish, but in contrast, the trans child is likely to be the one to be bullied and possibly harmed because of others who are not well informed in respect to transgender research. In addition, other rights and freedoms can be compromised for these children, especially for those who identify as non-binary. Attempts to join certain gendered after-school programs, sports teams, and camps can become a nightmare for both the child and their families, if a child does not identify as either male or female.

Another safety concern that has been discussed involves being screened at security points at the airport. It is a topic rarely mentioned but it could affect a child and their family when traveling. The scanning machines often flag if a trans child is "packing" or if a trans girl has not had bottom surgery. The results for some can cause extreme embarrassment, hostile harassment, and force them to deal with legal battles. This possible reality should be discussed before travel begins so that all individuals have a plan for how to protect the parties involved and what to do if a problem arises. It is highly recommended that each family member runs through exactly what they are going to say and do should a screener announce, "There is a bodily anomaly!" or some other similar degrading statement. It is critical for you to be aware of what legal rights your child and you, as a parent, have in every country you visit where a security screening may be necessary. Some trans children acquire a letter from a mental health or medical professional explaining that they are transgender with the proper wording, which may help them educate the screener if these challenges occur. In addition, some people elect to bring the phone numbers and email addresses of legal defense organizations or lawyers, in case they feel that they need immediate legal advice or assistance. If financially able, some parents have found obtaining Global Entry for their child is a way to avoid their child being required to do a full body scan. Should this be an option for the child, it is important to research which countries do not honor Global Entry policies, in order to have all of the facts. There are some families who choose not to travel to particular countries or investigate which documentation their child may need, in case they do experience a problem with the scanning procedures at the airport or at any other venue which has this practice.

While there are medical and mental health professionals who are aware of the transgender community and are well informed and supportive of a child's transition, there are many who are completely in the dark in reference to the process and can do much harm to children and their families if they do not have proper training. There are families who feel that they lose the privilege of being able to use the doctors whom they have gone to for years, due to the reality that their medical professional is not familiar with the specialized care they need to address as the child transitions. The more visible trans children are, the more essential it is for those in the medical field to educate themselves in order to remain current and have the ability to serve these patients.

Once children transition, they may experience changes in privilege in relation to work when they seek employment. For instance, depending on the politics of a country, all transgender individuals may not be able to serve in their country's military, for the mere fact that they are living in their affirmed gender. This loss of privilege can affect the trajectory of a child's life and their ability to fulfill a career choice. Some trans women state that they have experienced a loss of privilege and encountered misogyny due to the fact that companies often devalue cisgender women in the workplace by paying them less money, giving them fewer opportunities for advancement, and overlooking them when searching for leadership as a company grows. Furthermore, the role trans misogyny plays in the workplace can additionally marginalize trans women. Yet, trans men have shared that they may have gained male privilege in the workforce, for they can now be viewed as having more ability, possibly entitling them to a higher pay scale. Furthermore, they might be given greater opportunities to move up the ladder, simply because they are seen as male. Moreover, some trans children have expressed that they believe it is necessary to avoid working in certain fields, for fear they will not be hired if employers find out their trans status. The reality is that transphobia exists and sometimes trans people can be legally discriminated against in the workplace. Some countries, states, or provinces have laws that do not protect a person based on their gender and, as a result, trans youth can lose the freedom to freely seek employment. However, even though there are laws that clearly protect those in relation to their gender identity, sometimes both businesses and individuals elect to overlook these rights. As a result, trans people of all ages and their families can be forced to take legal action against these injustices to ensure the laws are enforced.

The subject of privilege for transgender children, their parents, and other family members can affect a plethora of circumstances, including public safety, especially in relation to bathroom and locker-room use and medical and health services. In addition, school challenges, legal rights, finances, inheritance, and the way friends and family interact or react to them individually and as a family can be quite difficult. The loss of privilege can be accompanied by shame, fear, anger, humiliation, confusion, and feelings of inferiority. In contrast, the gain of privilege can evoke feelings of pride, safety, joy, validation, empowerment, and guilt. No parent, child, or other family member can be prepared for all the possible encounters that may occur in relation to privilege. Nor can they understand how they will feel or react each and every time someone affects their loss or gain of privilege, as well as that of their child. The best way to approach these situations, which can be paralyzing, enraging, or empowering, is to have a plan.

It is suggested that you decide ahead of time how you will address the situation if you, your child, and other family members are mistreated or overlooked. Verbally rehearse what will be said if one of you is treated with less respect by school members, friends and family, medical professionals, religious community members, or others. Futhermore, when an unexpected privilege-related issue arises and you are unsure of what to say, perhaps you will have to put it aside and discuss what your best approach may be next time, should a similar scenario arise in the future. As emotionally challenging as it can be to ignore the action of another person's ignorance, it is always crucial to make safety your first concern. This is even more critical if your child is visibly trans or their gender can possibly be misread. The reality is that the loss and gain of privilege demands to be acknowledged in how it affects your family when the transition is now part of everyone's experience. It must especially be recognized that it plays a major factor, on a number of levels, in contributing to the self-worth, confidence, well-being, and lives of all involved!

GRAPHICS GALORE

Splash

When you think of privilege, what words come to mind? By creatively splashing words and short phrases, quickly attempt to express your answers randomly with as many responses as possible scattered on the paper.

GRAPHICS GALORE

Box

What societal privileges did you have prior to your child's transition, in relation to: sexual orientation, class, race, religion, ethnicity, ability, age, aesthetics, size, and gender? Record your responses below.
(You may try this exercise from the perspective of how these privileges have changed or may change for your child and other family members.)

Sexual orientation	Class	Race	Religion	Ethnicity

Ability	Age	Aesthetics	Size	Gender

REFLECTIVE RESPONSES

1. How do you feel that you, your child, and any other family member have lost and/or gained privilege in any way or in any area of your lives?

....

....

....

2. How do you feel privilege has been affected in relation to safety issues, bathroom use, and any other concerns for you, your child, and any other family member?

....

....

....

3. How is having your child viewed in their affirmed gender considered a loss or gain of privilege for you, your child, and other family members, if this applies in any way?

....

....

....

4. How do people at social events and activities (e.g. when at a public pool, restaurants) treat you, your child, and any other family member now that your child is considering transitioning, in transition, or has transitioned?

....

....

....

5. How do friends and family treat you, your child, and other family members in social circles, now that your child is considering transitioning, in transition, or has transitioned?

    . . . .

    . . . .

    . . . .

6. How do people in doctors' offices, hospitals, and the medical profession treat you, your child, and other family members, now that your child is considering transitioning, in transition, or has transitioned?

    . . . .

    . . . .

    . . . .

7. How do people who you, your child, and other family members bump into from the past treat you and other family members, now that your child is considering transitioning, in transition, or has transitioned?

    . . . .

    . . . .

    . . . .

8. How are gender roles and biased attitudes the same or different at home or in the presence of others for you, your child, and other family members, now that your child is considering transitioning, in transition, or has transitioned?

    . . . .

    . . . .

    . . . .

9. How do people in clothing or makeup departments treat you, your child, and other family members as they are there to assist the child as they use the store's services, now that your child is considering transitioning, in transition, or has transitioned?

. . . .

. . . .

. . . .

10. How does it feel if your child travels and may be faced with security both at the airport and in certain countries, now that your child is considering transitioning, in transition, or has transitioned?

. . . .

. . . .

. . . .

GRAPHICS GALORE

Bar Graph

To what degree do these concerns and related topics matter to you? Based on a scale from 1 to 10, with 1 being the lowest and 10 being the highest, color or shade in your response. This visual will illustrate where your greatest concerns lie and can be used as a tool to help you communicate your thoughts with your child and/or other family members, therapist, spiritual mentor, or for your own personal understanding. The bar graph results can vary as your child's transition progresses and your thoughts may shift.

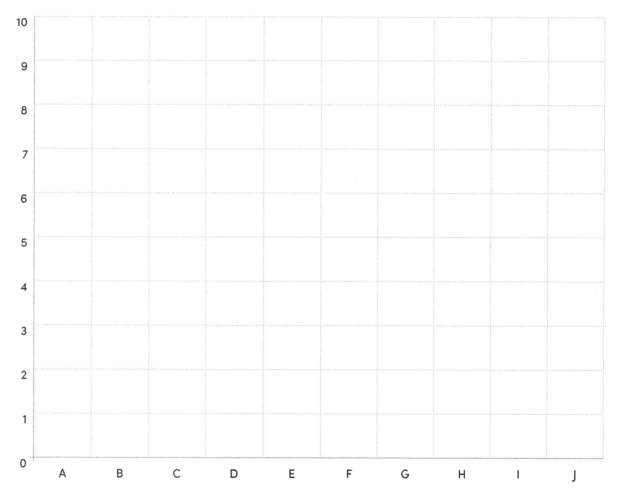

Use these ideas to fill in the bar graph or feel free to create your own!

A. The importance of the loss or gain of privilege in relation to safety issues for your child.

B. The importance of the loss or gain of privilege in relation to your child shopping or eating in restaurants.

C. The importance of the loss or gain of privilege in relation to your child in social circles with family and friends.

D. The importance of the loss or gain of privilege in relation to your child when receiving any medical treatment and with medical professionals.

E. The importance of the loss or gain of privilege in relation to inclusion of your child in the LGBTQ+ community.

F. The importance of the loss or gain of privilege in relation to your child's treatment in school.

G. The importance of the loss or gain of privilege in relation to your child's legal rights and the application of laws.

H. The importance of the loss or gain of privilege in relation to your child's current and future fertility and/or dating options.

I. The importance of the loss or gain of privilege in relation to your child's traveling and vacationing opportunities.

J. The importance of the loss or gain of privilege in relation to your child's current and future employment and career opportunities.

GRAPHICS GALORE

Pie Graph

To what degree are these concerns and related topics important to you? Decide how significant these issues are to you in relation to each other. Place the number that corresponds with a suggested topic within as many slices of the pie that convey how each one matters to you. Only one number should be placed in each slice. You do not need to use all the issues, but do fill in all the slices. Feel free to create your own topics and assign them their own number.

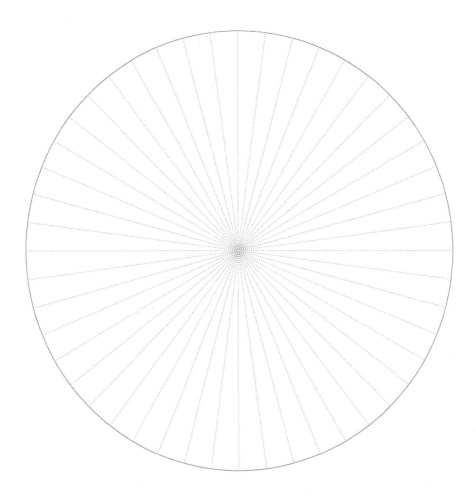

1. The importance of the loss or gain of privilege in relation to safety issues for your child.

2. The importance of the loss or gain of privilege in relation to your child shopping or eating in restaurants.

3. The importance of the loss or gain of privilege in relation to your child in social circles with family and friends.

4. The importance of the loss or gain of privilege in relation to your child when receiving any medical treatment and with medical professionals.

5. The importance of the loss or gain of privilege in relation to inclusion of your child in the LGBTQ+ community.

6. The importance of the loss or gain of privilege in relation to your child's treatment in school.

7. The importance of the loss or gain of privilege in relation to your child's legal rights and the application of laws.

8. The importance of the loss or gain of privilege in relation to your child's current and future fertility and/or dating options.

9. The importance of the loss or gain of privilege in relation to your child's traveling and vacationing opportunities.

10. The importance of the loss or gain of privilege in relation to your child's current and future employment and career opportunities.

DESERVING DE-STRESSING DELIGHT

ANECDOTAL AFFIRMATION

Change takes time,
So many changes.
Only time will tell,
How many changes,
And how much time.

Playtime

Play can be a time dedicated to pure happiness, laughter, and fun! How appealing can this be to any family member? For some, a light-hearted game of cards with friends can be the perfect remedy for possible isolation and/or any sadness that may be experienced during the heaviest moments of the mourning period. Even for those who are completely at peace with the transition, the interpersonal interactions with others can certainly be a pick-me-up experience that warms the soul. Playing board games with family members for hours or participating in a coloring club for adults could conjure up fun childhood memories. The goal is for family members not only to give themselves permission to play games or relive enjoyable childhood activities that soothe their heart, but also to schedule in what is lovingly coined "forced fun." It is recommended that whatever makes a parent and other family members feel free and smile will be optimal. Many family members may find that this time of "forced fun" can serve as a release of tension, fear, and anxiety or an opportunity to experience the gifts and joys in relation to your child's transition.

Journal your reaction to this Deserving De-Stressing Delight.

GRAPHICS GALORE

Web

Since your child's transition, what are some specific ways your life has been affected, if any, in relation to privilege?

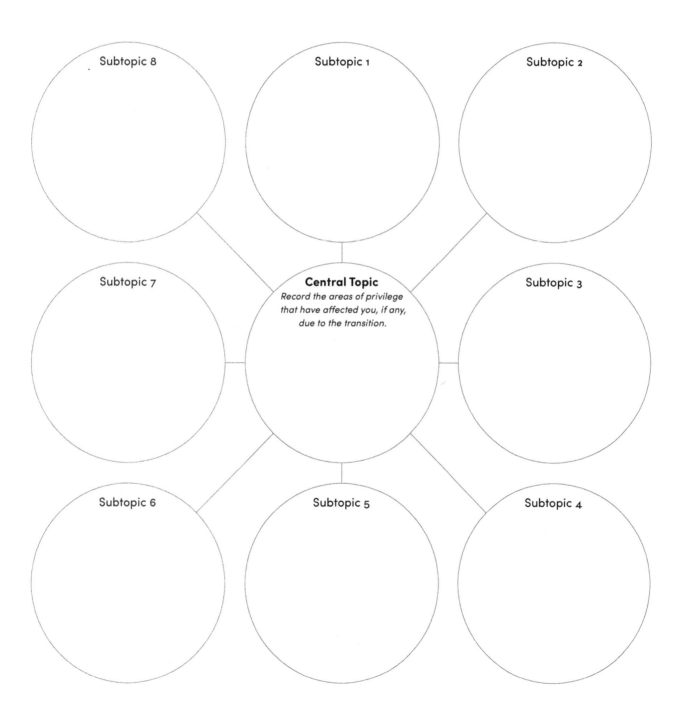

GRAPHICS GALORE

Venn Diagram

How has privilege played a role in your lives prior to your child's transition? Feel free to redo this exercise again during your child's transition and afterwards, when it may no longer be a major focus of your life.

1. Which privileges did you have or not have prior to your child's transition?

2. Which privileges did your child have or not have prior to their transition?

4.

7.

5.

6.

3. Which privileges did other family members have or not have prior to the child's transition?

EMPATHY-EMBRACING EXERCISE

Identifying what privilege means to any family member and then assessing whether your child's transition affects their privilege is an issue that is brought to the forefront by this exercise. It can be a subtle presence of positive or negative shifts. Many parents and other family members say that they see a change in privilege as an unexpected result of the child's transition, in relation to how others treat them.

Has there been a time in your life when you felt a loss or gain of privilege based on your gender, prior to your child's transition? If so, what was it and how did it affect your life? If it did not affect your life, why do you think this was the case?

> ANECDOTAL AFFIRMATION
>
> *One foot*
> *In front*
> *Of the other,*
> *The weight*
> *Of the world*
> *On my shoulders,*
> *I shift*
> *The load*
> *And forge ahead.*

. . . .

. . . .

. . . .

. . . .

. . . .

. . . .

. . . .

. . . .

. . . .

. . . .

. . . .

. . . .

. . . .

. . . .

. . . .

. . . .

. . . .

GRAPHICS GALORE

Timeline

Recording when you lost or gained any privilege throughout your child's transition, as an individual or as a family, can help you notice if the loss or gain of privilege has or is happening at a rapid or slow pace.

Date:	What privilege did you and/or another family member lose or gain today?	Did you lose or gain it personally or as a family?
Date:	What privilege did you and/or another family member lose or gain today?	Did you lose or gain it personally or as a family?
Date:	What privilege did you and/or another family member lose or gain today?	Did you lose or gain it personally or as a family?
Date:	What privilege did you and/or another family member lose or gain today?	Did you lose or gain it personally or as a family?
Date:	What privilege did you and/or another family member lose or gain today?	Did you lose or gain it personally or as a family?
Date:	What privilege did you and/or another family member lose or gain today?	Did you lose or gain it personally or as a family?
Date:	What privilege did you and/or another family member lose or gain today?	Did you lose or gain it personally or as a family?

GRAPHICS GALORE

T-Chart

How do you believe your individual privilege has been affected as a result of your child's transition? Feel free to answer this in relation to your relationship with your child and other family members, or not!

What are some positive changes you have experienced in relation to privilege?	What are some negative changes you have experienced in relation to privilege?	What areas have not changed in relation to privilege?

SAMPLER SHARES

All names have been changed to ensure anonymity in this section. The first initial designates an individual and the second initial identifies the relationship to the child, i.e. P = their parent, G = their grandparent, and S = their sibling.

How do you feel that you, your child, and/or any other family member have lost or gained privilege in any way or in any area of your lives?

CP: The world can be a scary place, more so for marginalized people. Some politicians are railing against trans people in the military and directing Health and Human Services to disallow people from identifying as transgender, thereby erasing them. Others are rolling back Obama-era guidance on trans students while knowing the harm that they are doing. It seems as if every day there is a new article or opinion piece published that reduces trans identities to nothing other than genitals and is about their value to society. My fears about my son's future and safety have yet to be resolved. There are times when I feel as if all I'm running on is adrenaline from that fear. My biggest fear and recognition of the loss of privilege took hold on a vacation. He was too old for me to "sneak" him into the ladies' room and I was terrified to let him in the men's room alone. This vacation spot does have family bathrooms, but those are usually in use by, well, families. Off to the men's room alone he went. A five-minute trip felt like five hours until I saw him come out of there unharmed. Today, I'm still afraid. I am afraid to attend protests that support my child's rights, while knowing those who oppose our views may incite violence, yet I am afraid not to participate. A lesson that we always taught him was to not allow fear to hold him back. Sometimes, we still feel we have to shout in the streets that all people are human and deserving of rights, respect, and dignity. *PARENT/CHILD: AFAB (Uses he/him/his pronouns)*

JS: Privilege is a spectrum. We all fall on different degrees of this spectrum based on how society sees us and many different things affect it. When I walk into a room with confidence, I am granted privilege as a white, cisgender, socially "competent" individual. Sadly, when people are perceived as different from the "norm," society often categorizes them as scary or dangerous and treats them as deserving of less respect, fewer protections, or having less worth. I think being a teenager is already hard and teenagers already have less privilege than adults who are more likely to be believed and who are given more rights, respect, and freedoms. In addition, teens may be ostracized by their peers for not having the right clothes, hair, mannerisms, self-confidence, or any number of things. When the exploration of sexuality and gender identity is added to the mix I can imagine kids may be further picked on and further lose the privileges of being respected by their peers and adults. My sibling is exploring "their" gender identity and I think it is incredible that we are living in a time when "they" are able to do this. Sadly, we are also living in a time when many people still do not like that "they" are able to do this, which leads to loss of privilege.

Though impossible to parse the exploration of gender identity from other aspects of who "they" are, I can only imagine this makes it harder for "them." My sibling once told me "they" wished that they could start school somewhere new where no one knew who "they" were and therefore "they" could start over, but I had this same thought when I was young without having ever questioned my gender. I can only hope that whether "they" determine that "they" are transgender, non-binary, or cisgender that "they" are accepted as "they" are by our family and community so that "their" physical health, safety, and mental health are not compromised. Those are what is at stake when one loses privilege. *SIBLING/GENDER QUESTIONING SIBLING: AFAB (Uses they/them/their pronouns)*

HP: I believe that we have come a long way when it comes to male/female equality in all aspects. Although, I still feel that it is a privilege to be a male in our society and that there are extra given opportunities for those gendered males in many venues. This is particularly true when it comes to the workforce and the amount of money individuals can potentially make in their life. Therefore, I feel that my son will definitely benefit more as a male than a female. His compassion and understanding the differences of being treated as a male versus female will allow him to do great things! *PARENT/CHILD: AFAB (Uses he/him/his pronouns)*

COMMUNICATION CORNER

When you speak spontaneously out of anger or fear about the unknown, without thinking it through, you can sometimes regret the way you phrased your words or the tone you used to express your feelings. Rehearsing what you want to ask or discuss with your child, and other family members, can help you before you actually communicate your thoughts. This gives you a moment to reflect and pause before you converse about emotional topics. You may choose to practice asking these questions with a trusted friend, family member, spiritual mentor, or therapist first. Explain your thoughts and feelings about these statements to one another verbally or in writing. It is important to note that some families elected to only address one question or two, while others preferred to answer them all. In order to recall the questions you answered, simply highlight and/or circle the ones you addressed as a family, yet acknowledging that you may return to discuss the others in the future. Decide what feels best for two or more family members and begin the conversation. Do you, your child, and other family members answer these questions in the same way or differently? Discuss your responses to understand how all of you view the answers to the questions and make time to celebrate all you learn from being willing to communicate with each other.

> ANECDOTAL AFFIRMATION
> *You taught me courage,*
> *I taught you*
> *Unconditional love!*

1. In what ways, if any, do you feel privilege may have changed for you in relation to safety concerns, due to your child's transition?

....

....

2. In what ways, if any, do you feel privilege may have changed for you in relation to shopping in stores and eating in restaurants with your child, due to your child's transition?

....

....

3. In what ways, if any, do you feel privilege may have changed for you in relation to your child's current or future fertility and/or dating options, due to your child's transition?

....

....

4. In what ways, if any, do you feel privilege may have changed for you in relation to medical treatment and with medical professionals, due to your child's transition?

....

....

5. In what ways, if any, do you feel privilege may have changed for you in relation to being part of the LGBTQ+ community, due to your child's transition?

....

....

6. In what ways, if any, do you feel privilege may have changed for you in relation to social circles of friends and family, due to your child's transition?

....

....

7. In what ways, if any, do you feel privilege may have changed for you in relation to your child's treatment in school, due to your child's transition?

....

....

8. In what ways, if any, do you feel privilege may have changed for you in relation to legal rights and the application of laws, due to your child's transition?

....

....

9. In what ways, if any, do you feel privilege may have changed for you in relation to your traveling or vacationing opportunities, due to your child's transition?

....

....

10. In what ways, if any, do you feel privilege may have changed for your child's current and future employment and career opportunities, due to your child's transition?

. . . .

. . . .

Chapter 11

LET'S TALK ABOUT FINDING A THERAPIST

VITAL VIGNETTE

ANECDOTAL AFFIRMATION

It comes
In waves.
Some days I get
Pulled under,
Other days
I am able
To ride them.
On the
Best days
I can hear
And see
The beauty!

Many times, feelings of concern or confusion are alleviated if a parent discovers a knowledgeable and experienced therapist. The search may not be difficult if you know how and where to look. As may be expected, it can be much easier to find a qualified therapist who is familiar with LGBTQ+ issues if you live in an urban or metropolitan area. The number of providers in this specialty is exploding. Training is occurring in many parts of certain countries, including rural areas. Some people who cannot find a trained provider in their area will travel great distances to work in person with a therapist. If this is not an option for you, parents and other family members may choose to speak remotely with a therapist or rely more on peer support through the internet, support groups, conferences, and so on.

Sometimes, there are LGBTQ+-experienced therapists who have very little training in regard to transition. Then, add in the fact that you are looking for a therapist who understands the unique experience of parents and families of someone who is in transition, and the pool can become narrower still. There are a multitude of things that you, as parents, should keep in mind when attempting to find a therapist who will suit your personal needs. It is strongly recommended that you interview the therapist on the phone as a first screening. Second, you can set up an initial in-person consultation, and use this opportunity to grasp the therapist's knowledge and awareness of the issues that matter most to you. Even if a therapist states that they are experienced in working with the LGBTQ+ community on a website or a referral list, this does not automatically mean they have had any specific training in transgender issues in working with parents and families who have a child or family member who is in transition. It could simply mean that they are open to providing services to those potential clients who identify as trans, and to their families. However, they may not have any professional experience or clinical training in relation to transgender matters or the needs of parents and families. It is completely acceptable to ask if the therapist is knowledgeable about vocabulary, inquire how many parents and families they have worked with or have as clients, and question their training and certifications that align with your needs. Equally important, you may have other core issues that must be addressed in addition to the transition, such as a history of abuse, addictions, trauma, panic attacks, or depression.

Sometimes the transition can unexpectedly trigger past trauma that has been buried, especially now that your child identifies differently from the gender they were assigned at birth. For instance, your child may now look more similar to you when you were their age and this could possibly trigger a memory that has either been suppressed or not completely processed. Furthermore, your child may have looked like you and no longer does or now resembles another family member (such as your parent, spouse, or sibling), and this brings up feelings related to your relationship with that family member.

Parents and other family members should be aware that their history of addictions or struggles with substances, including battles with food, can become more challenging throughout their child's transition process. In many cases, families may be seeking a therapist who has much experience not only with the unique factors that can be facing parents and other family members throughout the transition, but also other matters that are based on their own individual histories. It may be necessary to search for a therapist who is familiar with mental illness, trauma, or a myriad of critical issues, including matters related to identifying on the autism spectrum.

During your interviewing and initial consultation process, if at any time you feel that the therapist is inappropriate with their line of questioning or statements, such as shaming your actions of supporting your child's need to transition, blaming you for not stopping the transition process, or having a bias that contradicts your beliefs, you do not need to use this therapist. Trust your gut, and if any part of the interview feels uncomfortable, find a different therapist who fits your needs. However, it is vital to recognize that many difficult and unexpected issues can arise during therapy. You should question the therapist to clarify the communication. There can be miscommunication. Also, if you do not like the therapist after a first visit, there is no need to go back. But if you are uncomfortable with your current therapist, it is suggested that you discuss any issues with the therapist before terminating working with them. It is essential to realize that an experienced therapist whose cultural background, race, ethnicity, religion, gender, age, ability, size, or LGBTQ+ affiliations that may vary from yours, can bring a healthy array of dynamics and points of view into the therapeutic process, which could be worth considering. If the therapist's identity differs from yours, this does not mean that they do not have the professional skills required to treat you in therapy. You will have to decide to what degree these aspects matter to you, based on your preferences, needs, and issues.

If you are currently working with a trained provider who is helping you and you feel that they will continue to do so, even if they are not familiar with the LGBTQ+ topics that can arise, you may elect not to switch to a different therapist. This is something you will need to weigh and decide what matters most to you in order to have your needs met. However, if you are searching for a therapist, then keep in mind that besides training, you may want to consider these questions when selecting one:

- Are they able to provide guidance when you seek clarity?
- Do they make you feel accepted, respected, and understood?
- Are they a good listener?
- Are they willing to learn about topics that will help your sessions?
- Do you feel that they like you?
- Are they professional, on time, organized, and reliable?

It may take some time, but you can find a qualified therapist who is right for you. Once you do, they can become a major support and a welcome lifeline!

GRAPHICS GALORE

Splash

What are you looking for in regard to an individual and/or family therapist? By creatively splashing words and short phrases, quickly attempt to express your answers randomly with as many responses as possible scattered on the paper.

GRAPHICS GALORE

Web

Why might you want to begin and continue individual and/or family therapy now?

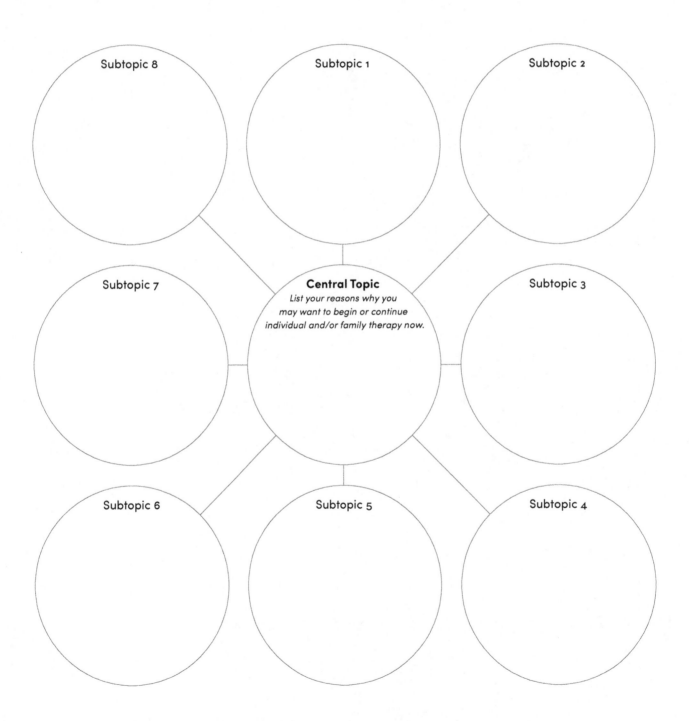

REFLECTIVE RESPONSES

1. Why do you feel that you should or should not be in individual therapy as your child begins their transition process?

    ·

    ·

    ·

2. Why do you feel that you should or should not be in family therapy as your child begins their transition process?

    ·

    ·

    ·

3. Why do you feel that your child and/or any other family member should or should not be in individual therapy as your child begins their transition process?

    ·

    ·

    ·

4. Can you think of anyone who is the parent or other family member of a child who has transitioned who could recommend a therapist they are using or have used?

    ·

    ·

    ·

5. Can you think of anyone you know that may be able to recommend a therapist to you, who is knowledgeable about transgender issues in relation to children and families?

. . . .

. . . .

. . . .

6. If you cannot find a therapist who is familiar with transgender issues, explain why you would or would not be willing to use a therapist who is open to helping you address your needs, but has little to no experience with transgender issues in relation to children and families?

. . . .

. . . .

. . . .

7. What, if any, support groups are there in your area that could recommend a therapist?

. . . .

. . . .

. . . .

8. Are you willing to call your insurance company, if you know they will keep this inquiry confidential, to find out what types of therapy your insurance pays for, if any, and what percentage or portion is your responsibility?

. . . .

. . . .

. . . .

9. If there is only one therapist in your area who is familiar with transgender issues, in relation to children, how will you and other family members decide whether this therapist will be for a family member's individual therapy or for family therapy?

. . . .

. . . .

. . . .

10. How will you elect to communicate with your or your child's individual therapist, if any of you are experiencing thoughts of wanting to change to a different individual therapist?

. . . .

. . . .

. . . .

11. How will you and other family members elect to communicate with your family therapist if you are experiencing thoughts of wanting to change to a different family therapist?

. . . .

. . . .

. . . .

12. What do you plan to do if you see your therapist at a conference, training, support group, or any social setting outside of therapy?

. . . .

. . . .

. . . .

13. How do you feel about possibly selecting a therapist, who identifies as trans, as your individual therapist?

. . . .

. . . .

. . . .

14. How do you feel about possibly selecting a therapist, who identifies as trans, as your family's therapist?

. . . .

. . . .

. . . .

15. How will you address the situation if your individual or family therapist is focusing more on your child's transition and not enough on your or your family's needs or issues, in respect to the possible transition?

. . . .

. . . .

. . . .

GRAPHICS GALORE

T-Chart

What are your thoughts about the therapist you interviewed?

What are their positive (+) aspects?	What are their negative (−) aspects?	Which aspects hold equal (=) weight?

GRAPHICS GALORE

Box

What issues or topics do you want to discuss in either individual or family therapy? Code with "I" for individual and "F" for family therapy. (You may or may not choose to ask your child and other family members what they want to discuss in family therapy.)

1. "I" or "F"	2. "I" or "F"	3. "I" or "F"	4. "I" or "F"	5. "I" or "F"
6. "I" or "F"	7. "I" or "F"	8. "I" or "F"	9. "I" or "F"	10. "I" or "F"
11. "I" or "F"	12. "I" or "F"	13. "I" or "F"	14. "I" or "F"	15. "I" or "F"
16. "I" or "F"	17. "I" or "F"	18. "I" or "F"	19. "I" or "F"	20. "I" or "F"
21. "I" or "F"	22. "I" or "F"	23. "I" or "F"	24. "I" or "F"	25. "I" or "F"
26. "I" or "F"	27. "I" or "F"	28. "I" or "F"	29. "I" or "F"	30. "I" or "F"

DESERVING DE-STRESSING DELIGHT

Clean and Organize

If life around you feels chaotic and out of your control during the transition or gender questioning, one of the things you can do to de-stress and give yourself a sense of order and structure is to organize something. The stability of arranging your environment may help you become grounded and peaceful.

Some people find that sorting out papers that have piled up or cleaning an overstuffed drawer or closet can give them a sense of calmness. Others have found that weeding through clothes may create a feeling of control by systemizing their belongings. The act of organizing can bring you comfort and is a mindless activity that can be useful. Some people have shared that they rearrange the furniture in a room, wash their car, or scrub their home from top to bottom. These simple acts help them be in control and do something that makes them feel better when it is over. Other parents who hate cleaning or physically organizing may decide to plan an event or schedule their weekly routine on paper. Completing or structuring a task can prove to be an extremely rewarding feat for numerous parents. By allowing themselves the time to organize something, parents can express the sense of achieving a tangible accomplishment and taking a visible action that feels as if they are contributing to the space around them. Many express that it gives them a greater sense of safety and familiarity that is obtainable and practical. So, go ahead and get organized!

Journal your reaction to this Deserving De-Stressing Delight.

. . . .

. . . .

. . . .

. . . .

. . . .

. . . .

GRAPHICS GALORE

Timeline

What did you discuss and discover about yourself or a situation in therapy today?

Date of service:	What did you discuss in therapy today?	As a result of the session today, what did you discover about yourself or the situation?
Date of service:	What did you discuss in therapy today?	As a result of the session today, what did you discover about yourself or the situation?
Date of service:	What did you discuss in therapy today?	As a result of the session today, what did you discover about yourself or the situation?
Date of service:	What did you discuss in therapy today?	As a result of the session today, what did you discover about yourself or the situation?
Date of service:	What did you discuss in therapy today?	As a result of the session today, what did you discover about yourself or the situation?
Date of service:	What did you discuss in therapy today?	As a result of the session today, what did you discover about yourself or the situation?
Date of service:	What did you discuss in therapy today?	As a result of the session today, what did you discover about yourself or the situation?

GRAPHICS GALORE

Venn Diagram

Deciding to begin family therapy is an important choice and could involve much negotiation and compromise between family members. It would be ideal if most, if not all, family members could find a therapist they could agree on as a team. It is critical to know and discuss your individual priorities when searching for a family therapist who could fulfill your needs as a family. What qualities matter to you in a family therapist?

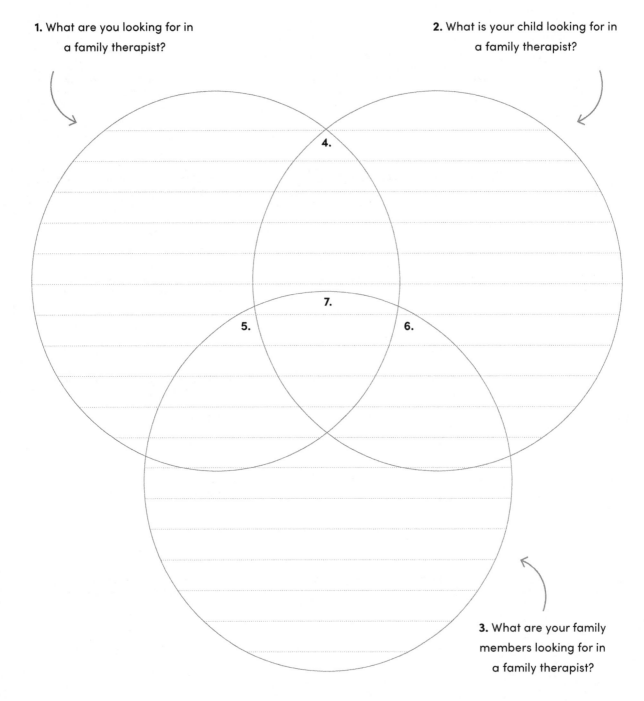

1. What are you looking for in a family therapist?

2. What is your child looking for in a family therapist?

4.

7.

5. 6.

3. What are your family members looking for in a family therapist?

EMPATHY-EMBRACING EXERCISE

Understanding the need your child has to transition is sometimes a challenge for parents and other family members. Trying to view the process through their lens may be an important step towards acceptance. Sometimes, the safest and most comfortable place to discuss and sort out all of these feelings is with a therapist, a support group, by attending a conference, or by searching the internet.

How do you think it would feel if you were asked to live your life not in your affirmed gender?

ANECDOTAL AFFIRMATION

A sea of people,
Which one is you?
I used to know,
I wish I still did!

GRAPHICS GALORE

Bar Graph

To what degree do these concerns and related topics matter to you? Based on a scale from 1 to 10, with 1 being the lowest and 10 being the highest, color or shade in your response. This visual will illustrate where your greatest concerns lie and can be used as a tool to help you communicate your thoughts with your child and/or other family members, therapist, spiritual mentor, or for your own personal understanding. The bar graph results can vary as your child's transition progresses and/or your thoughts may shift.

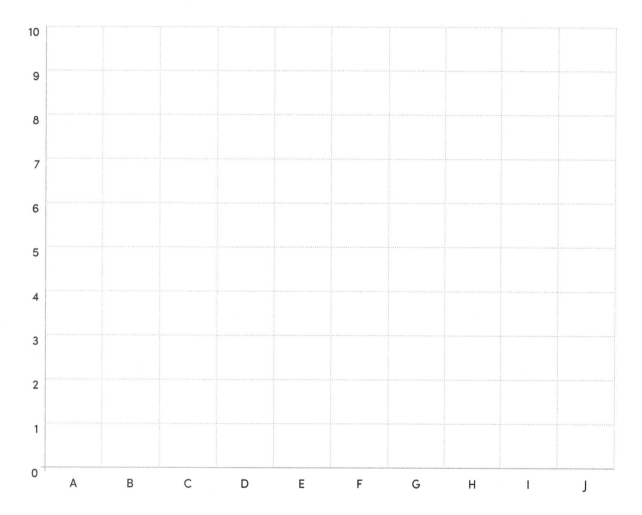

Use these ideas to fill in the bar graph or feel free to create your own!

A. The therapist identifies as part of the LGBTQ+ community.

B. Knowing the therapist is LGBTQ+ competent.

C. These aspects of the therapist's identity matter to you: age, race, religion, ethnicity, size, ability, aesthetics, or cultural background.

D. The therapist's gender matters to you.

E. The therapist takes your medical insurance.

F. The therapist's rate per session is affordable for you.

G. The location of the therapist's office is convenient in relation to your home/office.

H. The number of years the therapist has been in practice.

I. The areas of specialty the therapist has and any certification/s the therapist holds in relation to these areas.

J. The therapist is published on topics related to transgender issues for children.

GRAPHICS GALORE

Pie Graph

To what degree are these concerns and related topics important to you? Decide how significant these issues are to you in relation to each other. Place the number that corresponds with a suggested topic within as many slices of the pie that convey how each one matters to you. Only one number should be placed in each slice. You do not need to use all the issues, but do fill in all the slices. Feel free to create your own topics and assign them their own number.

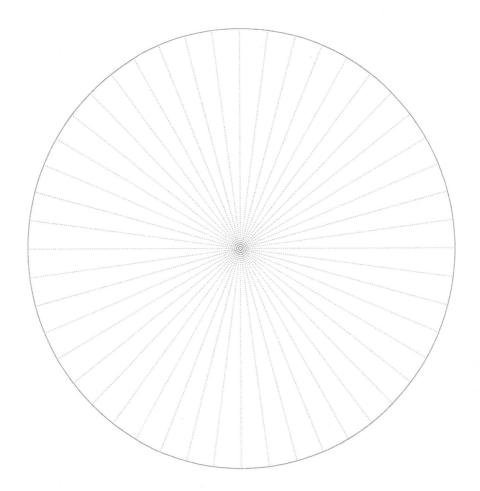

1. The therapist identifies as part of the LGBTQ+ community.
2. Knowing the therapist is LGBTQ+ competent.
3. These aspects of the therapist's identity matter to you: age, race, religion, ethnicity, size, ability, aesthetics, or cultural background.
4. The therapist's gender matters to you.
5. The therapist takes your medical insurance.
6. The therapist's rate per session is affordable for you.
7. The location of the therapist's office is convenient in relation to your home/office.
8. The number of years the therapist has been in practice.
9. The areas of specialty the therapist has and any certification/s the therapist holds in relation to these areas.
10. The therapist is published on topics related to transgender issues for children.

SAMPLER SHARES

All names have been changed to ensure anonymity in this section. The first initial designates an individual and the second initial identifies the relationship to the child, i.e. P = their parent, G = their grandparent, and S = their sibling.

Why do you feel that your child and/or any other family member should or should not be in individual therapy as your child begins their transition process?

GP: We started seeing a psychologist who would not allow me to go in for the session, so I was not aware of how the sessions were going. After a few months, I noticed how angry my child was getting. I decided to talk to the doctor alone. The doctor started telling me that my child was born a boy and I had to tell my child that they were a boy and that was it, period. That was completely against my beliefs and we never went back there. Later on, my daughter started sessions with a new, amazing therapist who understood what my child was going through. Since then, my daughter has grown stronger and stronger, becoming the person she really was meant to be! *PARENT/CHILD: AMAB (Uses she/her/hers pronouns)*

IS: Under no circumstances do I believe that therapy should suffice in this situation. I believe the best kind of therapy is full support from the family, since I feel only the family knows the full situation. *SIBLING/BROTHER: AFAB (Uses he/him/his pronouns)*

KP: I do feel therapy should be a part of the transition process. I think my child needs a qualified person they can talk to, who is not a family member or a friend. I found a therapist for my child by checking who takes our insurance. Many therapists do not take insurance, but will charge based on a sliding scale. My child started out in group therapy with other teens with similar issues, and they are currently in individual therapy, as well. Eventually, I will probably join them for family sessions. *PARENT/CHILD: AFAB (Uses they/them/their pronouns)*

HP: My son started to display great changes in his personality. He was always a very happy kid, who loved anything and everyone. Since birth, I called him "My Sunshine." I was paying close attention to him and all of my children, as a recently divorced parent. It was a phone call from his middle school counselor that made me realize something was wrong. She told me that another student/friend of my son had showed her pictures posted on social media of cutting marks. At this point, I still did not know that he was transgender, but it was the catalyst for him opening up to me. He told me that he had known he was transgender since the fifth grade and cutting was a way to deal with the pain and anxiety of feeling that he would be a disappointment to the people he loved—especially me, because he knew that I was so excited to have a girl. It was very clear to me that I needed to show him that I would love him as my child and not his assigned sex at birth. To this day, I am forever grateful that another student/friend had the courage and kindness in their heart to share their concern with a school faculty member. The feeling that my world was about to shatter ended up being a blessing in disguise. Finding a great therapist was the biggest gift to my son and our family. It allowed us to ask objective questions without making our son feel like we were singling him out. It also gave him the ability to feel that he could talk to someone in confidence. Initially, I felt awkward in using the wrong terms and was conscious about asking questions that could seem insensitive. For this reason alone, I felt that therapy sessions were of great need. I cannot imagine that therapy and group sessions would be considered anything but beneficial. *PARENT/CHILD: AFAB (Uses he/him/his pronouns)*

COMMUNICATION CORNER

When you speak spontaneously out of anger or fear about the unknown, without thinking it through, you can sometimes regret the way you phrased your words or the tone you used to express your feelings. Rehearsing what you want to ask or discuss with your child, and other family members, can help you before you actually communicate your thoughts. This gives you a moment to reflect and pause before you converse about emotional topics. You may choose to practice asking these questions with a trusted friend, family member, spiritual mentor, or therapist first. Explain your thoughts and feelings about these statements to one another verbally or in writing. It is important to note that some families elected to only address one question or two, while others preferred to answer them all. In order to recall the questions you answered, simply highlight and/or circle the ones you addressed as a family, yet acknowledging that you may return to discuss the others in the future. Decide what feels best for two or more family members and begin the conversation. Do you, your child, and other family members answer these questions in the same way or differently? Discuss your responses to understand how all of you view the answers to the questions and make time to celebrate all you learn from being willing to communicate with each other.

> ANECDOTAL AFFIRMATION
>
> *Find a quiet corner*
> *To reflect in silence.*
> *Listen to the message,*
> *There is space*
> *Enough for ME!*

1. Why or why not does it matter if the therapist identifies as part of the LGBTQ+ community?

. . . .

. . . .

2. Why or why not does it matter if the therapist is LGBTQ+ competent?

. . . .

. . . .

3. Why or why not do these aspects of the therapist's identity matter: age, race, religion, ethnicity, size, ability, aesthetics, or cultural background?

. . . .

. . . .

4.   Why or why not does the therapist's gender matter?

....

....

5.   Why or why not does it matter if the therapist takes your medical insurance?

....

....

6.   Why or why not does it matter if the therapist's rate per session is affordable for you?

....

....

7.   Why or why not does it matter if the location of the therapist's office is convenient in relation to your home/workplace?

....

....

8.   Why or why not does the number of years the therapist has been in practice matter?

....

....

9.   Why or why not do the areas of specialty the therapist has and any certification/s the therapist holds in relation to these areas matter?

....

....

10. Why or why not does it matter if the therapist is published on topics related to transgender issues for children?

....

....

Chapter 12

THE WORLD OF SCHOOLS

VITAL VIGNETTE

One overwhelming concern parents often have is not knowing if a school will address their child's needs. The issue of their child's safety is paramount, and the manner in which a school district approaches all that affects the student on a daily basis is based on policies and guidelines, which must be established in writing. The clarity and execution of these critical procedures will play a major role in the child's life throughout the years they attend school. It should come as no surprise that parents often lie awake at night, wondering if school will be a welcoming place for their child to enter, as they pursue the promise of an education.

> ANECDOTAL AFFIRMATION
>
> *School is a place to learn,*
> *Teach everyone to*
> *Embrace differences,*
> *Support and celebrate*
> *All gender identities.*

There is an abundance of issues that parents often inquire about connected to school district policies, some more essential than others. Navigating the topics of school safety, bathroom use, physical education classes, locker rooms, school records and documentation, peer bullying, training of all school personnel, after-school clubs, classroom policies and practices, socialization opportunities, and sibling pressures, plus much, much more, can become a full-time job for families. Every parent, and sometimes the child, may also need to consider these topics as they are grasping the pulse of the school's current climate and culture. All of these aspects must be addressed in order for a child to feel safe, comfortable, and heard during each school day.

Families are usually required to combat these obstacles and unknowns at the cost of relinquishing privacy, financial funds, job security, community support, daily safety, and loss of social circles, in addition to a myriad of other sacrifices. The awareness of all this is often draining, frustrating, and isolating. Furthermore, the strains and demands on the family dynamics and interactions may become insurmountable, especially when some parents are possibly being falsely accused and blamed for causing their child's gender-affirming needs, encouraging their child's wishes to transition, and not stopping their gender exploration.

When a child attends school, there is an inherent understanding that a school will provide an environment of safety to the best of their ability. This, too, must apply to students who identify on the transgender spectrum. Sometimes it is necessary for parents to approach most aspects of the transition from this perspective, knowing that this needs to be the platform from which all decisions and procedures are viewed. If the school district states policies that do not align with what you feel is best for your child, it is important for you to voice your objections.

It is imperative that all guidelines and school policies follow the most current laws. Though one would hope all those authoring these procedures would know the laws that will govern practices, this may not necessarily be the case. As a result, many parents have researched and learned the laws and rights that will affect the lives of their transgender children, in order to advocate for them in the best way possible. Some parents have hired experts in transgender rights and employed lawyers who are versed in the laws connected to transgender issues. Other parents have used free, available, knowledgeable advocates when attending school district meetings to ensure their child's needs are met. Still others have simply presented the legal facts they have acquired prior to such meetings and their singular voice has been enough to ensure that the school follows the law.

One main issue that often becomes very controversial is the use of bathrooms. Though the law takes precedent, some families find it acceptable to allow their child to use a separate designated bathroom. For other families, with the law on their side, this is completely unacceptable and insist that their child be allowed to use the bathroom which aligns with their affirmed gender. Even if this is not the law, many parents find this is the issue they will focus most of their energy on, until a satisfactory result is achieved. One question that must be addressed is that if your child is not legally permitted to use the bathroom that aligns with their affirmed gender, then how far is the distance of the bathroom they are assigned to use from where their schedule requires them to be most of the day? Some parents have shared that the bathroom was so far away their child soiled themselves as they rushed as quickly as they could to reach it. Others have told stories of their child being given a late warning to class, as a result of the fact that they had to race up and down stairs or travel half-way to the other side of the school to use the designated bathroom, leaving the child with very little time to arrive promptly in class. Whereas, some parents have stated that their child will avoid using the bathroom altogether, in order to not be late or endure the possible stigma of using a "separate but equal" bathroom. Not only can this cause medical challenges, such as urinary tract infections, but it may also prevent a child from being able to focus on their learning. Clearly, the use of a bathroom for a child is something that must be a priority and it is critical that the arrangements both follow the law and consider any problems that may arise from poor planning.

Each school district has its own policy in regard to changing school records and documents in reference to name changes, use of gender-affirming pronouns, and instituting the gender marker that aligns with a student's affirmed gender. Some will only recognize these changes if done legally, while others will respect the student's needs should their parents give permission to adjust them through written consent. There are schools that honor these changes, simply based on the student's request. Unfortunately, there are instances where schools have not respected any of these changes and parents and/or children have had to go to great lengths to have the child's school make these adjustments. It is critical that parents, children who can advocate for themselves, and schools know the laws and policies related to any changes in a child's name, pronouns, and gender marker.

Training for school personnel is a component that cannot be overlooked and it is most beneficial when the entire school is involved, not just for the sake of your child, that should be justification enough, but for the whole school population. Though your child's specific identity may be the catalyst for the training, you and your family should not be expected to either educate anyone associated with the school or find those who will be the trainers. Under most circumstances, these duties are the responsibility of the school or district. No child or family needs to "out" themselves or be required to do so. If your child and your family feel comfortable being part of the training or educating others, then it is important that you inform your child's school or district of this fact. However, your willingness to participate should not be in lieu of the school or district providing additional professional development for all those who interact with students throughout the school year. Furthermore, the law, school policies, and your wishes as a family must be the blueprint for what is required of the school or district to meet your child's needs.

GRAPHICS GALORE

Splash

Who are the people and categories of people who will interact with your child throughout the school year? By creatively splashing words and short phrases, quickly attempt to express your answers randomly with as many responses as possible scattered on the paper.

GRAPHICS GALORE

Web

Which school documents and records do you feel need to be changed? (It is advised that you consider consulting your child to decide which documentation they may elect to change. Perhaps, to ensure a collaborative effort, you may encourage your child to fill in this graphic alone, if age appropriate. Then, you can both share your thoughts with one another.)

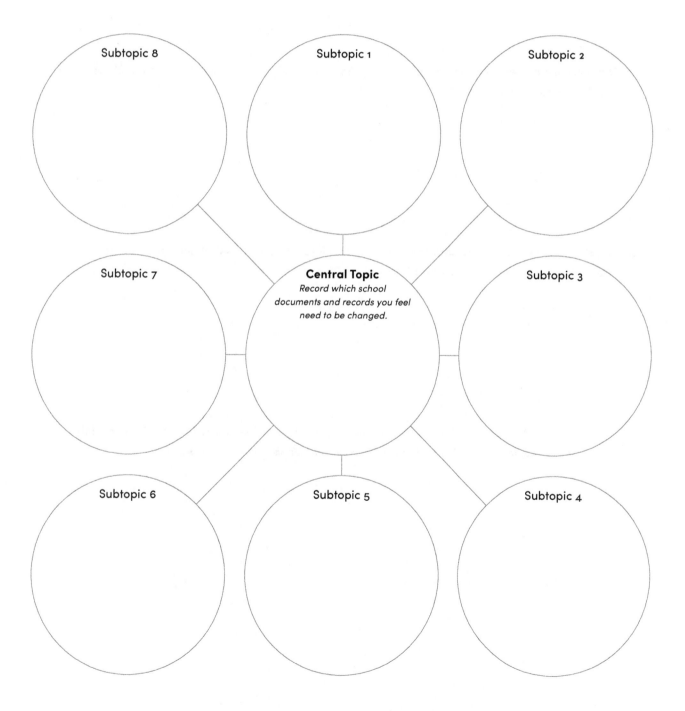

REFLECTIVE RESPONSES

1. Who is in charge of creating the school district policies that affect the protocol for trans children and what is the best way to correspond or meet with them directly?

....

....

....

2. What are the current laws that pertain to the gender needs of your child, while attending school, in relation to transgender issues?

....

....

....

3. What are the current policies implemented in your child's school district that pertain to children who identify on the transgender spectrum?

....

....

....

4. Who and/or what will determine which bathroom/s your child will be allowed to use? Explain if this outcome is acceptable to both you and your child in relation to your child's transition.

....

....

....

5. How will those directly responsible for your child's daily care, safety, and education at school be trained in relation to your child's transition?

. . . .

. . . .

. . . .

6. How will those directly responsible for your child's daily care, safety, and education at school communicate with you and you with them, should a concern, question, or relevant information need to be addressed in relation to your child's transition?

. . . .

. . . .

. . . .

7. What role are you comfortable playing, if at all, in training and answering the questions and/or concerns of others in relation to your child's transition?

. . . .

. . . .

. . . .

8. What role is your child comfortable playing, if at all, in training and answering the questions and concerns of others in relation to their transition?

. . . .

. . . .

. . . .

9. What role are other family members comfortable playing, if at all, in training and answering the questions and concerns of others in relation to your child's transition?

....

....

....

10. What is the current climate and culture of your child's school in relation to trans children?

....

....

....

11. What are your greatest wishes for your child during the time they are in the care of their school in relation to your child's transition?

....

....

....

12. What are your greatest fears or concerns for your child during the time they are in the care of their school in relation to your child's transition?

....

....

....

13. How can you find out if there are any peers or community members whose identity aligns similarly to your child and can serve as a mentor or advocate, or be a part of your support system, while your child is attending this particular school or another school within the school district's jurisdiction?

....

....

....

14. How will other students learn to understand your child's needs and who will discuss and teach them the appropriate ways to interact with, address, and treat your child in a manner that is acceptable to both you and your child in relation to your child's transition?

. . . .

. . . .

. . . .

15. How will your child's school deal with other parents, students, personnel, and additional community members if they do not align with and agree with the law, your child's needs, and school policies and procedures, especially when due to cultural and religious differences and/or beliefs in relation to your child's transition?

. . . .

. . . .

. . . .

16. Who will be the person or people available for your child, their siblings, and other students to reach out to for support during the day should an incident, concern, or question arise in reference to your child's transition, and how will the presence of these individual/s be communicated to both your child and others in relation to your child's transition?

. . . .

. . . .

. . . .

17. What has your child's teacher/s and other school personnel agreed to do to ensure your child's needs and safety issues are met on a daily basis in relation to your child's transition?

. . . .

. . . .

. . . .

18. How will documents, school records, and log-in procedures be implemented and changed to reflect your child's name, pronoun preference, and gender marker use in relation to your child's transition?

. . . .

. . . .

. . . .

19. What will be the school procedures and policies for communicating with after-school programs, visiting in-school programs, volunteers, and substitutes in relation to how to address the needs of trans children?

. . . .

. . . .

. . . .

20. How will you approach the need to ensure that the school curriculum be adjusted or strengthened to reflect the history, inclusiveness, experiences, and voices of transgender, gender questioning, and/or non-binary children?

. . . .

. . . .

. . . .

GRAPHICS GALORE

Venn Diagram

What school policies and guidelines are important to you, your child, and other family members?

1. What school policies are essential and ideal for you?

2. What school policies are essential and ideal for your child?

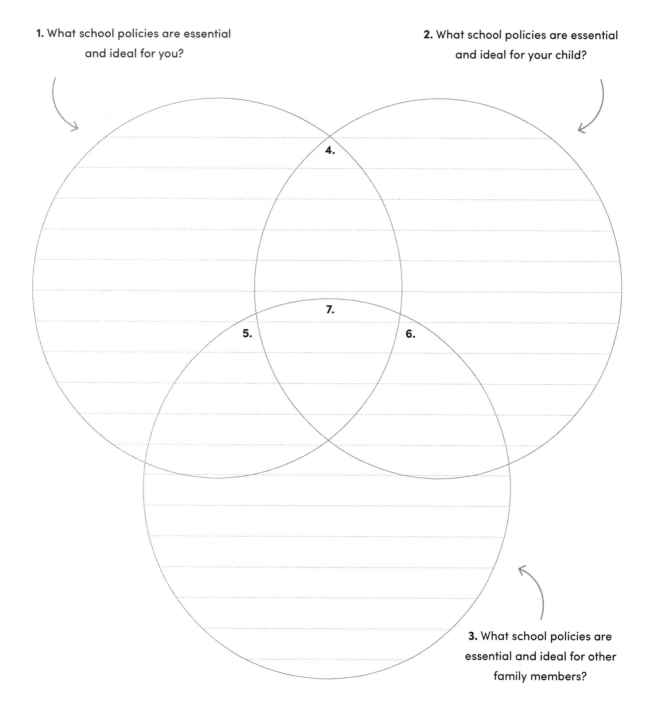

3. What school policies are essential and ideal for other family members?

GRAPHICS GALORE

Box

List any people who you would like to become part of your school district community support team for yourself, perhaps your child, and for other family members. You may elect to incorporate school personnel and community members, including students and their families, that you feel need to be aware of your child's transition. It is advised that you consider consulting your child before sharing any related information with any of the individuals or groups. Perhaps, to ensure a collaborative effort, you may encourage your child to fill in this graphic so that you can both share your thoughts with one another. Other family members can be welcomed by you and your child to do the same, when and if appropriate. Each square in the Box graphic organizer can be used for an individual contact and it is suggested you record their: name, title, agency and/or how you met them, address/location where they can be reached, email, and phone number with their extension. You can find an ally in teachers, other parents, a student's relative, siblings, an aide, school nurse, etc. Creating a support team within the school network will help you feel connected!

1.	2.	3.
4.	5.	6.
7.	8.	9.
10.	11.	12.

DESERVING DE-STRESSING DELIGHT

Pamper, Nurture, and Self-Care

What can be more loving than nurturing and pampering your body and soul? As a family member who supports a child's transition, you must embrace your own self-care because it is also critical for your personal health and emotional well-being. Pampering can be experienced in a multitude of ways and often finances may dictate the type of things you can afford. Regardless of your budget, pampering yourself during the transition is essential for coping and being present for yourself, your child, and other family members. For some, a massage can be the most calming and rejuvenating form of self-care. When low on funds, massage schools may offer services at a nominal fee or no cost when done by a trainee who needs to practice their skills. Another possibility is going to a nail salon and having an inexpensive ten-minute chair massage. Sometimes, requesting gift cards for holidays and special occasions, and then using those funds for a luxury massage can do the trick, too.

> ANECDOTAL AFFIRMATION
>
> *Ask not only*
> *What you*
> *Can do for*
> *Your child's school,*
> *But also ask*
> *What their school*
> *Can do*
> *For your child!*

Other ways people indulge in the nurturing of their body is having their hair cut and/or dyed, getting their nails done, or purchasing moisturizing creams and having someone you adore apply them on you. There are days that family members allow themselves to sleep longer or take a nap in the middle of the day. Some people find it liberating to dress up and go out to eat in a fancy restaurant with a family member, close friend, or simply by themselves. Included in self-care is giving yourself permission to shop, especially for clothing. Treating yourself with a special gift that is within your budget will remind you that you have value and worth.

One individual found being around dogs very comforting, but they did not own a dog, so they offered to dog-sit for friends free of charge. Taking care of your body by exercising can be extremely nurturing and a healthy expression of self-care. Another person enjoyed cooking. They would take the ingredients they had in their home and would challenge themselves to make a meal using only the components that were available. Many people have shared that they find free and thrifty ways to practice self-care by going for a meditative bicycle ride in their neighborhood, using a free-pass coupon to a gym, and taking a free open yoga class when special promotions are offered.

Caring for your own needs and focusing on your own body and soul are some of the kindest and most respectful ways a family member can honor themselves. As you journey through this process and learn how to satisfy your personal desires, lovingly pampering, nurturing, and caring for your own body must be at the top of the list!

Journal your reaction to this Deserving De-Stressing Delight.

....

....

....

....

....

....

....

....

....

....

....

....

....

....

....

....

....

....

GRAPHICS GALORE

T-Chart

What school policies are currently addressed in your child's school or district?

What do you KNOW are your child's school or district policies?	What do you WANT to change about your child's school or district policies?	What did you LEARN to assist in helping change your child's school or district policies?

GRAPHICS GALORE

Timeline

What steps can you take to change current school policies you, your child, and other family members feel need to be changed?

Policy:	Who did or do you need to talk to about changing this school policy?	What steps did or will you take?	What happened when you followed up on the last steps?
	Date:	Date:	Date:
Policy:	Who did or do you need to talk to about changing this school policy?	What steps did or will you take?	What happened when you followed up on the last steps?
	Date:	Date:	Date:
Policy:	Who did or do you need to talk to about changing this school policy?	What steps did or will you take?	What happened when you followed up on the last steps?
	Date:	Date:	Date:
Policy:	Who did or do you need to talk to about changing this school policy?	What steps did or will you take?	What happened when you followed up on the last steps?
	Date:	Date:	Date:
Policy:	Who did or do you need to talk to about changing this school policy?	What steps did or will you take?	What happened when you followed up on the last steps?
	Date:	Date:	Date:

EMPATHY-EMBRACING EXERCISE

ANECDOTAL AFFIRMATION

When I am not there,
Will you live in fear?
Please let those
At school care!

School can feel like a home away from home to some children, while it can be a place that is alienating and scary for others. Feeling accepted, respected, and included for being exactly who you are as a person is often the factor that determines which reality becomes a child's experience. Most family members can relate to one of these feelings, and it may even trigger memories from their past. Succeeding both academically and emotionally throughout school life is the desired outcome for all children who attend school. Unfortunately for many children who identify on the transgender spectrum, being asked to compromise who they are can become a daily struggle. However, sometimes learning to function and rise above such adversity has motivated people to overcome and thrive. Knowing that there is a support team that can provide a sense of community for trans children can make all the difference and it can save a life!

Can you remember a time when you were not accepted, respected, or included in school for any reason beyond your control? How did this make you feel? Were you able to overcome these feelings of rejection? If so, how did you do so, and did the support of others play any role in helping you be the person you are today?

....

....

....

....

....

....

....

....

....

GRAPHICS GALORE

Bar Graph

To what degree do these concerns and related topics matter to you? Based on a scale from 1 to 10, with 1 being the lowest and 10 being the highest, color or shade in your response. This visual will illustrate where your greatest concerns lie and can be used as a tool to help you communicate your thoughts with your child and/or other family members, therapist, spiritual mentor, or for your own personal understanding. The bar graph results can vary as your child's transition progresses and/or your thoughts may shift.

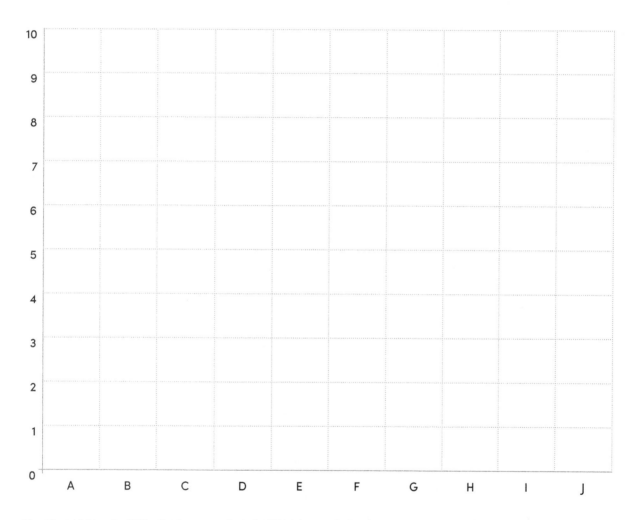

Use these ideas to fill in the bar graph or feel free to create your own!

A. Your child's safety as they use the bathroom and locker rooms at school based on their affirmed gender.

B. Your child's physical safety while at school other than in the bathroom and locker rooms.

C. The training of all school personnel in relation to your child's needs based on their affirmed gender.

D. Guarantee that all laws and school policies in relation to your child's gender identity will be honored at school.

E. Guarantee that the verbal use of your child's preferred name, pronoun/s, and gender marker by all those who have contact with your child at school will be honored.

F. Guarantee that the changing of your child's gender-affirming name, pronoun/s, and gender marker on all school documents and records will be honored.

G. Educating after-school programs and sports teams to both welcome your child and embrace their affirmed gender.

H. Educating the peers and their parents about acceptance of those who identify as transgender/non-binary/gender questioning.

I. Concerns of your child's siblings while attending school.

J. Fear that the school community and personnel will accuse you of harming your child by supporting their affirmed gender or causing their transgender identity, and blame you for not stopping the process.

GRAPHICS GALORE

Pie Graph

To what degree are these concerns and related topics important to you? Decide how significant these issues are to you in relation to each other. Place the number that corresponds with a suggested topic within as many slices of the pie that convey how each one matters to you. Only one number should be placed in each slice. You do not need to use all the issues, but do fill in all the slices. Feel free to create your own topics and assign them their own number.

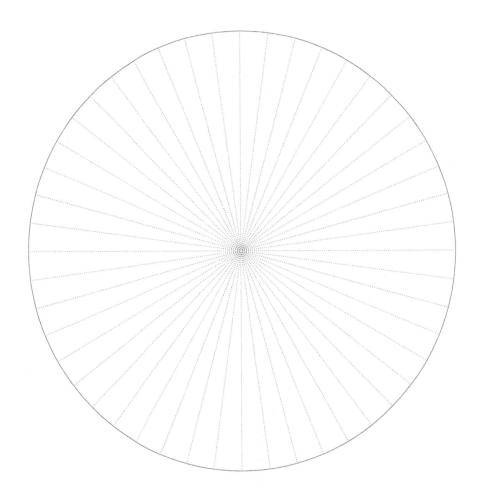

1. Your child's safety as they use the bathroom and locker rooms at school based on their affirmed gender.

2. Your child's physical safety while at school other than in the bathroom and locker rooms.

3. The training of all school personnel in relation to your child's needs based on their affirmed gender.

4. Guarantee that all laws and school policies in relation to your child's gender identity will be honored at school.

5. Guarantee that the verbal use of your child's preferred name, pronoun/s, and gender marker by all those who have contact with your child at school will be honored.

6. Guarantee that the changing of your child's gender-affirming name, pronoun/s, and gender marker on all school documents and records will be honored.

7. Educating after-school programs and sports teams to both welcome your child and embrace their affirmed gender.

8. Educating the peers and their parents about acceptance of those who identify as transgender/non-binary/gender questioning.

9. Concerns of your child's siblings while attending school.

10. Fear that the school community and personnel will accuse you of harming your child by supporting their affirmed gender or causing their transgender identity, and blame you for not stopping the process.

SAMPLER SHARES

All names have been changed to ensure anonymity in this section. The first initial designates an individual and the second initial identifies the relationship to the child, i.e. P = their parent, G = their grandparent, and S = their sibling.

Who and/or what will determine which bathroom/s your child will be allowed to use? Explain if this outcome is acceptable to both you and your child in relation to your child's transition?

GP: In the beginning my child was using the nurse's bathroom. Since the school had been so supportive and trying to accommodate my child the best way possible, I always felt that I didn't want to be too pushy about the bathroom issue. When my daughter began third grade, which was held in a different building within the school district, she decided that she wanted to use the girls' bathroom. She felt she belonged there. I remember that as she described the girls' bathroom her eyes lit up and she told me it was all pink and beautiful. The principal at the new building caught her using the girls' bathroom and told her that she couldn't use it anymore. After that, she refused to use the nurse's bathroom and was not going to the bathroom all day long until she got home. That's when I asked for a legal representative to come with me to the school and help me with this issue. After a few meetings, my daughter was finally allowed to use the girls' bathroom. *PARENT/CHILD: AMAB (Uses she/her/hers pronouns)*

HP: I allowed my son to guide me in the process and let him choose whichever he felt most comfortable with. It was a bigger concern that he was using the bathroom and not holding it all day. Therefore, by me not making a big deal about it, he worked it out. Luckily, his school has gender neutral bathrooms, and when we were in public, during his initial stages of transition, I would stay close by the restroom of his choice. *PARENT/CHILD: AFAB (Uses he/him/his pronouns)*

What role are you comfortable playing, if at all, in training and answering the questions and/or concerns of others in relation to your child's transition?

AP: I can first remember fear of how to navigate the clothing department. I didn't want her to wear something she didn't like but I also didn't want her clothing to create too much controversy in her classroom. I didn't pay attention too much to the transgender identity and how society would accept her at that point, but how the world was going to accept her eventually became my focus. All the fears any parent has for their children became compounded by the notion that she was transgender and would experience discrimination. Pushing the schools to be inclusive, and extending that knowledge further to the world at large would drive me for the next ten years. *PARENT/CHILD: AMAB (Uses she/her/hers pronouns)*

HP: It has been my goal to make sure that, besides family, his school and other outside environments are as secure and supportive as possible. It has been my experience that his artistic talents, LGBTQ support group, like-minded friends, and supportive teachers at school have held great weight in his happiness. *PARENT/CHILD: AFAB (Uses he/him/his pronouns)*

KP: My child began by working with the school social worker. My child expressed the desire to be called by their preferred name. I was instructed to write a letter requesting that the school use my child's preferred name on all school documents. Since we have not legally changed their name, they have to use their legal name on state tests and college entrance exams. The school has also allowed them to choose room assignments that make them comfortable on overnight trips. My child's school does not have gender neutral bathrooms. When necessary, they use the bathroom for the gender assigned at birth, but they generally try to avoid using the school bathrooms. *PARENT/CHILD: AFAB (Uses they/them/their pronouns)*

COMMUNICATION CORNER

ANECDOTAL AFFIRMATION

My child's safety
In school
Needs to be
The golden rule!

When you speak spontaneously out of anger or fear about the unknown, without thinking it through, you can sometimes regret the way you phrased your words or the tone you used to express your feelings. Rehearsing what you want to ask or discuss with your child, and other family members, can help you before you actually communicate your thoughts. This gives you a moment to reflect and pause before you converse about emotional topics. You may choose to practice asking these questions with a trusted friend, family member, spiritual mentor, or therapist first. Explain your thoughts and feelings about these statements to one another verbally or in writing. It is important to note that some families elected to only address one question or two, while others preferred to answer them all. In order to recall the questions you answered, simply highlight and/or circle the ones you addressed as a family, yet acknowledging that you may return to discuss the others in the future. Decide what feels best for two or more family members and begin the conversation. Do you, your child, and other family members answer these questions in the same way or differently? Discuss your responses to understand how all of you view the answers to the questions and make time to celebrate all you learn from being willing to communicate with each other.

1. What concerns, if any, do you have in relation to your child's safety as they use the bathroom and locker rooms at school based on their affirmed gender?

    . . . .

    . . . .

2. What concerns, if any, do you have in relation to your child's physical safety while at school, other than in the bathroom and locker rooms?

    . . . .

    . . . .

3. What concerns, if any, do you have in relation to the training of all school personnel in relation to your child's needs based on their affirmed gender?

    . . . .

    . . . .

4. What concerns, if any, do you have in relation to guaranteeing that all laws and school policies in relation to your child's gender identity will be honored at school?

. . . .

. . . .

5. What concerns, if any, do you have in relation to guaranteeing that the verbal use of your child's gender-affirming name, pronoun/s, and gender marker by all those who have contact with your child at school will be honored?

. . . .

. . . .

6. What concerns, if any, do you have in relation to guaranteeing that the changing of your child's gender-affirming name, pronoun/s, and gender marker on all school documents and records will be honored?

. . . .

. . . .

7. What concerns, if any, do you have in relation to educating after-school programs and sports teams to both welcome your child and embrace their affirmed gender?

. . . .

. . . .

8. What concerns, if any, do you have in relation to educating the peers and their parents in relation to acceptance of those who identify as transgender, non-binary and/or gender questioning?

. . . .

. . . .

9. What concerns, if any, do you have in relation to your child's siblings while they are attending school?

. . . .

. . . .

10. What concerns, if any, do you have in relation to the fear of the school community and personnel accusing you of harming your child by supporting their affirmed gender, causing their transgender identity, and blaming you for not stopping the process?

. . . .

. . . .

Chapter 13

CELEBRATIONS COME IN DIFFERENT SIZES

VITAL VIGNETTE

ANECDOTAL AFFIRMATION

We must
Teach others
So one day
Everyone
Will have
Learned!

There are dozens of ways to honor the milestones of the transition. For some families, the transition will be a time of celebration that will begin on day one without any hesitation, confusion, or feelings of grief. For others, the celebrating will evolve over time, little by little, and step by step. For a number of families, accepting or acknowledging the reality of the transition may be enough for your child at the time. For some parents, deep down, the possibility or reality of their child transitioning is such a loss for them that they are genuinely not able to celebrate. Furthermore, some will never celebrate and may remove themselves from the process. Knowing they will be absent from their child's transition process, they may elect to ask another family member or close friend to be the supportive adult assisting their child in this process. As has been stated many times, each parent's path is personal, based on their own needs and what feels comfortable for them.

For those parents who are able to celebrate, this can occur in an assortment of ways. A simple yet meaningful way could be hosting a party-like event to commemorate the transition. Another supportive act could be joining your child when they are shopping for new clothes or helping them learn how to apply makeup, after which they present themselves to the world as they deserve to be seen. One more unexpected but powerful act of care can be that you verbally correct a person who is inaccurately gendering your child if your child cannot find the words to do so for themselves. This may seem like a simplistic act of heroism, but it can mean a lot to your child. Some family members may offer to attend doctor appointments, be there when the child needs support at school, or to embrace the peace your child feels. These are all validating ways of celebrating your child's transition.

Financially contributing to a fund for future surgery and hormones, assisting in planning your child's purchasing of a binder, or being present when your child feels nervous about sharing their transition with a family member who may not receive the information well—these are all other ways some have shown love and support of the transition.

In addition to celebrating your child's transition, it is important that parents are celebrated as well. This celebration can be your child expressing appreciation by creating a special card acknowledging the many ways you were there for them, by cooking your favorite meal for you, or doing a task for you so you can have extra time for yourself to relax. They can also express their appreciation to you for being in their corner by encouraging you to pursue your own dreams, recognizing that your desires may have been placed on hold throughout the time that the transition needed to be the priority.

It may seem ironic that this next section appears in the celebrations chapter. However, learning and understanding how to use your experiences and voice, in solidarity with your child, is one of the greatest ways you can celebrate your own pride and courage. This chapter will discuss challenges some family members experience when dealing with inappropriate questions. Many family members are not sure if the inappropriate questions they receive are due to ignorance, curiosity, or insensitivity. Most do not believe intentional harm is meant, but the frequency of these inquiries may leave them feeling isolated, alone, and confused.

Something that has shocked family members is the abundance of these unanticipated questions and statements made on a regular basis. A common but pathetically baffling theme that repeatedly occurs is that others feel it is acceptable to ask the most intimate and insulting questions. The number of inquiries or statements that family members have to endure from pure ignorance and the inconsideration of others can feel insurmountable. Frequently, questions are often fixated on how the child's genitals will look, or people offer suggestions as to what they would do if their child was in transition or questioning their gender. Others feel it is their duty and right, to blame, shame, or judge a parent for supporting their child's transition. Some offer families their views without anyone even asking for their opinion. Many people have no ability to filter their thoughts and express their curiosities openly. Boldly, and with some misconstrued sense of entitlement, these people comment about the child's physical appearance and perceived levels or status of passing. These crude statements or intrusive questions can be asked by close and not-so-close friends, family members, co-workers, lawyers, medical professionals, and spiritual mentors—the list goes on and on.

Here are some practical suggestions offered to assist family members when these unforeseen situations occur. It is absolutely acceptable to state that a posed question is something that you are not comfortable answering. Some parents may choose to use a stronger stance and respond by saying the inquiry is inappropriate or none of the person's business, or let the person know that they are being offensive. Others refer people with questions to the internet, so that they can get the information from specific credible sites, articles, books, or organizations. It must be acknowledged that there are family members who are completely comfortable answering highly personal questions and are not insulted by insensitive statements or curious probes.

One strategy that has worked well when a child is gendered incorrectly is to restate your child's pronoun in the response: "Actually, he would prefer the vegetarian choice!" By stating it this way, there is no need to be confrontational, yet you can make your point without embarrassing anyone. Other times you could ask if the person inquiring would want you to ask the same question or make the same statement about them or their child. When posed like that, most people apologize and explain they hadn't realized the implications of what they said or asked—that is often the end of these queries!

In response to your child's transition, family members have been educated about the experience, learning ways to incorporate the new vocabulary, use of pronouns, and being appropriately respectful. You may need to recognize that you needed allowances to be made for you when you were learning, and so you can appreciate that other people will also need those same allowances for errors. Most people have to be taught how to use the proper language in relation to the transition, and gain an understanding of which inquiries and comments are appropriate. You will have to decide when, why, and for whom enough will be enough. This may take a while to figure out, be quite obvious to you immediately, or shift over time. The ideas discussed earlier can serve as a model of how to respond to challenging moments or unexpected social situations. How you react to what people may say or ask, and still retain your own dignity, needs to be addressed and understood by you. It is strongly suggested that you keep a record of what is stated by others and decide, in consultation with your child and other family members, some responses and rebuttals that feel comfortable to use in the future.

Celebrating all you have encountered since your child began to transition may be different for every parent. For some, the idea of celebrating is more aligned with acknowledging their own growth and knowing their child is at peace with living in their affirmed gender. Realizing that your voice matters, that there is support for you, and recognizing all you have learned from each experience in relation to the transition, are reasons enough to celebrate you!

GRAPHICS GALORE

Splash

What words would you use to describe how it feels to observe your child as they are living in their affirmed gender? By creatively splashing words and short phrases, quickly attempt to express your answers randomly with as many responses as possible scattered on the paper.

GRAPHICS GALORE

Web

Has anyone asked you, your child, or other family members any inappropriate questions or stated any inappropriate remarks? If so, record these questions and statements with the aim to help you review how you responded. Then reflect on your reply, in order to decide if there may be a better way to approach these inappropriate questions or remarks should they ever happen again in the future.

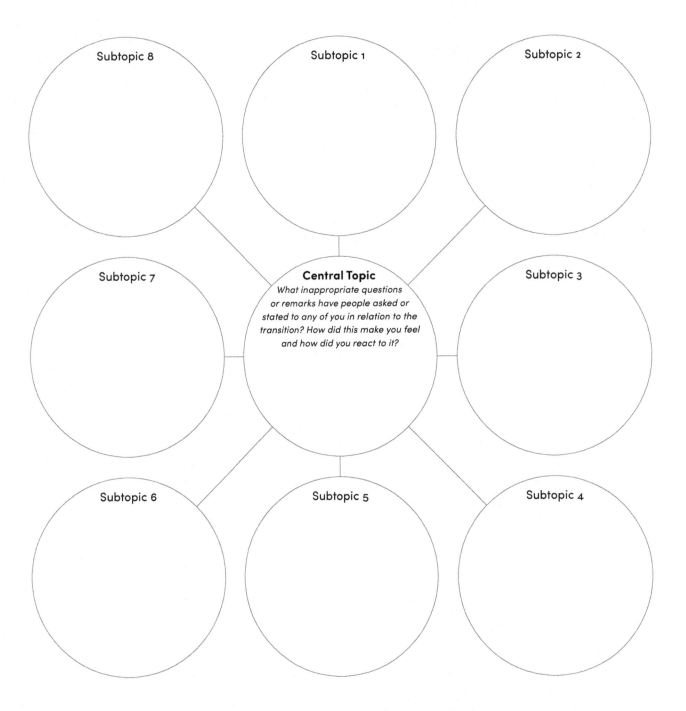

REFLECTIVE RESPONSES

1. In what ways have you demonstrated celebrating and/or supporting your child throughout their transition?

....

....

....

2. How, if at all, did your child's transition affect the parental or familial relationship with your child?

....

....

....

3. How, if at all, did your child's transition affect your friendships?

....

....

....

4. How, if at all, did your child's transition affect their self-confidence?

....

....

....

5. How, if at all, did your child's transition affect the communication between you and your child?

....

....

....

6. How, if at all, did your child's transition affect your relationships with other family members?

. . . .

. . . .

. . . .

7. How, if at all, did your child's transition affect your employment or career?

. . . .

. . . .

. . . .

8. How, if at all, did your child's transition affect your relationship with your spouse or significant other?

. . . .

. . . .

. . . .

9. What important changes, if any, have you noticed in your relationship with your child?

. . . .

. . . .

. . . .

10. What celebrations have not occurred yet, but need to be acknowledged privately?

. . . .

. . . .

. . . .

11. What celebrations have not occurred yet, but need to be acknowledged publicly?

....

....

....

12. How does it feel to see your child living in their affirmed gender?

....

....

....

13. How does it feel when you view others seeing your child living in their affirmed gender?

....

....

....

14. How do you think you will handle it when, or if, people ask you about or pose inappropriate questions in relation to your child's transition?

....

....

....

15. How is your contribution to your child's transition being celebrated by you and others?

....

....

....

GRAPHICS GALORE

Venn Diagram

What are some ways your child's transition can be celebrated? Consider answering this by keeping in mind that you, your child, and other family members deserve to be celebrated!

1. What are some ways you are comfortable celebrating your child's transition?

2. What are some ways your child is comfortable celebrating their transition?

4.

7.

5.   6.

3. What are some ways other family members are comfortable celebrating the transition?

GRAPHICS GALORE

T-Chart

How are the ways people reacted to your child's transition worth celebrating or not, in order to have these experiences documented and perhaps shared with others?

What were any of the positive (+) reactions people had in relation to your child's transition?	What were any of the negative (−) reactions people had in relation to your child's transition?	What were any of the neutral (=) reactions people had in relation to your child's transition?

DESERVING DE-STRESSING DELIGHT

Reading and Writing

There can be a stillness that takes over a person's entire body when they pick up a warm cup of tea or coffee and snuggle up with a good book. Reading allows some people to block out their worries by venturing into a land of make-believe. Some days, there is no better remedy than reading a book or writing your thoughts in a journal. Reading or writing can bring a person to a place of imagination and reflection that they find comforting. It is like being in the presence of a trusted friend who is simply there to listen and comfort you without any demands. When the transition begins for your child, reading and writing may be your first course of action and, even after a bit of time, it can still do the trick and help you de-stress. If reading or writing is comforting for you, it is suggested that you cuddle up with a book based on the genre of your liking, with a beverage or snack of choice, in a location that feels lovely to you. Should writing be more relaxing for you, feel free to use pages in this workbook or purchase a special journal with your favorite writing utensil and begin the soothing process of writing for yourself, just for fun and without any judgment. If both reading and writing appeal to you, then indulge in both and enjoy!

Journal your reaction to this Deserving De-Stressing Delight.

. . . .

. . . .

. . . .

. . . .

. . . .

. . . .

. . . .

. . . .

GRAPHICS GALORE

Box

Who would you want to celebrate for all the support that they have given you throughout your child's transition? (This could be done by a simple sincere thank you in person, by letter, online, or by phone.)

Friends	Family	Workplace associates
Medical people	Agencies	Others

GRAPHICS GALORE

Timeline

Record the ways you have celebrated your child's transition as they navigated their affirmed gender to feel whole. This will help you keep an in-depth track of each celebration once it has occurred.

Date:	State who, what, and how you celebrated:

Date:	State who, what, and how you celebrated:

Date:	State who, what, and how you celebrated:

Date:	State who, what, and how you celebrated:

Date:	State who, what, and how you celebrated:

Date:	State who, what, and how you celebrated:

Date:	State who, what, and how you celebrated:

EMPATHY-EMBRACING EXERCISE

ANECDOTAL AFFIRMATION

Inappropriate questions,
Let me introduce you
To...the internet!

Whether all family members support the process or not, there will most likely be at least one aspect worth celebrating. For those family members who are supportive, the celebrations will probably be abundant during the transition, even once it is no longer the focus of the family's interactions with the child.

It is important to recognize and document these necessary changes. For those who are not supportive, it may take much inner strength to find the bright side of the transition, but if you take the time to reflect, most likely there will be something that you learned about yourself, your child, and/or other family members during your child's transition. This question asks you to ponder and celebrate the positive.

Has there been a time in your life when you did something you dreamed of or needed to do for yourself which felt worthy of celebrating but may have had a major impact on another person's life? If so, what was it? How did it affect their life?

GRAPHICS GALORE

Bar Graph

To what degree do these concerns and related topics matter to you? Based on a scale from 1 to 10, with 1 being the lowest and 10 being the highest, color or shade in your response. This visual will illustrate where your greatest concerns lie and can be used as a tool to help you communicate your thoughts with your child and/or other family members, therapist, spiritual mentor, or for your own personal understanding. The bar graph results can vary as your child's transition progresses and/or your thoughts may shift.

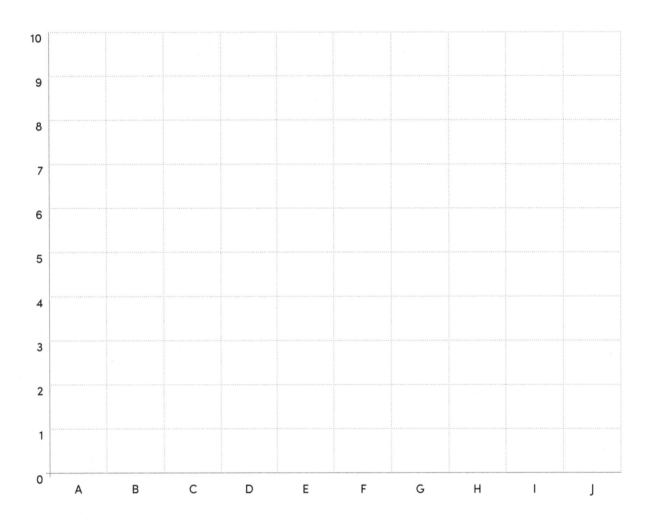

Use these ideas to fill in the bar graph or feel free to create your own!

A. Celebrating the role you have played throughout your child's transition.

B. Celebrating the role your child has played throughout their transition.

C. Celebrating the role your friends have played throughout your child's transition.

D. Celebrating the role your child's friends have played throughout your child's transition.

E. Celebrating the role your child's school has played throughout your child's transition.

F. Celebrating the role your other family members have played throughout your child's transition.

G. Celebrating the role your other family members' friends have played throughout your child's transition.

H. Celebrating the role your workplace associates have played throughout your child's transition.

I. Celebrating the role any support groups have played throughout your child's transition.

J. Celebrating the role any medical professional has played throughout your child's transition.

GRAPHICS GALORE

Pie Graph

To what degree are these concerns and related topics important to you? Decide how significant these issues are to you in relation to each other. Place the number that corresponds with a suggested topic within as many slices of the pie that convey how each one matters to you. Only one number should be placed in each slice. You do not need to use all the issues, but do fill in all the slices. Feel free to create your own topics and assign them their own number.

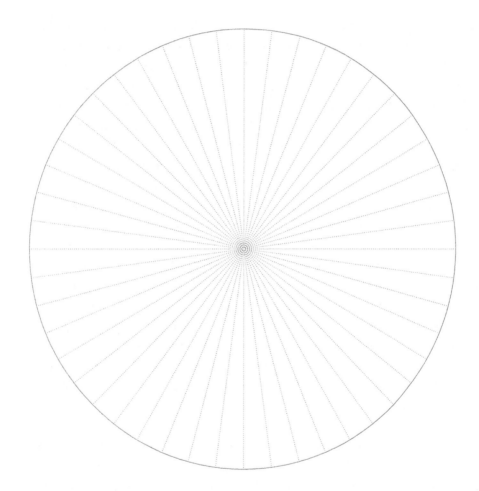

1. Celebrating the role you have played throughout your child's transition.

2. Celebrating the role your child has played throughout their transition.

3. Celebrating the role your friends have played throughout your child's transition.

4. Celebrating the role your child's friends have played throughout your child's transition.

5. Celebrating the role your child's school has played throughout your child's transition.

6. Celebrating the role your other family members have played throughout your child's transition.

7. Celebrating the role your other family members' friends have played throughout your child's transition.

8. Celebrating the role your workplace associates have played throughout your child's transition.

9. Celebrating the role any support groups have played throughout your child's transition.

10. Celebrating the role any medical professional has played throughout your child's transition.

SAMPLER SHARES

All names have been changed to ensure anonymity in this section. The first initial designates an individual and the second initial identifies the relationship to the child, i.e. P = their parent, G = their grandparent, and S = their sibling.

In what ways have you demonstrated celebrating and/or supporting your child throughout their transition?

CP: If you were to ask him, my son would say that the biggest form of support we gave him was just being there with him at all of his doctor appointments, all the legal documents needing to be changed, and just being 100 percent behind him. There were, and still are, lots of little ways that we celebrate and support him. For his first Christmas after coming out we bought him a new "birth" ornament. It says, "It's a Boy," with his name and the year he began his transition on it. When his legal name change came in the mail we went out and celebrated his "Name Day." We have attended and spoken at rallies. When a group had a public referendum on our state ballot looking to rescind rights for trans people by using fear, I placed lawn signs outside my house urging people to vote yes to keeping those rights. I hung both a rainbow and trans pride flag outside my house. I spoke to people about why their vote was so important. I tried to educate people online about the dangers of rolling back those protections and about how this group only had fear on their side, but not actual evidence. I've gone to conferences, one in New York that ended on the first day of June, the first day of Pride Month. That evening we went to Washington Square Park and from there we walked over to Christopher Park and stood outside The Stonewall Inn. He was able to visit the place where Pride began. We've walked together in a Pride Parade, and have attended others near our home. We celebrate who our son is, not who we think he should be. We were not "given" him to create a smaller version of ourselves, but to guide him to become his most authentic self. *PARENT/CHILD: AFAB (Uses he/him/his pronouns)*

HP: On my son's initial starting of testosterone, I videoed, documented how he felt, and took a picture with his medical doctor. Along the way, I have bought him things to put in his room that represent the LGBTQ community. Also, his monthly group meetings have given us another way to share our progress. *PARENT/CHILD: AFAB (Uses he/him/his pronouns)*

JS: I want to give my sibling support through the exploration of "their" gender identity but it is a hard balance since teenagers overall often have strong opinions without much life experience. I try to discuss "their" views and feelings on any topic with open-ended questions and without judgment, while pointing out inconsistencies I see and other viewpoints to make "them" think outside "their" own worldview. "They" have never brought up the topic of "their" gender identity with me and I have not pushed "them" to discuss it with me. I try to remember to use "their" chosen name since hearing it from other family members, even though my sibling has never said anything to me about "their" chosen name or gender. When we are together, I refrain from introducing "them" and try to allow "them" to introduce "themselves." While I want to be supportive of "their" exploration process, I don't want to speak for "them." I try to be supportive by being respectful and loving "them" no matter what without demanding answers from "them" because I don't know that "they" have the answers figured out and I don't want to push for answers "they" aren't ready to give. I will always be here to listen when "they" need me. *SIBLING/GENDER QUESTIONING SIBLING: AFAB (Uses they/them/their pronouns)*

How do you think you will handle it when, or if, people ask you about or pose inappropriate questions in relation to your child's transition?

CP: A family member would always refer back to when our children were young with statements like "when the girls were little," or "when it was her graduation," or "when 'deadname' was a baby." We would always correct her and move on, but she didn't respond to it, or correct herself. One evening after correcting her for what felt like the hundredth time, she responded with "whatever." My husband in that moment lost all the cool he had and told her, "You will not 'whatever' my son, his name is **** and he is a boy and he has always been a boy, and if you can't accept that then you don't need to call me anymore." That is one extreme example of family members; others are much more subtle and easier to deal with. I've had people who have known my son since childhood ask questions about his use of testosterone and if that will cause him problems "sexually." I respond to that by telling them that if I'm not privy to my son's sex life (other than the obvious safe sex and sexuality discussions), why should they be? I've had other "friends" tell me that we shouldn't be allowing him to transition and should be teaching him to love his body as it is. We are not friends anymore. They couldn't understand that that's not how dysphoria works. I've had other people make statements like "I wouldn't let my kid mutilate themselves." I would quickly respond, "Well, it's a good thing that's not what I'm doing!" Then there are also statements and questions that don't even deserve a response. I try to determine if a question or statement is coming from a place of genuinely wanting to learn, but the asker is ignorant to the fact that what they have said is hurtful or inappropriate; in that situation, I'll try to educate the person on why it is, and if I can answer it, I will. *PARENT/ CHILD: AFAB (Uses he/him/his pronouns)*

HP: My responses are based on the feeling that I am getting from the person who has approached me. If I feel that answering their question will help to educate them and keep them from doing the same to another person, I will answer. Otherwise, my normal response is vague or non-responsive. It has been very apparent in certain situations that nothing could be said to change a person's mind. *PARENT/CHILD: AFAB (Uses he/him/his pronouns)*

COMMUNICATION CORNER

When you speak spontaneously out of anger or fear about the unknown, without thinking it through, you can sometimes regret the way you phrased your words or the tone you used to express your feelings. Rehearsing what you want to ask or discuss with your child, and other family members, can help you before you actually communicate your thoughts. This gives you a moment to reflect and pause before you converse about emotional topics. You may choose to practice asking these questions with a trusted friend, family member, spiritual mentor, or therapist first. Explain your thoughts and feelings about these statements to one another verbally or in writing. It is important to note that some families elected to only address one question or two, while others preferred to answer them all. In order to recall the questions you answered, simply highlight and/or circle the ones you addressed as a family, yet acknowledging that you may return to discuss the others in the future. Decide what feels best for two or more family members and begin the conversation. Do you, your child, and other family members answer these questions in the same way or differently? Discuss your responses to understand how all of you view the answers to the questions and make time to celebrate all you learn from being willing to communicate with each other.

> ANECDOTAL AFFIRMATION
> *Live, confusion, live,*
> *Cry, laugh, cry,*
> *Love, celebrate, love!*

1. How, if at all, do you think your child's transition has affected your relationship with your child?

   . . . .

   . . . .

2. How, if at all, do you think your child's transition has affected your relationships with other family members?

   . . . .

   . . . .

3. How, if at all, do you think your child's transition has affected your friendships?

   . . . .

   . . . .

4. How, if at all, do you think your child's transition has affected your own self-confidence and in turn had an effect on your relationship with your child?

. . . .

. . . .

5. How, if at all, do you think your child's transition has affected your communication with your child and/or other family members?

. . . .

. . . .

6. How, if at all, do you think your child's transition has affected your employment/career?

. . . .

. . . .

7. What is the hardest change, if any, that you have noticed in your relationship with your child and/or other family members?

. . . .

. . . .

8. What is the most important change, if any, that you have noticed in your relationship with your child and/or other family members?

. . . .

. . . .

9. What celebrations have not occurred yet, but need to be acknowledged privately?

. . . .

. . . .

10. What celebrations have not occurred yet, but need to be acknowledged publicly?

. . . .

. . . .

Chapter 14

WHERE ARE YOU NOW?

VITAL VIGNETTE

> ANECDOTAL AFFIRMATION
>
> *You found you,*
> *I lost part of me.*
> *Finding you happy*
> *Is how it must be!*

Welcome! This is the chapter that focuses on the future of your relationship with yourself, your child, and with your other family members, while acknowledging the growth and changes experienced as a result of your child's transition. It is a time to take the pulse of how your life moves from this place. All families will get here—some will remain together as a unit as they reach this destination, whereas others may not.

Critical issues that contributed to the current status may be based on personal beliefs, unexpected expectations, costs, parental wishes, levels of communication, stress, and the health of family relationships prior to the knowledge of the transition. And other factors could have played a role in why some families have remained intact and others have not.

It is essential for each parent to honestly sort through and re-evaluate their thoughts, feelings, concerns, and confusions by journaling. Parents are now asked to embrace their future and examine how their own lives have transitioned due to their child's transition. For those whose family has not remained intact, learning how to interact again with one another can be filled with fear of the future and sadness for what is not possible. The hope is, by using the tools of journaling and by providing a space for reflective self-exploration, which is what this workbook has offered, you will see that both your child's welfare and yours must be paramount.

For those families who have remained intact, it is time to get reacquainted or meet one another again in different ways. Take small, slow steps with patience to navigate the path the relationships will now travel. Map it out together, with each of you expressing your individual needs and your needs as a family. Where do you, as individuals and as a unit, desire to go from here? This can be addressed by using the exercises, questions, and journaling from this workbook, and seeking the advice of professionals and those who have been where you are now.

Most likely, there is an extra special bond that has developed among all of you, due to the experience of the transition process. Now is the moment to recognize this, by embracing and celebrating all you have been through. There may still be some rocky roads ahead, as you figure out how to move forward and adjust along the way. This is the journey for all families, but throughout the transition you have developed a language and unique skills of communication that will help you endure what may lie ahead. Patience and honesty filled with compassion and empathy can enable these relationships in more ways than you may know now.

Whether you are still living as the same unit or not, you can choose to discuss or reassess all the things that may have been put on hold as a result of the focus on the transition. Maybe the things that took a back seat during the transition could still come to fruition, such as finally earning the college degree you can now explore, finding the job of your dreams, or buying that house you always wanted to purchase. The energy and effort that was funneled into the transition, coupled with the decisions that needed to be made, can now be redirected to help you feel whole again.

You may choose to make additional space to nurture outside friendships or other family relationships that may have been neglected or exhausted and require tender loving care. These people will also need to be willing to see you, your child, and other family members as you are today and not necessarily as you were once seen. Important conversations may have to occur, perhaps involving your child and other family members, reassuring everyone that life has moved forward past the transition. It is to be hoped that they can respect your wishes. Perhaps you will form new friendships based on acceptance. This, too, may be a learning curve and, again, you have a choice as to whether to engage in these friendships and family dynamics or not.

For all intents and purposes, the physical, emotional, and financial needs of the transition, on most levels, will now have been discussed and a plan will be in place. At this stage, it does not matter if you have entered this chapter of your life as someone who is still part of the same family configuration or not. What does matter are your answers to the questions: What is next? Where do you go from here? Where do we go from here as a family? For weeks, months, and perhaps even years, the primary topic has been the transition in all its forms. Can you do this? Can your child do this? How will we all do this as a family? The "confusing cans" and "wondering hows" are now answered. "Did you?" or "Who did not?" are insignificant at this point. Whatever the outcome is, you are there now. There is no judgment or expectation of the choices that you found worked best for your future and the lives of your family members, especially for your child who needed to feel whole. The wish is that you have come out of this experience stronger and knowing yourself and your family much better. This finish line simply celebrates a new beginning and cheers for all the possibilities of desire, dreams, and fortitude that are now lining up together, awaiting you and your family with open arms!

GRAPHICS GALORE

Splash

What are some of your favorite things to do or that you dream of doing one day? By creatively splashing words and short phrases, quickly attempt to express your answers randomly with as many responses as possible scattered on the paper.

GRAPHICS GALORE

Venn Diagram
What are the things you would like to do and focus your energy on now, alone or with another person?

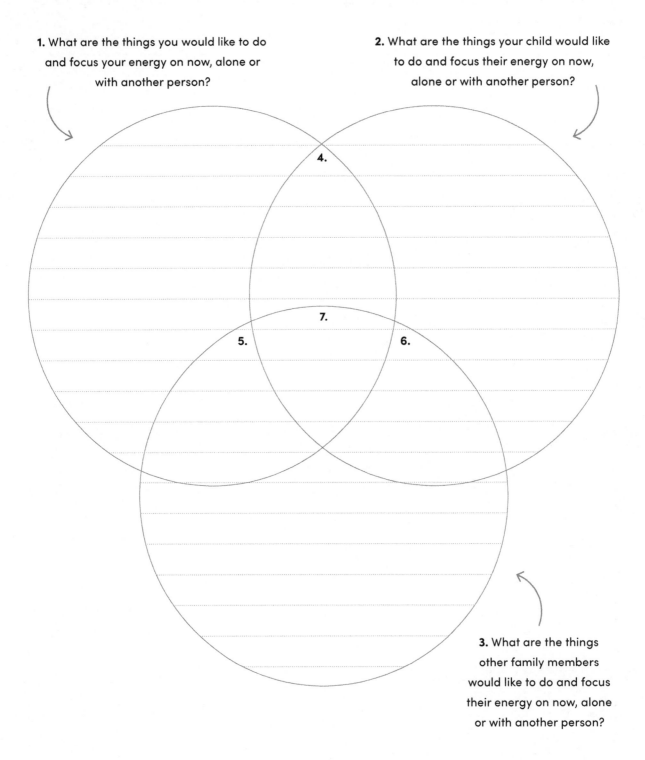

1. What are the things you would like to do and focus your energy on now, alone or with another person?

2. What are the things your child would like to do and focus their energy on now, alone or with another person?

4.

7.

5.

6.

3. What are the things other family members would like to do and focus their energy on now, alone or with another person?

REFLECTIVE RESPONSES

1. How can you get to know your family again, now that your child's transition may not necessarily need to be the focus of your time?

    ....

    ....

    ....

2. What can you do to get to know yourself again, now that your child's transition may not necessarily need to be the focus of your time?

    ....

    ....

    ....

3. What interests do any of you have in common? (Use the Venn Diagram tool above to help answer this.)

    ....

    ....

    ....

4. Which friends do you want to spend time with now that your child's transition may not necessarily need to be the focus of your time?

    ....

    ....

    ....

5. Will you feel comfortable becoming an advocate as a result of your own experience or would you prefer to have a low profile in the Transgender community?

. . . .

. . . .

. . . .

6. What do you foresee for yourselves in the future as a family, now that your child's transition may not necessarily need to be the focus of your daily lives?

. . . .

. . . .

. . . .

7. What are any medical or emotional follow-ups you need to address for yourself, now that your child's transition may not necessarily need to be the focus of your daily lives?

. . . .

. . . .

. . . .

8. What are any medical or emotional follow-ups that need to be addressed for any of your children and/ or other family members, now that your child's transition may not necessarily need to be the focus of your daily lives?

. . . .

. . . .

. . . .

9. What are any medical or emotional follow-ups that you need to address as a family, now that your child's transition may not necessarily need to be the focus of your daily lives?

....

....

....

10. Where are you financially, as an individual and as a family, now that your child's transition may not necessarily need to be the focus of your daily lives?

....

....

....

11. Do you want to remain in the same job/career?

....

....

....

12. Do you still want to remain in the same home and neighborhood?

....

....

....

13. Are there any other worries, concerns, or fears you still have and need to address?

....

....

....

14. How do you think your needs and your family's needs will be negotiated, now that your child's transition may not necessarily need to be the main focus of your daily lives?

....

....

....

15. Have you found a way to balance your own personal life that embraces the changes you have all experienced?

....

....

....

16. Is there anything you know now about yourself or others that you did not know before your child's transition and that still upsets you?

....

....

....

17. Is there anything you know now about yourself or others that you did not know before your child's transition and that comforts you?

....

....

....

18. Is there anything you know now about yourself or others that you did not know before your child's transition and that still surprises you?

· ·

· ·

· ·

19. What positive and/or negative effects has your child's transition had on your family?

· ·

· ·

· ·

20. Are there any bits of advice or suggestions you would offer a parent and/or other family members whose child recently told them they are considering transitioning and/or questioning their gender?

· ·

· ·

· ·

GRAPHICS GALORE

Web

What is one personal goal you have put on hold during your child's transition that you would like to consider trying to achieve at this time? Record this goal in the center of the web. Then write the steps you plan to do in the subtopic circles in order to achieve this goal.

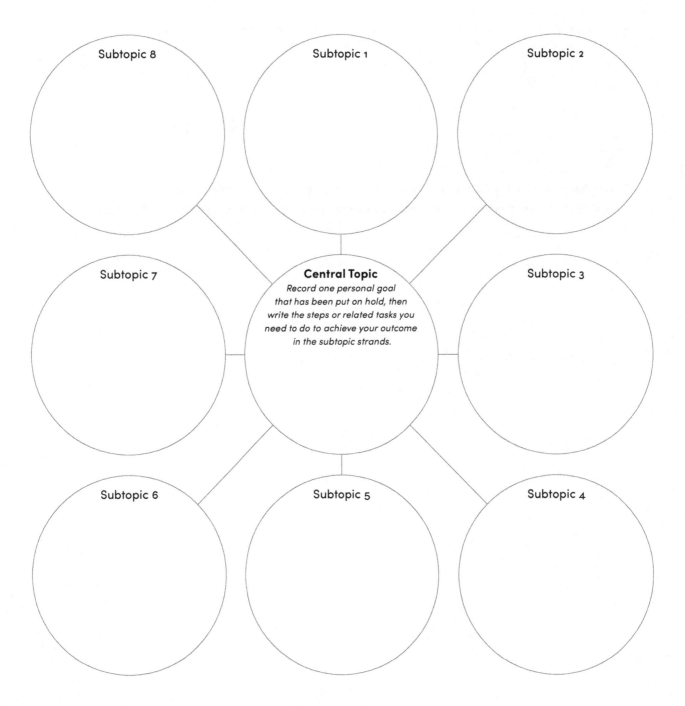

GRAPHICS GALORE

Timeline

What is the timeframe for beginning these goals?

Goal:	What do you need to get started?	Start date:	Completion date:

DESERVING DE-STRESSING DELIGHT

Volunteering

If you want to focus your energy on something independent of your child's transition, to gain additional self-worth and more compassion, then volunteer somewhere. Helping others can be a very humbling experience and may allow you to see the gifts you already possess. Some parents can reach a point during their child's transition when they wonder if it is acceptable to address something else while they are navigating their own journey. Volunteering can help you understand and observe the various ways others cope with the unexpected, adversity, or things that are out of their control, as well as embrace and celebrate all that life has to offer!

> ANECDOTAL AFFIRMATION
> *Change is scary,*
> *Change never stops,*
> *Change is hard!*

These experiences can teach parents and other family members life lessons that few other circumstances can provide. Many organizations and activism groups regularly seek volunteers. Some require weekly commitments and training or a specific set of skills. If this is too much of a commitment for you at this point in your life, then there are other options.

Being of service to another person, outside your home, does not always have to be a structured form of volunteering. Maybe a single parent in your area needs a free babysitter for one evening or a neighbor who uses a wheelchair wants help changing a ceiling lightbulb. Perhaps taking the time to simply volunteer to drive a recently widowed relative to a family function or offering your companionship by joining them for a movie matinee could feel quite rewarding.

Volunteering, formally or not, may not only help another person, but might also show and teach you things about yourself. Doing so can prove to be invaluable at a time when you may feel alone or unsure of your own thoughts. Maybe working with a particular organization or person will open doors or possibilities to you that you never even considered before you volunteered. Perhaps volunteering will shed a little light on your daily life and assist you in viewing your specific uncertainties from a different perspective. You may never know until you try!

Journal your reaction to this Deserving De-Stressing Delight.

. . . .

. . . .

. . . .

. . . .

GRAPHICS GALORE

Box

Do any of these suggested ideas seem enjoyable to you? Create your own or use these! After you try the activities stated below, feel free to document your experience below.

Movies that you have been meaning to see! (With someone else or not.)	Places you hope to visit one day! (With someone else or not.)	Your favorite ways to feel pampered! (With someone else or not.)
Activities you would like to try or do again! (With someone else or not.)	Friends or other family you would enjoy visiting! (With someone else or not.)	Concerts you would like to attend one day! (With someone else or not.)

GRAPHICS GALORE

T-Chart

What are the ways you can grow and improve your daily lifestyle?

How can you grow academically or improve your current work status?	How can you nurture or improve your living space and environment?	How can you improve your social life and expand your social circle?

EMPATHY-EMBRACING EXERCISE

ANECDOTAL AFFIRMATION

*I long
For yesterday,
But welcome
Tomorrow.*

Understanding your next steps once your child's transition is no longer front and center enables family members and all other relationships to move forward. This exercise grants parents the freedom to examine all the possibilities that are open to them, now that most of your own energy is not focused primarily on the transition. As parents, you can decide this on your own or consult others; regardless, embrace it and soar!

Now that your child's transition may not necessarily need to be the focal point of your daily life, what seems to be the most important topic affecting you alone and/or your current relationships with other family members or friends? Do you feel your child and other family members will support you in spending the majority of your time and energy on your own needs and dreams?

. . . .

. . . .

. . . .

. . . .

. . . .

. . . .

. . . .

. . . .

. . . .

. . . .

. . . .

. . . .

GRAPHICS GALORE

Bar Graph

To what degree do these concerns and related topics matter to you? Based on a scale from 1 to 10, with 1 being the lowest and 10 being the highest, color or shade in your response. This visual will illustrate where your greatest concerns lie and can be used as a tool to help you communicate your thoughts with your child and/or other family members, therapist, spiritual mentor, or for your own personal understanding. The bar graph results can vary as your child's transition progresses and your thoughts may shift.

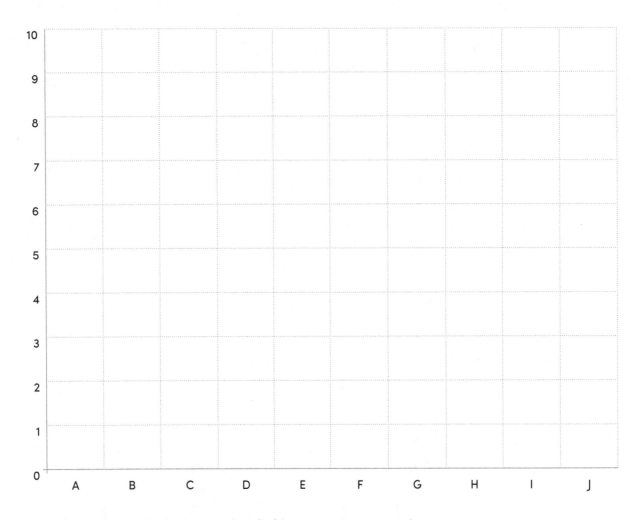

Use these ideas to fill in the bar graph or feel free to create your own!

A. Focusing on furthering your own education and growth.

B. Focusing on your leisure and fun activities.

C. Focusing on your career, business ideas, and finances.

D. Focusing on your medical, emotional, and health needs.

E. Focusing on your relationships with friends and family.

F. Focusing on your home and living environment.

G. Focusing on figuring out what it is you want to focus on now but do not know yet.

H. Focusing on new parenting/pregnancy or on any of the children you already parent.

I. Focusing on your relationship with your spouse/partner or meeting someone else.

J. Focusing on advocacy for the LGBTQ+ community.

GRAPHICS GALORE

Pie Graph

To what degree are these concerns and related topics important to you? Decide how significant these issues are to you in relation to each other. Place the number that corresponds with a suggested topic within as many slices of the pie that convey how each one matters to you. Only one number should be placed in each slice. You do not need to use all the issues, but do fill in all the slices. Feel free to create your own topics and assign them their own number.

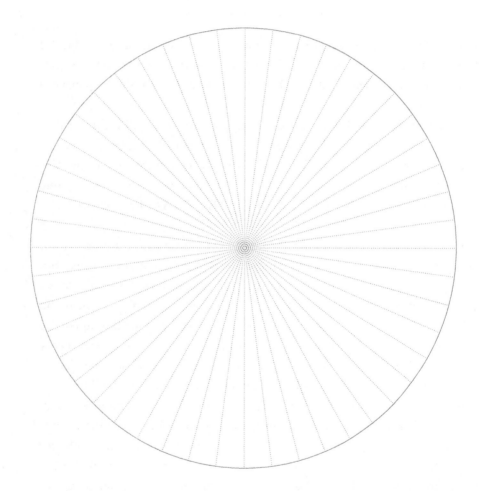

1. Focusing on furthering your own education and growth.
2. Focusing on your leisure and fun activities.
3. Focusing on your career, business ideas, and finances.
4. Focusing on your medical, emotional, and health needs.
5. Focusing on your relationships with friends and family.
6. Focusing on your home and living environment.
7. Focusing on figuring out what it is you want to focus on now but do not know yet.
8. Focusing on new parenting/pregnancy or on any of the children you already parent.
9. Focusing on your relationship with your spouse/partner or meeting someone else.
10. Focusing on advocacy work for the LGBTQ+ community.

SAMPLER SHARES

All names have been changed to ensure anonymity in this section. The first initial designates an individual and the second initial identifies the relationship to the child, i.e. P = their parent, G = their grandparent, and S = their sibling.

Are there any bits of advice or suggestions you would offer a parent and/or other family members whose child recently told them they are considering transitioning and/or questioning their gender?

DP: Bottom line for me: my child is now happy. I truly do not care what he looks like. He is finding himself as a new young man, has a lot of the same friends and some new ones. All I want is a happy and healthy child. *PARENT/CHILD: AFAB (Uses he/him/his pronouns)*

HP: See if their school offers an after-school group support, and look online for websites and resources that can help answer questions. Listen to what your child is telling you. Pay attention to the changes in their personality, to the best of your ability, and be objective and try not to initially make it about you as a parent. Look for a respected therapist who works in the Transgender community. *PARENT/CHILD: AFAB (Uses he/him/his pronouns)*

FP: LOVE YOUR CHILD! Forget your original hopes and dreams for your child, and create new ones. As I once told my husband: I understand this is not what you wanted, but *this is not about you!* Your child can live a lie for the rest of their life, but it would have a devastating impact on their livelihood and that of those around them forever. Be proud of your child for being courageous enough to be themselves, and provide the supportive environment necessary to do it as painlessly as possible. They will have to deal with plenty of negativity and intolerance in society as a whole, but home should be their safe haven. It is not an easy journey, especially if you do not have a clue. So, *educate yourself!* It is your duty as a parent to learn what you do not already know. Just think for a minute, if your child was to ever feel as if life is no longer worth living, as mine has at times, wouldn't you rather know that you are a part of the solution and not the cause of the problem? Your acceptance and love of your child may just save their life. Finally, it is important to make sure that those around you (neighbors, grandparents, aunts, uncles, nephews, etc.) are on board, or they should hit the road. *Your child is your priority!* As long as you stay firm in your support of your child, the rest will eventually follow. So, believe me, it gets easier with time. *PARENT/CHILD: AFAB (Uses he/him/his pronouns)*

COMMUNICATION CORNER

ANECDOTAL AFFIRMATION

Being seen
And respected
For who you are
Is the greatest
Gift of all!

When you speak spontaneously out of anger or fear about the unknown, without thinking it through, you can sometimes regret the way you phrased your words or the tone you used to express your feelings. Rehearsing what you want to ask or discuss with your child, and other family members, can help you before you actually communicate your thoughts. This gives you a moment to reflect and pause before you converse about emotional topics. You may choose to practice asking these questions with a trusted friend, family member, spiritual mentor, or therapist first. Explain your thoughts and feelings about these statements to one another verbally or in writing. It is important to note that some families elected to only address one question or two, while others preferred to answer them all. In order to recall the questions you answered, simply highlight and/or circle the ones you addressed as a family, yet acknowledging that you may return to discuss the others in the future. Decide what feels best for two or more family members and begin the conversation. Do you, your child, and other family members answer these questions in the same way or differently? Discuss your responses to understand how all of you view the answers to the questions and make time to celebrate all you learn from being willing to communicate with each other.

1. As part of a family unit and as an individual, what actions can you take to help you focus on furthering your education and growth?

    . . . .

    . . . .

2. As part of a family unit and as an individual, what actions can you take to help you focus on your interests connected to leisure and fun activities?

    . . . .

    . . . .

3. As part of a family unit and as an individual, what actions can you take to help you focus on furthering your careers, business ideas, and finances?

    . . . .

    . . . .

4. As part of a family unit and as an individual, what actions can you take to help you focus on your own medical, emotional, and health needs?

....

....

5. As part of a family unit and as an individual, what actions can you take to help you focus on your relationships with friends and family?

....

....

6. As part of a family unit and as an individual, what actions can you take to help you focus on your home and living environment?

....

....

7. As part of a family unit and as an individual, what actions can you take to help you figure out what you all want to focus on now, but do not know yet?

....

....

8. As part of a family unit and as an individual, what actions can you take to help you focus on new parenting/pregnancy or on any of the children you already parent?

....

....

9. As part of a family unit and as an individual, what actions can you take to help you focus on your relationship with your spouse/partner or moving on and meeting someone else?

....

....

10. As part of a family unit and as an individual, what actions can you take to help you focus on advocacy work for the LGBTQ+ community?

. . . .

. . . .

Chapter 15

YOU ARE NOT ALONE (RESOURCES, GLOSSARY, AND ANSWER KEYS)

VITAL VIGNETTE

If you would like to reach out to the author and share your thoughts in reference to this workbook, or to learn more about her workshops, retreats, and speaking engagements, contact D. M. Maynard at dmmaynardworkbook@gmail.com.

ANECDOTAL AFFIRMATION

Seeing you happy
Makes my day brighter!

I realize that resources are a crucial aspect of any book, so I am providing you with the ones I felt were relevant at the actual time of writing. Since resources and information are rapidly being updated and changed on a daily basis, I recognize that some sources or recommendations listed today can be outdated within a month's time. In addition, there may be very valuable resources that could have arisen while this workbook was in production or that I was not familiar with at the time this workbook was created. Should any reader know of a credible resource that is or was useful to them during their journey and it is not listed below, kindly email me the source. If after I review the information and am able to confirm that the suggestion aligns with the purpose of this workbook, I would be happy to share it with parents and other family members. That being said, here is the list parents, families, and I found useful.

RESOURCES/REFERENCES

ARTICLES

Amy Hillier and Elisabeth Torg (2019) "Parent Participation in a Support Group for Families with Transgender and Gender-Nonconforming Children: Being in the Company of Others Who Do Not Question the Reality of Our Experience." *Transgender Health* 4(1): 168–175. Published online Aug 12, 2019. doi: 10.1089/trgh.2018.0018.

Jeff Schwaner (2017) "Understanding These Gender Terms Is Easy." Accessed on May 15, 2018 at www.newsleader.com/story/news/2017/09/20/understanding-these-gender-terms-easy/679663001.

Simon Van Der Weele (2017) "Mourning Moppa: Mourning without Loss in Jill Soloway's Transparent." *TSQ: Transgender Studies Quarterly* 4(3–4): 608–626.

CHILDREN'S BOOKS

Jennifer Carr (2010) *Be Who You Are* (AuthorHouse).
Nick was born in a boy's body, but has always felt like a girl inside. Nick's family supports him when he says he no longer wants to be called a boy or dress like a boy: "Always remember to be who you are Nick. Remember that we love you, and we are so proud of you" (p.17). Nick's parents find a group for families like theirs. With their support, Nick expresses a desire to be addressed as "she," and then to be named "Hope." Based on the author's experiences with her children.

Jessica Herthel and Jazz Jennings (2014) *I Am Jazz* (Dial Books).
The story of a transgender child based on the real-life experience of Jazz Jennings, who has become a spokesperson for trans kids everywhere and now has a television series on TLC. From the time she was two years old, Jazz knew that she had a girl's brain in a boy's body. She loved pink and dressing up as a mermaid and didn't feel like herself in boys' clothing. This confused her family, until they took her to a doctor who said that Jazz was transgender and that she was born that way. Jazz's story is based on her real-life experience and she tells it in a simple, clear way that will be appreciated by picture book readers, their parents, and teachers. For info on the television series: www.tlc.com/tv-shows/i-am-jazz.

Colt Keo-Meier (2017) *Stacey's Not a Girl* (self-published).
This children's book takes us on a gender journey with Stacey who does not feel like a girl, but is not so sure they are a boy either. This book introduces us to ideas of gender beyond the binary. The first book of its kind with all-transgender contributors: author, illustrator, and designer. Elements from each contributor as well as close friends and family are woven into Stacey's story.

Cheryl Kilodavis (2010) *My Princess Boy* **(Aladdin).**
Dyson loves pink, sparkly things. Sometimes he wears dresses. Sometimes he wears jeans. He likes to wear his princess tiara, even when climbing trees. He's a Princess Boy. This is a heart-warming book about unconditional love and one remarkable family. Inspired by the author's son, and by her own initial struggles to understand, this is a call for tolerance and an end to bullying and judgments. The world is a brighter place when we accept everyone for who they are.

Kyle Lukoff (2019) *When Aiden Became a Brother* **(Lee & Low Books).**
When Aidan was born, everyone thought he was a girl. His parents gave him a pretty name, his room looked like a girl's room, and he wore clothes that other girls liked wearing. After he realized he was a trans boy, Aidan and his parents fixed the parts of his life that didn't fit anymore, and he settled happily into his new life. Then Mom and Dad announce that they're going to have another baby, and Aidan wants to do everything he can to make things right for his new sibling from the beginning—from choosing the perfect name to creating a beautiful room and picking out the cutest onesie. But what does "making things right" actually mean? And what happens if he messes up? With a little help, Aidan comes to understand that mistakes can be fixed with honesty and communication, and that he already knows the most important thing about being a big brother: how to love with his whole self. This heart-warming book will resonate with transgender children, reassure any child concerned about becoming an older sibling, and celebrate the many transitions a family can experience.

Robb Pearlmann (2018) *Pink is for Boys* **(Running Press Kids).**
An empowering and educational picture book that proves colors are for everyone, regardless of gender. Pink is for boys...and girls...and everyone! This timely and beautiful picture book rethinks and reframes the stereotypical blue/pink gender binary and empowers kids—and their grown-ups—to express themselves in every color of the rainbow. Featuring a diverse group of relatable characters, this book invites and encourages girls and boys to enjoy what they love to do, whether it's racing cars and playing baseball, or loving unicorns and dressing up. Vibrant illustrations help children learn and identify the myriad colors that surround them every day, from the orange of a popsicle, to the green of a grassy field, all the way up to the wonder of a multicolored rainbow. Parents and kids will delight in the author's sweet, simple script, as well as its powerful message: life is not color-coded.

Brook Pessin-Whedbee (2016) *Who Are You? The Kid's Guide to Gender Identity* **(Jessica Kingsley Publishers).**
This brightly illustrated children's book provides a straightforward introduction to gender for anyone aged five to eight. It presents clear and direct language for understanding and talking about how we experience gender: our bodies, our expression, and our identity. An interactive three-layered wheel included in the book is a simple yet powerful tool to clearly demonstrate the difference between our body, how we express ourselves through

our clothes and hobbies, and our gender identity. It is ideal for use in the classroom or at home, and a short page-by-page guide for adults at the back of the book further explains the key concepts and identifies useful discussion points. This is a one-of-a-kind resource for understanding and celebrating the gender diversity that surrounds us.

Sarah Sage and Fox Fisher (2017) *Are You a Boy or Are You a Girl?* **(Jessica Kingsley Publishers).**
Tiny prefers not to tell other children whether they are a boy or girl. Tiny also loves to play fancy dress, sometimes as a fairy and sometimes as a knight in shining armor. Tiny's family don't seem to mind, but when they start a new school some of their new classmates struggle to understand.

Theresa Thorn (2019) *It Feels Good to Be Yourself: A Book About Gender Identity* **(Henry Holt & Co).**
A picture book that introduces the concept of gender identity to the youngest reader. Some people are boys. Some people are girls. Some people are both, neither, or somewhere in between. This sweet, straightforward exploration of gender identity will give children a fuller understanding of themselves and others. With child-friendly language and vibrant art, this book provides young readers and parents alike with the vocabulary to discuss this important topic with sensitivity.

CONFERENCES

Gender Conference NYC—New York, USA
Gender Conference NYC has its roots in Gender Conference East (GCE), which began in 2014 in Baltimore, Maryland. The seed was planted in 2008 when mothers in both Maryland and New York were eager for support and community. They found each other, and with the help of PFLAG Columbia-Howard County, PFLAG NYC, The Ackerman Institute's Gender & Family Project, and Gender Spectrum, GCE was born. After a move to Newark in 2016, GCE continued to grow. By 2018, the increasing number of families in need resulted in the founders of GCE creating events in two locations, and Gender Conference NYC was born. We are forever grateful to PFLAG Howard County and Gender Spectrum for their efforts and guidance.
www.genderconference.nyc

Gender Odyssey—San Diego, California and Seattle, Washington, USA
An international conference focused on the needs and interests of transgender and gender diverse children of all ages, their families and supporters, and the professionals who serve them. Their conference is packed with thought-provoking workshops, including medical information and consultation opportunities, professional education, discussion groups, networking, children and youth programming, and social events. This one-of-a-kind annual gathering attracts people from all over the world for an uplifting weekend of connection, support, and community. It is an international conference focused on the

needs and interests of transgender and gender diverse children of all ages, their families and supporters, and the professionals who serve them.
www.genderodyssey.org

Philadelphia Trans Wellness Conference—Philadelphia, Pennsylvania, USA
This Philadelphia-based conference, as part of the Mazzoni Center's mission, offers education and information for healthcare professionals and the trans community, including friends and family, by addressing a myriad of health and well-being issues, while promoting networking and providing an inclusive environment, which welcomes gender diversity and expression through supporting all voices.
https://web.cvent.com/event/64535734-3ab3-4aca-a0ee-0352fff0b806/summary

DOCUMENTARIES/FILMS
Gun Hill Road (2011)
1 hour 26 minutes (film). Directed by Rashaad Ernesto Green, produced by SimonSays Entertainment, A Small Production Company, and The Princess Grace Foundation.
An ex-con returns home to the Bronx after three years in prison to discover his wife estranged and his child exploring a gender transformation that will put the fragile bonds of their family to the test.
www.imdb.com/title/tt1525838

Ma Vie En Rose/My Life in Pink (French subtitles in Belgium) (1997)
1 hour 28 minutes (film). Directed by Alain Berliner, produced by Carole Scotta and Canal+, Eurimages, CNC.
A 1997 Belgian drama that tells the story of Ludovic, a child who is seen by family and community as a boy, but consistently communicates being a girl. The film depicts Ludovic's family struggling to accept this transgressive gender expression.

The Most Dangerous Year (2018)
90 minutes (documentary). Directed by Vlada Knowlton, produced by Vlada Knowlton, Lulu Gargiulo, and Chadd Knowlton.
In 2016, a group of Washington State families with transgender children banded together with activists and like-minded lawmakers and fought tooth and nail against the wave of anti-trans rights legislation that swept the nation and their home state. This is their story.
www.siff.net/festival/the-most-dangerous-year

Trans in America: Texas Strong (2018)
18 minutes (Emmy-winning documentary). Directed by Daresha Kyi, produced by the ACLU & Little By Little Films, with an LGBT-led team.
An intimate portrait of Kimberly and Kai Shappley, a mother who has to confront her religious community while her young transgender daughter navigates life at school, where she's been banned from the girls' bathroom.
www.youtube.com/watch?v=cuIkLNsRtas&t=5s

ORGANIZATIONS

Ackerman Institute's Gender & Family Project

The Gender & Family Project (GFP) empowers youth, families, and communities by providing gender affirmative services, training, and research. GFP, founded in 2010, promotes gender inclusivity as a form of social justice in all the systems involved in the life of the family.

www.ackerman.org/gfp

FORGE

A progressive organization whose mission is to support, educate, and advocate for the rights and lives of transgender individuals and SOFFAs (significant others, friends, family, and allies). It is dedicated to helping move fragmented communities beyond identity politics and forge a movement that embraces and empowers our diverse complexities. It is a national transgender, anti-violence organization, founded in 1994. Since 2009, it has been federally funded to provide direct services to transgender, gender nonconforming, and gender non-binary survivors of sexual assault. Since 2011, FORGE has served as the only transgender-focused organization federally funded to provide training and technical assistance to providers around the country who work with transgender survivors of sexual assault, domestic and dating violence, and stalking. Their role as technical assistance providers reveals the key continuing and emerging challenges many agencies are experiencing in serving sexual assault survivors of all genders.

https://forge-forward.org

Gender Spectrum

This organization offers information and training for families, educators, professionals, and organizations, helping them to create gender-sensitive and inclusive environments for all children and teens.

www.genderspectrum.org

GLSEN (Gay, Lesbian and Straight Education Network)

Championing LGBTQ issues in K–12 education since 1990, this organization works to ensure that LGBTQ students are able to learn and grow in a school environment free from bullying and harassment. It transforms US schools into the safe and affirming environment all youth deserve as it believes that every student has the right to a safe, supportive, and LGBTQ-inclusive K–12 education. It has a national network of educators, students, and local GLSEN chapters working to make this right a reality, and its research and experience have shown that there are four major ways schools can cultivate a safe and supportive environment for all of their students, regardless of sexual orientation, gender identity, or gender expression.

www.glsen.org

Human Rights Campaign

The Human Rights Campaign represents a force of more than three million members and supporters nationwide. As the largest national lesbian, gay, bisexual, transgender, and queer civil rights organization, the Human Rights Campaign envisions a world where LGBTQ people are as sured of their basic equal rights, and can be open, honest, and safe at home, at work, and in the community. The Human Rights Campaign Foundation's Welcoming Schools is the nation's premier professional development program, providing training and resources to elementary school educators on a range of issues, including how to support transgender and non-binary students. The Human Rights Campaign's Transgender Children and Youth page includes resources for families, community members, school officials, and more. Co-published with the American Academy of Pediatrics and the American College of Osteopathic Pediatricians, the Human Rights Campaign Foundation's *Supporting & Caring for Transgender Children* is a groundbreaking resource that explains how families and healthcare professionals can help transgender and gender-expansive children thrive.

www.hrc.org/resources/topic/parenting

www.hrc.org/resources/resources-for-people-with-transgender-family-members

The Jim Collins Foundation

This foundation, in memory of Jim Collins, offers financial assistance towards gender-affirming surgeries.

https://jimcollinsfoundation.org

Lambda Legal

This national LGBT organization offers legal services, impact litigation, education, and public policy work.

www.lambdalegal.org

LGBTQ+ Centers

There are locations, often within large cities, which house LGBTQ+ Centers, in the United States and countries worldwide. These centers can sponsor community events, meetings, and workshops for the transgender community. Occasionally, some of these meetings or workshops may even host support groups that focus on the unique needs and challenges that parents and families face. If these centers do not yet have meetings or workshops geared toward supporting parents and families, they are often open to welcoming such programs. This can be viewed as an opportunity to create a series for parents and families by individuals who are knowledgeable on transitioning, based on the needs of the parents and families, and then form a network or support program. You can search the internet for LGBTQ+ Centers in your area.

https://en.wikipedia.org/wiki/List_of_LGBT_community_centers_in_the_United_States

National Center for Transgender Equality (NCTE)

This organization was founded in 2003 by transgender activists who recognized the urgent need for policy change to advance transgender equality. With a committed board of directors, a volunteer staff of one, and donated office space, NCTE set out to accomplish what no one had yet done: provide a powerful transgender advocacy presence in Washington, DC. Today, it is a team of hard-working staff members supported by a nationwide community of transgender people, allies, and advocates with an extensive record of winning life-saving change for transgender people.

https://transequality.org

PFLAG (Parents and Friends of Lesbians and Gays)

A national non-profit organization with thousands of members and supporters and more than 400 chapters across the United States. This vast grassroots network is cultivated, resourced, and serviced by the PFLAG National Office, located in Washington, DC, the national board of directors, and 13 regional directors. This organization promotes the health and well-being of gay, lesbian, bisexual, and transgender people, their families, and friends through support, education, and advocacy. As an extended family of the LGBTQ+ community, PFLAG families, friends, and allies work together with those who are lesbian, gay, bisexual, transgender, and queer+ to provide opportunities for dialogue about sexual orientation and gender identity. They act to create a society that is healthy and respectful of human diversity. PFLAG has local chapters across the United States, including groups specifically for families with transgender children.

https://pflag.org/transgender

www.pflaghoco.org

The Family Acceptance Project® (FAP)

FAP has collaborated with Child and Adolescent Services at San Francisco General Hospital/University of California, San Francisco (UCSF) and with community providers to develop a new family-oriented model of wellness, prevention, and care for LGBT children and adolescents, based on research. This new family-related approach helps ethnically and religiously diverse families to decrease rejection and increase support to prevent risk and promote their LGBT children's well-being. It provides training on its family intervention approach and using its research-based resources to providers, families, and religious leaders across the United States and in other countries. FAP is currently implementing its family support model in collaboration with several agencies and communities around the country. This includes a partnership to integrate the approach into services provided by the Ruth Ellis Center in Wayne County, Michigan.

http://familyproject.sfsu.edu

The Trans Youth Equality Foundation

This foundation provides education, advocacy, and support for transgender and gender nonconforming children and youth, and their families. It shares information about the

unique needs of this community, partnering with families, educators, and service providers to help foster a healthy, caring, and safe environment for all transgender children. In addition, this organization offers programs that include camps, retreats, support groups, and a popular Tumblr blog for youth.
www.transyouthequality.org

Welcoming Schools

Creating safe and welcoming schools for all children and families, HRC Foundation's Welcoming Schools is the Nations premier professional development program providing training and resources to elementary school educators to embrace all families, create LGBTQ and gender inclusive schools, prevent bias-based bullying, and support transgender and non-binary students.
www.welcomingschools.org

World Professional Association for Transgender Health (WPATH)

A non-profit, interdisciplinary professional and educational organization devoted to transgender health. Members engage in clinical and academic research to develop evidence-based medicine and strive to promote a high quality of care for transsexual, transgender, and gender-nonconforming individuals internationally. Please note: The Standards of Care Information is available on the WPATH website. In addition, this site also offers an opportunity to search for medical and mental health providers who are members of the association.
www.wpath.org

PROFESSIONAL BOOKS

Diane Ehrensaft, PhD (2016) *The Gender Creative Child: Pathways for Nurturing and Supporting Children Who Live Outside Gender Boxes* (Experiment).
In this up-to-date, comprehensive resource, Dr. Ehrensaft explains the interconnected effects of biology, nurture, and culture to explore why gender can be *fluid*, rather than binary. As an advocate for the gender affirmative model and with the expertise she has gained over three decades of pioneering work with children and families, she encourages caregivers to listen to each child, learn their particular needs, and support their quest for a true gender self.

Laura Erickson-Schroth (ed.) (2014) *Trans Bodies, Trans Selves: A Resource for the Transgender Community* (Oxford University Press).
This encyclopedic resource guide, written by professionals and community members who share their stories and expertise, covers major topics and current information that addresses the lives of those who are transgender or questioning individuals, and others who are affected by these issues.

Elisabeth Kübler-Ross and David Kessler (2005) *On Grief and Grieving:*
Finding the Meaning of Grief Through the Five Stages of Loss (Scribner).
Elisabeth Kübler-Ross's last book, written in collaboration with David Kessler, concludes
her journey exploring the famous five stages of grief and loss. The authors discuss a vast
multitude of issues affecting the varied processes of mourning and grieving.

Arlene I. Lev and Andrew R. Gottlieb (eds) (2019) *Families in Transition: Parenting*
Gender Diverse Children, Adolescents, and Young (Harrington Park Press, LLC).
This is a collection of clinically oriented articles, research, and case material authored by
mental health and medical experts, both nationally and internationally known, as well as
first-person narratives written by parents and families, exploring the complexities faced
by parents and caretakers attending to the needs of their children in a largely hostile
world. The professional articles are positioned side by side with the voices of the parents
themselves—each complementing the other—adding up to a richly complex, original
tapestry. This text is designed for mental health professionals—clinicians, educators,
and researchers; medical providers; parents and caretakers of gender diverse children,
adolescents, and young adults—and is suitable for graduate and doctoral level coursework
in a range of subject areas, including gender, sexuality, and family studies.

Elijah C. Nealy, PhD, MDiv, LCSW (2017) *Transgender Children and Youth:*
Cultivating Pride and Joy with Families in Transition (W. W. Norton & Company).
Elijah C. Nealy, therapist and former deputy executive director of New York City's LGBT
Community Center, and himself a trans man, has written the first-ever comprehensive
guide to understanding, supporting, and welcoming trans kids. This book is full of best
practices to support trans kids, covering everything from family life to school and mental
health issues, as well as the medical, physical, social, and emotional aspects of transition.

Rylan Jay Testa, PhD, Deborah Coolhart, PhD, LMFT, and Jayme Peta,
MA, MS (2015) *The Gender Quest Workbook: A Guide for Teens and Young*
Adults Exploring Gender Identity (Instant Help; Workbook edition).
This comprehensive workbook will help young people navigate gender identity and expression at home, in school, and with peers. The activities in this book will help transgender
and gender nonconforming (TGNC) teens explore their identity internally, interpersonally,
and culturally. And along the way, TGNC teens will learn how to effectively express
themselves and make informed decisions on how to navigate their gender with family,
friends, classmates, and co-workers. The book also includes chapters on sex and dating,
balancing multiple identities, and how to deal with stressful challenges when they arise.
This workbook incorporates skills, exercises, and activities from evidence-based thera-
pies—such as cognitive behavioral therapy—to help TGNC teens address the broad range
of struggles they may encounter related to gender identity, such as anxiety, isolation, fear,
and even depression.

VIDEOS AND WEBSITES

On the internet, you will find endless videos and websites that can be an incredible resource. It is important to know that each video is usually one person's journey or experience, which may or may not help you in your time of need and/or confusion.

Dear Parents of Trans Youth (2016) Sam Collins

Q&A video to help parents of trans kids. It is a candid interview that answers questions based on the experiences of a mom and her trans child.
www.youtube.com/watch?v=gIgs3YrQGaU

Dear Transphobic Parents (2018) ThatEmoKidAlex

Though the title may deter some parents to view this video, the message is important and relevant.
www.youtube.com/watch?v=X8a3-qHWcbE

Gender Dysphoria Affirmative Working Group

A discussion space for medical and mental health professionals, academics, researchers, activists, and allies supporting transgender and gender nonconforming youth.
www.gdaworkinggroup.com

HealthyTrans

This website suggests some questions which pertain to transgender issues that can be asked at medical appointments.
www.healthytrans.com

Parents and Transgender Children Read Powerful Affirmations (2017) Iris

Parents are asked to read affirmations to their transgender children.
www.youtube.com/watch?v=t9h7jWYJa5w

To the Parents of Trans Kids (2016) From buzzfeed LGBT on Facebook

This positive video discusses positive ways transgender kids were and/or can be supported.
www.youtube.com/watch?v=LVdB2TjneEk

Trans America Videos for Parents of Trans Kids

This is an excellent way to find resources using the key words: trans, America, trans, and kids.
www.youtube.com/results?search_query=trans+America+parents+of+trans+kids

Transgender: a mother's story—Susie Green (2017) TEDxTruro

Susie Green shares the inspirational story of her transgender daughter, who told her when she was four that she should have been born a girl. Susie is the CEO of Mermaids, a charity that supports gender variant children, young people, and their families. Susie

became involved with Mermaids when she needed support for her daughter, Jackie. Susie has expanded the charity's capacity and funding, as well as developing the services it offers. She campaigns for the provision of more services and respectful media representation of transgender people. This talk was given at a TEDx event using the TED conference format but independently organized by a local community.
www.youtube.com/watch?v=2ZiVPh12RQY

Transgender Children Talk About Being Raised by their Families (2017)
Transgender children and their families discuss challenges of growing up in today's world.
www.youtube.com/watch?v=ZLNdExzuKwc

Transgender kids are just kids after all—Amber Briggle (2016) TEDxTWU
A self-identified feminist mom tells her story of coming to recognize her son for who he is rather than who she assumed he was based on his sex assigned at birth. Gender nonconformity is something often championed by feminists, but trans identity is something else entirely. Amber Briggle is a small business owner, a community volunteer, a political junkie, and the mother of two incredible children—Lulu (age three) and MG (age eight)—who have brought many surprises along the way, including MG's revelation at the age of two that he was mislabeled at birth and identified not as a girl, but as a boy. Through trial by fire, Amber has quickly and earnestly become an advocate for transgender rights, helping her son navigate the world of boy/girl while simultaneously challenging society's gender stereotypes. She is also a board member of the League of Women Voters of Texas and a proud member of Rotary International, and she has a rescue dog named Bluebell who still hasn't figured out how to fetch Amber a glass of wine, but they're working on it. This talk was given at a TEDx event using the TED conference format but independently organized by a local community.
www.youtube.com/watch?v=t_gCASi58Ps

Transgender Myths (2016) Kovu Kingsrod
Kovu Kingsrod discusses myths in relation to transgender voices.
www.youtube.com/watch?v=sduSt9LqFS8&list=PLHHj7HICtRLNiZ8hifS6ApPHBUyobLpH1

TransGenderPartners.com: Resources for significant others, friends, family and allies of transgender people
This website offers resources for significant others, friends, family, and allies of transgender people. Though this website has *partners* in the title, it also offers many resources for parents and families.
www.transgenderpartners.com/resource-for-partners-2

EMPATHY-EMBRACING EXERCISE

ANECDOTAL AFFIRMATION
*Breathe,
Research,
Embrace!*

Movies and theater have always been a source of information that can both educate and entertain. As the world is beginning to learn about the Transgender community, more and more movie, theater, and television studios are willing to incorporate transgender characters and storylines that address the needs and realities that affect the lives of transgender children and their families. Although parents and families are not necessarily the focus of many plots or scripts, some movies, theater, and television shows can enlighten those who are in the dark. In time, the hope is that the needs and realities of parents and families will be portrayed in a way that brings both respect and an understanding of what their daily lives can look like throughout the transition process.

The more parents and families become aware of transgender issues, the more they often notice their relevance or lack of presence in the world around them. As you begin to observe places where transgender topics are discussed or absent, you may want to document these realities and share your experiences with others. It is important for parents and families of trans children to have their journey and voice recognized in the arts, media, and literature in everyday situations. Should you find materials that honor the parents, families, and children's experience, it is both critical and responsible for you to share it with others. It is equally important to state if the portrayal of the parents, families, and children's experience appears accurate and realistic. When it does not, state it, and when it does, applaud it! This will be key in educating others!

Can you think of any TV show or series, movies, plays, musicals, books, or internet resources that focus on the transition from the point of view of the parents, families, and children?

....

....

....

....

....

....

....

....

COMMUNICATION CORNER

Which resources, if any, would you like to invite your child, other family members, and/or friends to review or research with or without you and which resources would you prefer to review or research alone?

<table>
<tr><td>ANECDOTAL AFFIRMATION

You are a
Silent Angel
Of the transition.</td><td>1. Which additional article references/resources do you know of or want to research?

. . . .

. . . .</td></tr>
</table>

. . . .

2. Which additional children's book references/resources do you know of or want to research?

. . . .

. . . .

3. Which additional conference references/resources do you know of or want to research?

. . . .

. . . .

4. Which additional documentary/film references/resources do you know of or want to research?

. . . .

. . . .

5. Which additional LGBTQ+ Center references/resources do you know of or want to research?

. . . .

. . . .

6. Which additional organization references/resources do you know of or want to research?

. . . .

. . . .

7.   Which additional professional book references/resources do you know of or want to research?

. . . .

. . . .

ANECDOTAL AFFIRMATION

Let love
Fill our hearts,
Let laughter
Fill our souls,
Let happiness
Fill our days!

8.   Which additional support group references/resources do you know of or want to research?

. . . .

. . . .

. . . .

9.   Which additional video references/resources do you know of or want to research?

. . . .

. . . .

. . . .

10. Which additional website references/resources do you know of or want to research?

. . . .

. . . .

GLOSSARY

agender Someone who does not identify with any gender.

androgynous Someone who possesses both masculine and feminine characteristics.

asexual Someone who does not feel sexual attraction to others.

bigender Someone who experiences themselves as both masculine and feminine.

bilateral mastectomy A surgical procedure that removes breast tissue from both sides of the chest and can include the construction of a male-appearing chest.

binary The belief that there are only two genders, male and female.

binding A practice of using material or clothing to constrict the breasts that enables a person to flatten their chest.

bisexual (bi) A person who is attracted to both masculine and feminine people.

bottom surgery A surgical procedure that permanently changes the genitals or internal reproductive organs.

cisgender (cis) Someone whose gender assigned at birth and gender identity are aligned.

cisgender privilege The advantages granted by society to people whose gender aligns with the gender assigned at birth.

deadname A term that describes the name assigned to a person at birth, which they no longer use, for it does not align with their affirmed gender and can also be referred to as their old name.

dilate A prescribed routine post-vaginoplasty where a person inserts medical equipment into the neovagina in order to maintain the creation of the vaginal canal.

drag Enacting gender for the purpose of performance and/or show.

endocrinologist A medical doctor who specializes in glands and hormones.

facial feminization surgery A variety of plastic surgery procedures to create a more feminine appearance to the features of the face.

FTM (female-to-male)/F2M/MTM An abbreviation that describes a person who now identifies as male gendered but was assigned a female gender at birth.

gatekeeper A mental health or medical professional who controls access to medical treatment such as hormones and surgery.

gender How a person internally experiences themselves as male, female, masculine, feminine, some combination of these, or none of them; aspects of these can be culturally defined.

gender-affirming surgery (GAS) Surgery that brings the individual's body into alignment with their gender identity.

gender dysphoria The uncomfortable, distressing, anxiety-provoking, and/or sometimes depressing feelings that occur in people when aspects of their body and behavior are not congruent with their gender identity.

gender expression The manner in which a person demonstrates their masculinity or femininity that can include clothing, body, behavior, speech, gestures, and other forms of appearance.

gender fluid A gender identity and expression that encompasses a variety of aspects related to femininity and masculinity that could change over time.

gender identity One's internal sense of being masculine-identified, feminine-identified, neither, or both.

gender marker The legal designation of one's gender on official documentation or records.

gender nonconforming A term for people who do not meet common gender norms.

genderqueer A gender that is not exclusively masculine or exclusively feminine and is outside the gender binary.

GnRH (Gonadotropin Releasing Hormone) A medical term for the hormone that is released by the hypothalamus governing the production of LH (Luteinizing Hormone) and FSH (Follicle-Stimulating Hormone) by the pituitary gland, which causes the gonads to produce estrogen and testosterone.

intersex A group of medical conditions where someone can be born with ambiguous genitalia and/or internal sex organs or chromosomal differences that are not clearly male or female.

LGBTQQIA+ An all-encompassing abbreviation which stands for lesbian, gay, bisexual, transgender, queer, questioning, intersex, allies, plus others.

metoidioplasty A gender-affirming bottom surgery which releases the micro phallus and can include urethra lengthening.

misogyny A disdain, hatred, or mistrust of all people female and feminine.

monogamous A type of relationship where a person is sexually and/or romantically involved with only one person at a time.

MTF (male-to-female)/M2F/FTF An abbreviation that describes a person who now identifies as female gendered but was assigned a male gender at birth.

non-binary A gender that is not exclusively male or exclusively female and is outside of the gender binary.

orchiectomy A type of bottom surgery that involves the removal of testicles.

outing The act of disclosing someone's sexuality and/or gender identity without their knowledge and/or permission.

packing The use of prosthetics and/or other materials to enable an individual to possess the appearance and feeling of having a penis and testicles.

pan hysterectomy A type of bottom surgery that usually includes removing the uterus, ovaries, and fallopian tubes and which could involve the removal of the cervix.

pansexual Someone who is attracted to people of various genders.

passing The ability for a person to be read as their affirmed gender by those who are unaware the individual's identity is transgender.

phalloplasty A type of bottom surgery that entails the construction of a penis and can include the construction of testicles and the implant of an erection device.

polyamorous A type of relationship where a person is sexually and/or romantically involved with more than one person at the same time.

preferred gender pronouns The practice of using or referring to a person in the way an individual desires to be addressed, when pronouns are involved.

puberty blockers A term for a medicine that blocks the hormone GnRH (Gonadotropin Releasing Hormone).

queer A word that refers to a sexual orientation that is not heterosexual and/or anything that is non-heteronormative.

questioning The act of a person who is attempting to figure out their own sexuality and/or gender.

scrotoplasty A surgical procedure that creates a scrotal sac and can include testicular implants.

sexuality The pattern of thoughts, feelings, and arousal that determines sexual preferences.

stealth A word used for a transgender person who chooses to keep their trans status private.

Tanner stages A system to classify the development of puberty in children.

they A word that may also be used as a gender-neutral pronoun to describe a single individual.

top surgery A surgical procedure made to create a masculine-appearing chest or to have breast implants.

tracheal shave A surgical procedure that reduces the thyroid cartilage, which makes up the Adam's apple.

transgender/trans-identified An overarching word, which can be used for people whose gender expression and/or gender identity does not align with their sex assigned at birth.

transitioning The social and/or medical actions a person takes to explore and affirm their gender identity.

transmisogyny A term coined by Julia Serano to describe a form of misogyny that is focused on trans women.

transphobia Prejudice, fear, disdain, or discrimination in respect to gender nonconforming and transgender people.

transsexual A person who identifies within the gender binary (either male or female) and may have medical procedures to bring their body in line with their identity. However, not all transgender people who have medical transitions identify as transsexual.

two-spirit An Indigenous North American identity embraced by some individuals who incorporate a variety of gender roles, identities, and expressions by embodying both masculine and feminine spirits and traits.

vaginoplasty The surgical construction of a vagina.

ANSWER KEYS

Answer Key for Matching Pre-Test #1

Vocabulary Number	Definition Letter	Vocabulary Number	Definition Letter
1	D	7	L
2	G	8	B
3	A	9	F
4	K	10	I
5	H	11	J
6	E	12	C

Answer Key for Matching Pre-Test #2

Vocabulary Number	Definition Letter	Vocabulary Number	Definition Letter
1	J	7	F
2	G	8	A
3	E	9	K
4	L	10	I
5	B	11	C
6	H	12	D

Answer Key for Matching Pre-Test #3

Vocabulary Number	Definition Letter	Vocabulary Number	Definition Letter
1	H	7	K
2	A	8	J
3	L	9	D
4	B	10	E
5	I	11	G
6	F	12	C

Answer Key for Matching Pre-Test #4

Vocabulary Number	Definition Letter	Vocabulary Number	Definition Letter
1	F	7	J
2	G	8	B
3	H	9	C
4	K	10	D
5	A	11	E
6	L	12	I

Answer Key for Matching Pre-Test #5

Vocabulary Number	Definition Letter	Vocabulary Number	Definition Letter
1	B	7	I
2	F	8	D
3	A	9	J
4	G	10	L
5	K	11	H
6	C	12	E

Answer Key for Word Search

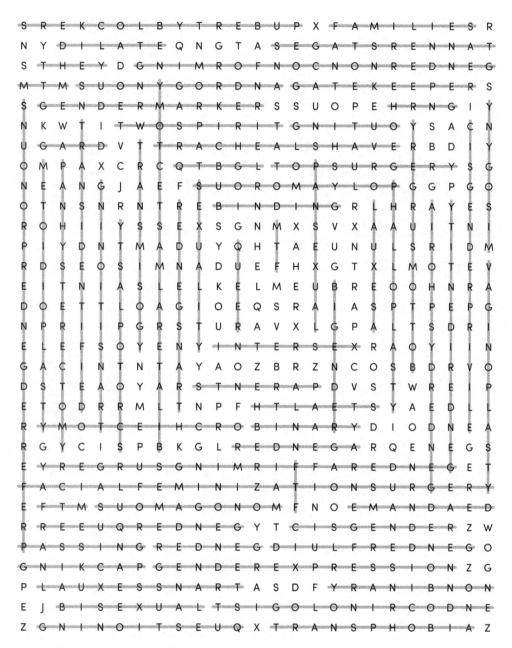

agender	facial feminization	genderqueer	parents	top surgery
androgynous	surgery	GnRH	passing	tracheal shave
asexual	families	intersex	phalloplasty	trans-identified/
bigender	FTM/MTM	LGBTQ	polyamorous	transgender
bilateral mastectomy	gatekeeper	metoidioplasty	preferred gender	transitioning
binary	gender	misogyny	pronouns	transmisogyny
binding	gender-affirming	monogamous	puberty blockers	transphobia
bisexual	surgery	MTF/FTF	queer	transsexual
bottom surgery	gender dysphoria	non-binary	questioning	two-spirit
cisgender	gender expression	orchiectomy	scrotoplasty	vaginoplasty
cisgender privilege	gender fluid	outing	sexuality	
dilate	gender identity	packing	stealth	
drag	gender marker	pan hysterectomy	Tanner stages	
endocrinologist	gender nonconforming	pansexual	they	

Answer Key for Crossword Puzzle

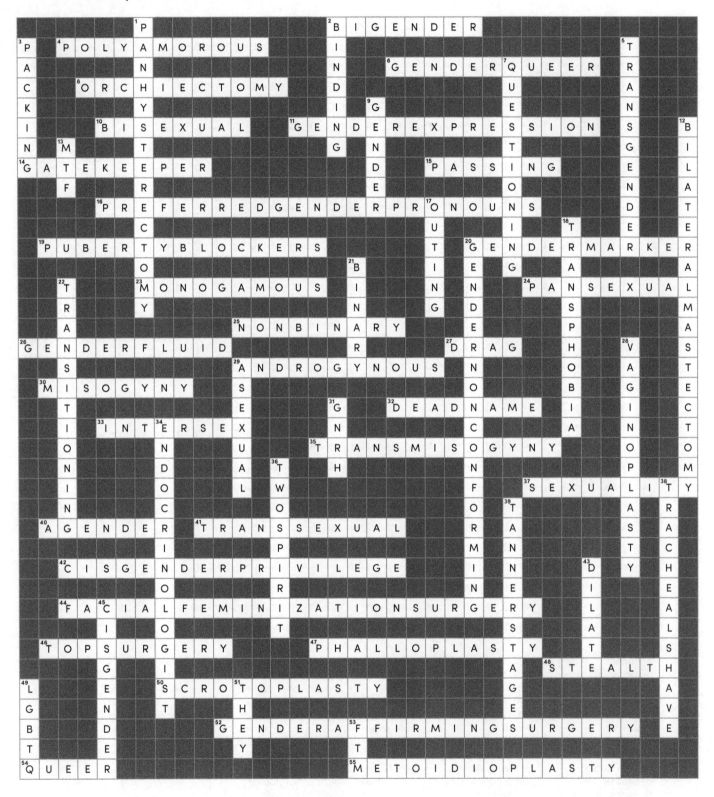

MISSING: BOTTOM SURGERY, GENDER DYSPHORIA, GENDER IDENTITY, AND TRANS-IDENTIFIED
(BONUS WORD INCLUDED: QUEER)

Answer Key for Crossword with Clues

ACROSS

2 BIGENDER: An 8-letter word that means someone who experiences themselves as both masculine and feminine.

4 POLYAMOROUS: An 11-letter word that means a type of relationship where a person is sexually and/or romantically involved with more than one person at the same time.

6 GENDERQUEER: An 11-letter word that means a gender that is not exclusively masculine or exclusively feminine and is outside the gender binary.

8 ORCHIECTOMY: An 11-letter word that means a type of bottom surgery that involves the removal of testicles.

10 BISEXUAL: An 8-letter word that means a person who is attracted to both masculine and feminine people.

11 GENDER EXPRESSION: A 16-letter term that means the manner in which a person demonstrates their masculinity and/or femininity and which can include clothing, body, behavior, speech, gestures, and other forms of appearance.

14 GATEKEEPER: A 10-letter word that means a mental health or medical professional who controls access to medical treatment such as hormones and surgery.

15 PASSING: A 7-letter word that means the ability for a person to be read as their affirmed gender by those who are unaware that the individual's identity is transgender.

16 PREFERRED GENDER PRONOUNS: A 23-letter term that means the practice of others using or referring to a person in the way an individual desires to be addressed, when pronouns are involved.

19 PUBERTY BLOCKERS: A 15-letter term that means a medicine that blocks the hormone GnRH (Gonadotropin Releasing Hormone).

20 GENDER MARKER: A 12-letter term that means the legal designation of one's gender on official documentation or records.

23 MONOGAMOUS: A 10-letter word that means a type of relationship where a person is sexually and/or romantically involved with only one person at a time.

24 PANSEXUAL: A 9-letter word that means someone who is attracted to people of various genders.

25 NON-BINARY: A 9-letter word that means a gender that is not exclusively male or exclusively female and is outside the gender binary.

26 GENDER FLUID: An 11-letter term that means a gender identity and expression that encompasses a variety of aspects related to femininity and masculinity that could change over time.

27 DRAG: A 4-letter word that means enacting gender for the purpose of performance and/or show.

29 ANDROGYNOUS: An 11-letter word that means someone who possesses both masculine and feminine characteristics.

30 MISOGYNY: An 8-letter word that means a disdain, hatred, or mistrust of all female and feminine people.

32 DEADNAME: An 8-letter word that means a term that describes the name assigned to a person at birth, which they no longer use, for it does not align with their affirmed gender and can also be referred to as their old name.

33 INTERSEX: An 8-letter word that means a group of medical conditions where someone can be born with ambiguous genitalia and/or internal sex organs or chromosomal differences that are not clearly male or female.

35 TRANSMISOGYNY: A 13-letter word coined by Julia Serano to describe a form of misogyny that is focused towards trans women.

37 SEXUALITY: A 9-letter word that means the pattern of thoughts, feelings, and arousal that determine sexual preferences.

40 AGENDER: A 7-letter word that means someone who does not identify with any gender.

41 TRANSSEXUAL: An 11-letter word that means a person who identifies within the gender binary (either male or female) and may have medical procedures to bring their body in line with their identity. However, not all transgender people who have medical transitions identify as transsexual.

42 CISGENDER PRIVILEGE: An 18-letter term that means the advantages granted by society to people whose gender aligns with the one assigned at birth.

44 FACIAL FEMINIZATION SURGERY: A 25-letter term that means a variety of plastic surgery procedures made to create a more feminine appearance to the features of the face.

46 TOP SURGERY: A 10-letter term that means a surgical procedure made to create a masculine-appearing chest or to have breast implants.

47 PHALLOPLASTY: A 12-letter word that means a type of bottom surgery that entails the construction of a penis and can include the construction of testicles and the implant of an erection device.

48 STEALTH: A 7-letter word that is used for a transgender person who chooses to keep their trans status private.

50 SCROTOPLASTY: A 12-letter word that means a surgical procedure that creates a scrotal sac and can include testicular implants.

52 GENDER-AFFIRMING SURGERY: A 22-letter term that means surgery that brings the individual's body into alignment with their gender identity.

54 QUEER: A 5-letter word that refers to a sexual orientation that is not heterosexual and/or anything that is non-heteronormative.

55 METOIDIOPLASTY: A 14-letter word that means a gender-affirming bottom surgery which releases the micro phallus and can include lengthening of the urethra.

DOWN

1 PAN HYSTERECTOMY: A 15-letter term that means a type of bottom surgery that usually includes removing the uterus, ovaries, and fallopian tubes and which could involve the removal of the cervix.

2 BINDING: A 7-letter word that means a practice of using material or clothing to constrict the breasts that enables a person to flatten their chest.

3 PACKING: A 7-letter word that means the use of prosthetics and/or other materials to enable an individual to possess the appearance and feeling of having a penis and testicles.

5 TRANSGENDER: An 11-letter overarching word which can be used for people whose gender expression and/or gender identity does not align with their sex assigned at birth.

7 QUESTIONING: An 11-letter word that means the act of a person who is attempting to figure out their own sexuality and/or gender.

9 GENDER: A 6-letter word that means how a person internally experiences themselves as male, female, masculine, feminine, some combination of these, or none of them; aspects of these can be culturally defined.

12 BILATERAL MASTECTOMY: A 19-letter term that means a surgical procedure that removes breast tissue from both sides of the chest and can include the construction of a male-appearing chest.

13 MTF: A 3-letter abbreviation that describes a person who now identifies as female gendered but was assigned a male gender at birth.

17 OUTING: A 6-letter word that means the act of disclosing someone's sexuality and/or gender identity without their knowledge and/or permission.

18 TRANSPHOBIA: An 11-letter word that means prejudice, fear, disdain, or discrimination in respect of gender nonconforming and transgender people.

20 GENDER NONCONFORMING: A 19-letter term that means people who do not meet common gender norms.

21 BINARY: A 6-letter word that means the belief that there are only two genders, male and female.

22 TRANSITIONING: A 13-letter word that means the social and/or medical actions a person takes to explore and/or affirm their gender identity.

28 VAGINOPLASTY: A 12-letter word that means the surgical construction of a vagina.

29 ASEXUAL: A 7-letter word that means someone who does not feel sexual attraction to other people.

31 GNRH: A 4-letter acronym which stands for Gonadotropin Releasing Hormone and means a medical term for the hormone that is released by the hypothalamus governing the production of LH (Luteinizing Hormone) and FSH (Follicle-Stimulating Hormone) by the pituitary gland, which causes the gonads to produce estrogen and testosterone.

34 ENDOCRINOLOGIST: A 15-letter word that means a medical doctor who specializes in glands and hormones.

36 TWO-SPIRIT: A 9-letter word that means an Indigenous North American identity embraced by some individuals who incorporate a variety of gender roles, identities, and expressions by embodying both masculine and feminine spirits and traits.

38 TRACHEAL SHAVE: A 13-letter term that means a surgical procedure that reduces the thyroid cartilage, which makes up the Adam's apple.

39 TANNER STAGES: A 12-letter term that means a system to clarify the development of puberty in children.

43 DILATE: A 6-letter word that means a prescribed routine post-vaginoplasty where a person inserts medical equipment into the neovagina in order to maintain the creation of the vaginal canal.

45 CISGENDER: A 9-letter word that means someone whose gender assigned at birth and gender identity are aligned.

49 LGBTQ: A 5-letter abbreviation which stands for lesbian, gay, bisexual, transgender, and queer.

51 THEY: A 4-letter word that may also be used as a gender-neutral pronoun to describe a single individual.

53 FTM: A 3-letter abbreviation that describes a person who now identifies as male gendered but was assigned a female gender at birth.